Oglethorpe in America

JAMES EDWARD OGLETHORPE,
founder of the Colony of Georgia in America
(Courtesy of the Georgia Department of Archives and History.)

Phinizy Spalding

Oglethorpe in America

The University of Chicago Press

Chicago and London

To Margie

The University of Chicago Press, Chicago 60637
The University of Chicago Press, Ltd., London

Phinizy Spalding is associate professor of history
at the University of Georgia and editor of the
Georgia Historical Quarterly. He is a contrib-
utor to the forthcoming *History of Georgia*
and the *Encyclopedia of Southern History*.

Library of Congress Cataloging in Publication Data

Spalding, Phinizy.
    Oglethorpe in America.

    Bibliography: p.
    Includes index.
    1. Oglethorpe, James Edward, 1696-1785. 2. States-
men—Georgia—Biography. 3. Georgia—History—Colonial
period, ca. 1600-1775. I. Title.
F289.0367   975.8'02'0924 [B]   76-8092
ISBN 0-226-76846-5

Contents

Preface and Acknowledgments

It has been forty years since the publication of Amos Aschbach Ettinger's biography of James Edward Oglethorpe, and no work has since been written that can compare with it. Georgia and Oglethorpe students will always be deep in debt to Ettinger for his detective work and scholarly integrity. One of the few regrets the careful reader has, however, is that Ettinger was not able to treat in enough detail Oglethorpe's American career.

Since the appearance of Ettinger's biography in 1936, numerous primary sources have come to light. The Phillipps Collection of Egmont Papers, with its store of information on colonial Georgia, is now available to scholars at the University of Georgia Library; a new Egmont journal has been published; the journals of William Stephens from 1741 to 1745, long presumed lost, have been found and are now printed; accounts by Georgia officials Thomas Christie and Peter Gordon, recorder and first bailiff respectively, illuminate the *Anne*'s crossing to America in 1732–33, as well as the early days of the colony of Georgia, have surfaced; quantities of information touching upon the Salzburgers are now being carefully translated and edited by George Fenwick Jones; and the copybook of John Brownfield, an early Moravian merchant in Savannah, has recently come to the attention of Georgia scholars. All these sources deal extensively and importantly with James Oglethorpe.

In South Carolina, the Letterbooks of Robert Pringle and Eliza Lucas Pinckney, as well as the Council Journals and Journals of the Upper House of Assembly provide rich sources. And finally the Boswell Papers at Yale contain valuable insights by Oglethorpe and about Oglethorpe in his latter days. His rambling conversations and his correspondence with Boswell reveal a new Oglethorpe.

In addition to the primary sources not available to Ettinger, there has been some fine secondary work done since 1936 as well as several excellent dissertations. Among the works important for a study of colonial Georgia are books by Trevor Reese, E. Merton Coulter, Albert Saye, and Kenneth Coleman, and articles in the *Georgia Historical Quarterly* and the *William and Mary Quarterly*. Research and writing by Margaret Davis Cate, Geraldine Meroney, Paul Taylor, H. B. Fant, Richard Dunn, Verner Crane, and John Tate Lanning have brought sensible focus to many aspects of the Trusteeship period. The work by M. Eugene Sirmans on South Carolina's first hundred years and Richard Sherman's biography of Robert Johnson touch Oglethorpe briefly as do a number of books on the Indians and Indian policy. Larry Ivers has produced a work concerned with Georgia's early military history, but no scholar of the period has done an in-depth study of Oglethorpe since Ettinger's day.

In almost all the early secondary literature concerning Oglethorpe two things are apparent: the majority of these works are uncritical, and they use the strict chronological approach. It was the first point that caused the literary historian Moses Coit Tyler to describe the traditional image of Oglethorpe as "somewhat nauseating in its sweetness." And it is, in part at least, the fault of the chronological approach, which can make the narrative an end in itself, that authors dealing with Georgia's founder often seem reluctant to interrupt the narrative's flow to take stock. It is hoped the present volume has escaped both these pitfalls.

I am not saying that a topical approach contains qualities inherently superior to the chronological narrative, but I *am* saying that such an approach makes it easier for me to reach judgments at appropriate places. And this is the basic weakness of the literature about Georgia's founder: no thorough and scholarly treatment of his career has ever seriously considered whether the man was really worthy of the admiration accorded him. Should Oglethorpe take his place among effective and successful colonial founders such as Winthrop, Smith, Raleigh (whom Oglethorpe apparently idolized), and Penn?

It should be made clear that this book makes no claim to be a complete account of the activities of James Edward Oglethorpe in America. On the contrary, rather than attempt to follow every step Oglethorpe took in the New World, a conscious effort has been made to avoid such an approach. For example, in the chapter on Oglethorpe as colonizer only the early experiences on board ship and in Savannah have been examined in detail, and these for fairly specific reasons. I felt that the voyage of the *Anne*, illuminated by the availability of new sources, provided an opportunity to observe Oglethorpe as he led his colonists to the shores of America. Furthermore, Savannah, being the first permanent British settlement in Georgia, was not only the most important early colonizing effort but was fairly typical in plan and organization of other nonmilitary towns later established by Georgia's founder. I have therefore considered Savannah in some detail but not the villages and hamlets clustered about it, and I have touched only lightly upon the basically military settlements, because these were chosen for strategic considerations and not as sites especially suited for permanent non-military occupation. Most of these outposts did not last beyond victory over or agreement with Britain's enemies. Even Frederica, that expensive settlement on St. Simons Island, could not long survive the withdrawal of Oglethorpe's regiment.

Similarly, in the section concerning Georgia's various laws I have not aimed so much at a minute recounting of the rise of opposition to these regulations as at an assessment of their feasibility in the light of eighteenth-century opinion and the frontier reality in Georgia. Oglethorpe's ability to enforce the laws and to administer the colony properly is considered at some length.

Since Oglethorpe's military exploits are best comprehended in narrative, this traditional approach has been followed in the chapters dealing with them.

The Epilogue is almost wholly subjective in that here I try to come to grips with Oglethorpe the man and to assess his achievements and comprehend his actions, particularly as they relate to his American experience.

The staff at the University of Georgia Library in Athens has shown an unfailing interest in my manuscript, particularly John

W. Bonner, Mrs. William Tate, Susan Aldrich, and Tony Dees, all in Special Collections. I would also like to express my thanks to Carroll Hart, director of the Georgia Department of Archives and History, Pat Bryant, Deputy Surveyor General of Georgia, and Lilla M. Hawes, retired director of the Georgia Historical Society.

Of specific faculty members, mention should be made of Fletcher M. Green and Hugh T. Lefler, formerly members of the history department at the University of North Carolina, Chapel Hill, and of E. Merton Coulter of the University of Georgia, the "youngest" of all emeritus professors. I owe a deep debt to Kenneth Coleman, scholar and friend. My thanks go also to Professor and Mrs. Frederick Pottle of the Boswell Papers at Yale University, to Patricia Hill of Clemson University, to Mr. John Talmadge of Athens, and to the American Philosophical Society, which aided my research by a generous grant.

In addition to the pleasant, but usually anonymous, people at the British National Library, the British Public Record Office, and other depositories in England, I would like to single out Jill Beck in the Guildford Muniment Room, Guildford, Surrey, Betty Wood of Girton College, Cambridge, Alan Patillo of London, and the staff at London University's Institute for Historical Research. Mrs. Helen Forsyth has helped trace contemporary likenesses of Georgia's founder, and Trevor R. Reese stimulated my thought in more than one way until his tragically early death in June 1976.

For the approval to use and to draw quotations from certain manuscript collections, I would like to express my sincere gratitude to the Earl of Cholmondeley (the Cholmondeley [Houghton] Manuscripts); the Archives of the Moravian Church, Bethlehem, Pennsylvania (Copy Book of John Brownfield); Colonel Arthur B. Lloyd-Baker (Granville Sharp Papers); Mr. James More-Molyneux (the Loseley Manuscripts); the Papers of James Boswell and McGraw-Hill, Inc. (the Private Papers of James Boswell).

For Mrs. Beth Abney I save extra thanks for cheerfulness, sensible recommendations, and sound advice. But it is my wife,

Margaret Roscoe Spalding, who has suffered or celebrated through every phase of the book. It simply could not have been done without her. My appreciation.

1   Voyage and Settlement

From the decks of the *Anne,* off the South Carolina coast at Charles Town early in 1733, James Edward Oglethorpe gratefully observed that the trees he saw on the horizon were "No disagreeable sight to those who for seven weeks have seen nothing but Sea and Sky." Still, the voyage from England had been a relatively easy one. The ship, with her cargo of supplies and settlers, had been steered southward "to avoid the fury of the North west Winds that generaly rage in the Winter."[1] The stratagem had worked. It had been "a very favourable Passage," and Oglethorpe and his colonists, carefully picked to be the nucleus of the province of Georgia, arrived in American waters at almost full strength on 13 January 1733.[2] Two children had died during the passage and were buried at sea,[3] but to have escaped so lightly was considered a stroke of good fortune. Once Oglethorpe got ashore, Governor Robert Johnson of South Carolina and his political friends and allies hastened to assure him of their vital interest in and concern for the new province. Aid and cooperation from Carolina were promised; all the omens seemed good.[4]

The controlled excitement in Oglethorpe's opening letter from America can be easily understood. He was a trifle impatient to get on with the business of settlement. It was time for that colonial vision, which had long enchanted Englishmen of public spirit, to be brought to reality. And who, more than the highly considered Oglethorpe himself, might have a better chance of bringing the vision to reality and making it an object of universal respect and admiration?

Oglethorpe, of a distinguished and volatile Jacobite family, inherited from both his parents an almost unbounded enthusiasm and zest for life, qualities that were to remain with him until he died in 1785 at an advanced age. These same qualities stood him in good stead during his American years. Although he had been involved before with issues that demanded his undivided attention, of all his interests the cause of Georgia was to concern him longest and closest. Never in his writing or conversation did he clearly articulate what bordered upon a fixation with Georgia, but to criticize Georgia was to criticize Oglethorpe. Had he been a seventeenth-century New England colonist, Oglethorpe might have confided to a diary, but Oglethorpe kept no diary, and history is the poorer for it. He himself must surely have been aware of his hypersensitivity, and his enemies certainly were. They soon learned that barbs cast at Oglethorpe's role as colonizer and founder seemed especially sharp. Even at his death the needlers could not resist:

> ONE HUNDRED TWO! Methusalem in age,
> A vigorous soldier, and a virtuous sage;
> He founded GEORGIA, gave it laws and trade;
> He saw it flourish, and he saw it fade![5]

On the surface, it would seem difficult to find a man better qualified than Oglethorpe for colonial leadership. Born in 1696, he had been a member of Parliament since 1722 as representative from the borough of Haslemere. In the Commons he had demonstrated his volubility as a frequent speaker and had shown a keen interest in imperial affairs. His name gradually became noted and remembered, and though not everyone thought his abilities first rate, he was respected by his colleagues, who recognized in him an honest and independent spirit.[6]

To be respected as an independent was no small feat for one whose mother, Eleanor Wall Oglethorpe, was an inveterate Jacobite plotter. His sisters had married into the French aristocracy and lived in exile rather than risk the horrors of life in an England no longer controlled by the Stuarts.[7] It is a comment on the kind of society enjoyed by early eighteenth-century Britain that Oglethorpe could be accepted as an active member of the body politic even as his activist mother and sisters lived and did their best to bring down that same system.

Oglethorpe was typical of members of his family in that he was aggressive, determined, and endowed with a powerful moral sense. Like his father, Theophilus, he had a highly developed sense of duty and justice. He had also a powerful notion of his own rectitude and a finely honed conception of what constituted religion and morality. Although a staunch advocate of Protestantism, Oglethorpe's beliefs may well have been tempered by the consideration that his brothers-in-law, nephews, and nieces were Roman Catholic. The closely knit family group of which James Edward was a member was not dubbed "the loyal Oglethorpes" without foundation. His broad compassion is reflected in the issues which, besides Georgia, are most closely linked with his name: sailors' rights, improvement of conditions in the jails insofar as they related to debtors, and slave reform. His generosity with his own money was well known.

The Oglethorpe ambition was well known too. Where his mother and sisters spent their time seeking what favors they could from the exiled courts of the Stuarts, James, after a brief flirtation with the Jacobites, sought recognition from the powerful in England. As a member of the House of Commons, he gained his recognition by hard work and close attention to affairs of state. These traits were to serve him well in the New World with its many problems.

By the time of Georgia's settlement in 1733 Oglethorpe had developed into a man keenly aware of his own powers, and though he was not the sort of person who could have his head turned by soft words, still he had grown rather used to flattery. As the youngest child and, finally, as the only surviving son of Theophilus and Eleanor Oglethorpe, he had been coddled and pampered and prepared for a role in life. It was only natural, then, that James Oglethorpe thought highly of his own abilities and never doubted for a moment that his training and experience would triumph over any problems he might face across the sea.

It should also be borne in mind that Georgia's founder had an almost naive faith that the environment can make, or remake, a man. If given an opportunity an individual who might have failed in his first chance could possibly succeed in his second. Hence Oglethorpe's emphasis on prison reform. He had a firm belief in the validity of the legal process and a thorough respect for British traditions and the common law. Social evils, his actions seemed to say, can be ameliorated; man's plight can be improved. If English institutions such as the monarchy, Parliament, committees—such as his own celebrated committee to inquire into the condition of the jails—and even charitable corporate bodies like the Georgia Trustees were made to operate effectively, society would be uplifted. Oglethorpe and a small group of influential men acted consistently with this deeply rooted conviction in the validity of English institutions in order to work within the system and eradicate some of the worst evils of society. The Georgia experiment was, in the final analysis, an act of faith in the British way concocted by those whose vision was lofty and idealistic.

Oglethorpe, it should be emphasized, aimed only at eliminating some of the most obvious evils in the system. He had no frame of reference from which to develop ideas leading in the direction of political reform that might change the nature of Parliament itself. (If any such reform were to come about, Oglethorpe would very likely have lost his own seat, for which he paid a goodly sum.)[8] But he most sincerely desired, with Parliament's leave, to aid significant segments of English society. At first, sailors and jailed debtors received his attention, but his vision became more inclusive and grew to embrace peripheral groups as the Georgia scheme widened in scope. Various elements of the unemployed, small farmers, and modest storekeepers began to be included in his purview. Ultimately he also included victims of economic and religious oppression such as the Salzburgers, the Moravians, and the Jews.

There is little doubt that where American affairs were concerned Oglethorpe knew more than the average person of his interests and, for that matter, more than the average member of Parliament. It is also certain that he knew less than Bishop George Berkeley, who had actually been to the New World and had personally tasted some of the disappointment and frustration attendant upon colonial schemes.[9] But Oglethorpe, who became well acquainted with Berkeley, was more hardheaded and less idealistic than the bishop. Admittedly Viscount Percival (later Earl of Egmont) had more facts and figures at his disposal than did Oglethorpe, but he never seriously entertained the notion of going to America himself. With all his knowledge and careful scholarship, however, Egmont was to learn the lesson that a colony could not be run from Old Palace Yard, Westminster, no matter how often disinterested philanthropists met and pored over mind-dizzying reports from America.

The conclusion should not be drawn that Oglethorpe, though better prepared to lead a colonial venture than most of his contemporaries, necessarily knew quite enough about either America or human nature to be a wholly successful founder. His contention, in his 1733 *New and Accurate Account of the Provinces of South-Carolina and Georgia*, that huge lakes northwest of the Appalachian Mountains successfully warmed the winter gales and prevented them from being offensive to Georgia, hardly fills the modern reader with confidence. Similarly, his notion that the Gulf of Mexico cooled the summer winds and kept Georgia moderate at that time of year is at best an inaccurate description of a Georgia summer.[10] He also maintained that to clear timber only a "half a Dozen Strokes of an Ax" around the base of a tree would effectively kill it. After "a Year or two" the rain would have soaked the trees in the colonist's field to the point that "a brisk Gust of Wind fells many Acres for you in an Hour, of which you may then make one bright Bonfire." It was reluctantly conceded that "Strangers" might be prone to have a slight "Ague, or Sort of a Fever; but then 'tis very slight." Fatefully, at least insofar as the history of Georgia during the Trusteeship period was concerned, Oglethorpe maintained that the only thing keeping the region's people from perfect health was intemperance brought on by the availability of rum, "a fatal Liquor" to whites as well as Indians.

Oglethorpe was familiar with John Archdale's *Description of South Carolina;* he had read the latest literature in the London periodicals as well as the most recent pamphlets on the subject of colonization. His narrative of the early settlement efforts by the French and Spanish in the general vicinity of Georgia is usually concise and self-assured, and the account of various Carolina colonizing ventures carries the ring of authority. Above all, *A New and Accurate Account* exudes the confidence felt by the author. Oglethorpe's plan to settle a colony of persecuted Protestants and "unfortunate People in the Kingdom of reputable Families" appeared logical.[11] The nation's trade would benefit and Georgia would supply Britain with such products as silk and wines for which hitherto she had had to look elsewhere. Its location, south of Carolina, would make Georgia a protection to the older colony. With the financing and the leadership the new colony was promised, how could it fail?

If Oglethorpe was guilty of "colonizing by latitudes," he was no more misleading than the other "specialists" of his day. His enthusiasm for olives, wines, silks, and flax caused his image of what Georgia should be to slip out of focus temporarily, but once he understood the reality of Georgia's climate and soil he never, for example, seriously pushed for implementation of the Trustees' requirements that the colonists plant specified numbers of mulberry trees per acre. Here, to be sure, he showed a certain malleability that, in other instances, was lacking in his conduct.

On the whole, Oglethorpe had enormous zest and ebullience, together with the considerable knowledge necessary for the founder of a colony. Also, he was eager to attempt such a daring experiment; he was unattached, independently wealthy, and still at thirty-five, a fairly young man. If mistaken in his colonial assumptions he could profit from his misconceptions and alter his plans to meet the realities.

Oglethorpe's intensity, combined with Egmont's connections, paid off in June 1732 when the Georgia Trustees received the royal charter they had requested some years before.[12] Oglethorpe had chafed at the various vexatious delays. He suspected the real stumbling block to be not the king, who was blamed by the ministry, but Robert Walpole himself. Because Egmont was at this time still a political ally of Walpole, he questioned the first minister's brother, Horace, as to the reasons for the charter's delay. The latter denied that the ministry slowed the Georgia request, but at the same time Egmont was asked not to repeat what he had heard to Oglethorpe and the others as "they were warm men."[13] Certainly Oglethorpe, who earlier in his life had shown distressing tendencies to lose his temper,[14] was "warm" about the delay. Goaded by Oglethorpe and the Georgia faction, Robert Walpole later personally expedited the issue of Georgia's basic constitutional document.[15] When the way was finally cleared, Oglethorpe could not contain his eagerness that the business of colonizing should be organized and dispatched as soon as possible.

Warnings came from America that haste should be made slowly. In April 1732, Governor Jonathan Belcher of Massachusetts wrote Thomas Coram, English philanthropist and Georgia Trustee, to emphasize that the southern areas of the North American continent "have been graves to the people of England."[16] Governor Johnson of South Carolina also counseled against hasty action and sadly wrote of a recent fever that had hit his colony and robbed him of a son and three servants,[17] but even had Johnson's sobering letter arrived before Oglethorpe's departure, it is not likely to have deterred him.

With Oglethorpe pushing relentlessly, the first expedition was selected and equipped. His decision personally to lead the colonists into the wilderness soothed some of the misgivings of the Trustees and doubtless those of the settlers as well. So on 17 November 1732 final farewells were taken at Gravesend as the two-hundred-ton galley *Anne*, loaded with settlers, provisions, and good beer, put off down the Thames to sea.[18] Egmont, who had urged caution as he relaxed at Bath, had not been in such a rush, but he did not return to London until 27 October.[19] By then it was too late to stop what was already well in motion.

The voyage across the Atlantic demonstrated Oglethorpe's capacity for leadership. It also demonstrated that he was a good sailor, for the day after leaving Gravesend, Oglethorpe wrote that many of the colonists were seasick but that he had thus far escaped.[20] Fortunately for Oglethorpe he adjusted easily to shipboard life, a quality that proved an asset on subsequent voyages, particularly in the stormy crossing to England in 1736–37. During the later voyage his ship was nearly wrecked on the Welsh coast and was saved only when he and Richard Tanner, a young Surrey friend who accompanied him, tended the lines that the regular sailors had abandoned.[21]

On board the *Anne* Oglethorpe took infinite pains to see that the colonists were as comfortable as could be expected. Nothing seemed too small to concern him, a characteristic appreciated by his shipmates. It not only helped give them confidence in what they were doing but also inspired respect for the man who had given up a life of ease to lead such a venture.

Peter Gordon, named by the Trustees as one of the first officials of the new colony,[22] left a partial record of the crossing of the *Anne*. Unfortunately, he was taken sick less than a month into the voyage and reported in detail only a few events before the sighting of the Carolina coastline. Gordon indicates that during his confinement Oglethorpe, the Reverend Henry Herbert, and Captain John Thomas attended him "constantly" in his cabin and made certain that he received everything he needed.[23] Thomas Christie, chosen recorder for the new colony, kept a rudimentary diary of the crossing in which he gives a sketchy but flattering picture of Oglethorpe. Once at sea, Christie says, Oglethorpe made a point of visiting the settlers "in the hold" where their spaces were located; he acted as godfather to the Warrens' son, born at sea and happily christened Georgius Marinus; he organized his people to render them helpful and to keep their minds off the tedium of life on the main, and issued orders to make sure that lights were out by eight and to prevent smoking "unless with a Cap on the Pipe & then on the Deck." On the misty evening of 24 November a dog belonging to Oglethorpe was lost, presumably "flung Over board by some of the Sailors."[24] Oglethorpe ordered that his own stores be relied upon should shortages become a problem on the *Anne*.

A month out Oglethorpe "caught a Dolphin." When he heard that "some Big-bellyd. Women" on the *Anne* had admired his prize he presented it to them "withot. tasting any himself."[25] Later, a fishing party comprised of Oglethorpe, Thomas, Herbert, and others huddled together in the ship's longboat "undr. an Umbrella" for protection against the distinctly un-English sun. In celebration of Oglethorpe's thirty-sixth birthday, "a sheep and some other fresh provissions was dress'd for our people, and a quantity of liquor given to drink the health of the day. After dinner we were diverted with cudgell playing and riding of skimingtons on account of Mrs. [Anne] Coles having beat her husband."[26]

There were very sober days as well. Samuel Clark, a child who had died on board, was buried at sea, and after the funeral Oglethorpe found it necessary to resort to extraordinary means to maintain order. For a reason not entirely clear, there was an incident at the end of the services when someone offered—or threatened—"to throw water on them." Oglethorpe took the situation into his own hands and "came behind him & gave him a good kick on ye arse."[27] After calming another controversy later, he prescribed "a pint of Bumbo" for everyone "to Drink & be friends together."[28]

Even Oglethorpe must have been on edge by 13 January, when land off Charles Town finally came into view and guns were fired as a signal for a pilot to come out to the *Anne*.[29] Oglethorpe did not stay long in the Carolina port city, although the town had put on its best face to greet him. During his brief stop, however, Oglethorpe made friends with Governor Johnson and the legislative leaders and was assured by them that whatever Carolina could do for the new province would, indeed, be done.[30] Oglethorpe, fully grasping the importance of having the older colony oversee the younger and realizing that Carolina's help might prove essential in the early stages, gladly accepted the offers of provisions, financial aid, and various other kinds of assistance.[31] But the burden for the ultimate success or failure of the project rested on Oglethorpe, and he knew it. Georgia's future settlers were permitted to watch from the ship but not to land at Charles Town. The *Anne* went on to Port Royal before the weary travelers were allowed to test their land legs.

While his new Georgians recovered from their journey at Port Royal, Oglethorpe reconnoitered Yamacraw Bluff; he found it enormously to his liking. In spite of Carolina's conviction that

the Altamaha River was the best site for a first settlement, the
decision to locate Georgia's pioneer outpost on the bluff,
overlooking the lazy Savannah River as it meandered to the sea,
was a fairly obvious one. The place was healthy, on high
ground, had access to a goodly supply of fresh water, was
relatively easily cleared, had superior communication links with
the internal waterways around the coastal islands, was accessible
to oceangoing ships, was known to the Indians and Indian
traders, and finally, was close to Carolina should war break out
with the Spanish or French.

When the various debits and assets of the bluff are weighed,
its suitability as a location for a settlement was probably superior
to any other mainland site chosen as an original settlement
south of St. Mary's City in Maryland. The site, in fact, can
be favorably compared to almost any of the original English
continental settlements. As Oglethorpe pointed out in letters to
the Trustees, the location was some forty feet above river level
and about ten miles from the point where the Savannah
emptied into the ocean. From this vantage point the settlers had
a "very agreeable" view. The overlook was useful for more than
just aesthetic purposes: potential enemies could be tracked with
relative ease.[32] Savannah, thanks to Oglethorpe's choice, stood
aloof from successful attack until British forces wrested it from
the rebellious Americans late in 1778.

The bluff had been used as a sort of loading and unloading
spot for Carolina Indian traders, and the presence in the
immediate neighborhood of a small tribe of natives added to
the appeal of the place. Oglethorpe hastened to make friends
with the old Yamacraw leader, Tomochichi, who had reconciled
himself to the news that the English were coming to his territory
in force and intended to remain there permanently. Indeed, he
had no option. His tribe was weak and accustomed to English
ways and English goods. To fight the intrusion would be
foolish; to withdraw from the bluff and return to the heartland
of the Lower Creeks from which he was an exile was equally
unthinkable. Tomochichi therefore threw himself, in effect, on
the mercy of James Oglethorpe. It is one of the pleasanter
aspects of this history that the trust confided was never violated.

The two men developed a deep respect for each other; Oglethorpe's sadness at the old mico's death in 1739 was real.

Finding his reception on the bluff to be satisfactory, Oglethorpe went back to Carolina and rejoined his colonists. On 30 January, over one hundred strong, they all left the barracks at Port Royal in eight large boats accompanied by a detachment of soldiers. Ten days ashore and good food had refreshed the voyagers, and after two nights en route the little flotilla reached the future location of Savannah on the afternoon of 1 February 1733.

As they approached Yamacraw Bluff they were greeted by Captain Francis Scott and a contingent of armed men who fired a welcoming salute to Oglethorpe and his settlers. Scott and his troops, who had been left there by Oglethorpe after his first visit, had gone so far as to build steps up the face of the bluff to make it easier for the colonists to climb to the site of the town. His salute was gallantly returned and the expectant settlers debarked.[33]

Roughly an hour after their landing, Chief Tomochichi of the Yamacraws, his Queen, and John Musgrove, an Indian trader and interpreter, came to welcome them.[34] The Indians, decked out in all their finery, were preceded by "a Man dancing in Antick Postures"[35] with a huge feather fan and "ratles in his hands (something like our casternutts)."[36] He was prancing and singing as he came. Oglethorpe moved with dignity a short distance from his pitched tent to meet the natives. The ceremonial dance continued for more than fifteen minutes as the Indian "waved his Fans over him [Oglethorpe] & Strok'd him on every Side with them." After the dance Oglethorpe invited the red men to enter his tent, where he seated Tomochichi on his right, with Musgrove "standing between them."[37] There was an amicable quarter-hour discussion, after which the Indians returned upriver to their town. Oglethorpe with his colonists then spent their first evening on Georgia soil.

That night there occurred an unfortunate incident in the Yamacraw village. Because he was still recovering from his illness and, presumably, had been told to avoid sleeping in the night air (there had not been time to pitch his tent), Peter

Gordon went to Musgrove's Indian post to pass the evening. The natives were in high good spirits, and to show it entertained by dancing. One "Doctor Lyons," a figure about whom little is known beyond what Gordon reports, joined the group at the Indian town. Although he was "One of the oldest of our people" Lyons had sneaked away from the Savannah camp and joined in the Indian revels. Gordon discreetly notes that Lyons had "gott a litle in drink." Upon being informed of the situation, Bailiff Gordon told Lyons to quit his foolishness and return to camp; if he persisted then Oglethorpe must be told. Lyons promised he would dance no more, but he was so inspired by the occasion that he joined in again. Gordon then ordered Lyons carried back to Savannah "by force." It was, he remarked, a bad example for the Indians to view an older white man cavorting in such a way.[38] The Indians admired their own elders and they would never gain the proper respect for Georgia if the colony seemed to represent a society where the older men acted the fool. Gordon read Oglethorpe's thoughts concerning Anglo-Indian relations perfectly.

On the following day Oglethorpe presented the natives with their first gifts from the colony.[39] They were well received. A good start had been made, and the Lyons episode passed without repercussions.

Preliminaries out of the way, Oglethorpe and his colonists plunged into the serious business of blocking out a town, fortifying it, cutting trees, and generally regulating the new colonial society tenuously perched atop Yamacraw Bluff and called Savannah.[40] Oglethorpe, it was reported, "is both great & Good." The colony was off to such a harmonious and successful start "owing to his good Conduct only."[41]

On 7 February, the settlers began "to digg trenches for fixing palisadoes" in case of Indian or Spanish attack; on the next day, each family was given "an iron pott, frying pan, and three wooden bowls, a Bible, Common Prayer Book, and Whole Duty of Man," and the sawing and splitting of boards to make "clapp board houses" was begun. On 9 February every able bodied person was given "a musket and bayonett, cartrige box and belt" to defend himself and his family. That same day

William Bull from Carolina, who had come to Georgia bringing with him "Four Labourers" to lend assistance in the construction work, helped Oglethorpe delineate "the Square, the Streets, and 40 Lotts for Houses."[42] The inhabitants were "drawn up under owr arms for the first time" on 11 February, and Oglethorpe officially divided them into four tithings of ten men each. That night Gordon set up the first guard from his tithing and the clapboard guardhouse, put "upon the most convenient part of the Bluff, for commanding the river both wayes," was manned.[43] In another week Oglethorpe felt so confident that he left Savannah to investigate a proposed location for a settlement by Carolinians on Tybee Island.[44]

There was so much to do that Oglethorpe found himself writing the Trustees scarcely ten days after establishing Savannah that he was "so taken up" by the myriad of "necessary things" that he was desperately short of time. A more detailed report, he promised, would soon follow.[45] But as time went on, Oglethorpe discovered that he had less time rather than more, and his frantic effort to keep abreast of events became a recurring theme in his correspondence.

He soon learned that expenses were going to be more of a problem than he or the Trustees had anticipated. In spite of the rice that had been given by South Carolina Oglethorpe had to purchase more as the quantity sent had not been "near sufficient."[46] A refrain from this letter, or one very much like it—"I have been obliged to make many expences here"—was to become only too familiar to the Georgia Board in London. In addition to rice, Oglethorpe had to lay out funds "for Intelligence, Rewards for taking Outlaws and Spies," and "many other Articles of Expence."[47] All this in Georgia's earliest infancy.

Still, Oglethorpe seemed to be everywhere. There were houses to be built, land to be surveyed, lots to be granted, tithings to be arranged, Indians to be parlayed with, and Spaniards and French to watch. Oglethorpe was at his incisive best during these early weeks of the Savannah settlement; he let nothing stand in the way of the proper ordering of the colony. Where many colonial leaders might have looked to their safety and comfort first, Oglethorpe was content to spend the few relaxing hours he permitted himself in a tent under a clump of pines at the top of Savannah's bluff.[48]

Samuel Eveleigh, prominent Charles Town trader, came to Savannah in mid-March and brought Oglethorpe ''a great bundle of Asparagus.'' To Eveleigh's astonishment Oglethorpe directed that this delicacy be given to a pregnant woman ''without reserving any for himself.''[49] Whether Eveleigh was irked by Oglethorpe's generosity or whether the latter disliked asparagus is not the point. The important thing is that Oglethorpe, by his gesture, showed a keen awareness of the problems some of his colonists were experiencing in the New World. In Charles Town it was reported that he was ''indefatigable,'' and ''extreamly well beloved by all his People: The general Title they give him, is FATHER.''[50]

With the arrival of spring, hopes ran high. Probably by this time Savannah had begun to show the first feeble indications of a communal life of its own. Cordial relations were established with Tomochichi, who now attended church and asked Oglethorpe to assume the education of his nephew and heir, Toonahowi. Oglethorpe reported that he himself was so popular with the Indians that the Creeks and Uchees had asked him to arbitrate between them.[51] Many of the influential men of the Creeks had come to Savannah to test Oglethorpe's mettle and had stayed to negotiate friendly relations with the province.[52] The natives had been impressed.

A sobering note was sounded when the colony's physician, Dr. William Cox, died ''much lamented'' on 6 April 1733. He was the first of the original shipload of settlers to succumb in Georgia. With the colony still under rigid discipline, Oglethorpe directed Cox be accorded a military funeral. The tithings were called upon and small arms and minute guns were fired with the colony's bell ''constantly toling.''[53] It was an impressive and moving experience but one too often repeated during the subsequent months when the heat and the fevers ravaged Georgia's first settlers.

During May, Oglethorpe was in Charles Town and with

pardonable pride sent a "cask of Seeds ..., some Bear Oyle and some druggs as the first fruits" of Georgia to the Trustees.[54]

With Georgia moving along nicely in the spring of 1733, it might have been the appropriate moment to relax some of a founder's vigilance and let natural forces take over. Instead of working the colonists under close supervision, Oglethorpe might well have given them free rein to see what they could do on their own. Much of the labor done in the early days had been done in common, and partly as a result of forced work schedules and the need to post a watch over the town, individual initiative had been neglected. Many of the colonists had developed a tendency to rely too heavily upon the Trustees for their necessities rather than upon the products of their own labor. Oglethorpe, though he must have been aware of this trend, did nothing to counteract it. He continued to make all the important decisions himself, and it was only after he began to think seriously about his return to Great Britain that he concentrated on the problem of how to establish a local power structure to fill the void when he was gone.

He designated 7 July 1733 as the day when the inhabitants were to come together to witness the implementation of the Trustees' commission to Oglethorpe to appoint the local officials and to constitute a court of record. The court was to be comprised of Savannah's three bailiffs, the recorder, and the registrar of the colony. All civil and criminal matters were to be decided by this body in consultation with a twelve-man jury summoned by the recorder. Additional local officers could be appointed by the magistrates if they saw fit.[55] The judicial body was to go "by the Name and Stile of the Town Court."[56] It was anticipated that the court was to meet at six-week intervals and the English system of petty and grand juries was to be utilized. In Georgia, however, lawyers were forbidden "to plead for Hire." The Trustees as well as Oglethorpe evinced a distinct dislike for the legal profession. It was hoped that the custom would develop, as "in old times in *England,*" where each man would plead "his own Cause."[57] Here Oglethorpe and the Trustees were to be sorely disappointed, for lawyers soon entered Georgia and rendered themselves indispensable to the colonists—much to Oglethorpe's and the Trustees' grief. These unwanted lawyers, acting in concert with the town court, were to try to take over control of Savannah when Oglethorpe left the colony.

As Peter Gordon said in criticism of the inadequate arrangement for local government, control was entrusted to hands that had little or no legal experience. In general, the people of Savannah acquiesced in the court's and the magistrates' decisions "in the litle matters," but on the larger issues they did not always agree, and their only appeal was to the Trustees in Great Britain—a long, costly, and not necessarily rewarding process.[58]

Such dissension undermined what little prestige the court and the magistrates had. When, as Gordon pointed out, the Georgia officials were so inadequately grounded in the workings of English law, how could they be looked upon as "people of concequence enough or suffitiently qualified for so great a trust"?[59] The questioning of the magistrates' decisions was not only a blow to the authority of the colonial officials, but it led to the development of cabals and discontent with Trustee rule.

That Oglethorpe reveled in being the source of power and decision making in Savannah is implicitly clear from his reluctance to share either. Although Oglethorpe complained about having to make all the decisions, the Reverend Samuel Quincy struck home when he wrote the Georgia leader that his attention to minutiae could not properly be called "Hardships" because of "the real Pleasure You took in them."[60] As the only person in the colony with any real experience in legal principles and parliamentary procedure, Oglethorpe could have taken it upon himself to impart to his magistrates a basic knowledge of the problems which, in normal circumstances, they might be expected to face, but he did not. It seems clear that Oglethorpe should have set up a court and put Georgia's officials effectively to work almost immediately, certainly no later than a week after the founding of the original settlement. He could have gradually exposed the magistrates to civil and criminal procedures and a training period might have been provided. Oglethorpe's years in Parliament could have been a sound foundation from which to train these men, and his experiences at Gray's Inn, where he registered in 1729, would have helped give maturity and strength to Savannah's civil structure.[61]

Oglethorpe did not choose to follow this course. He acted a bit impatiently in creating the court from nothing and expecting it to spring full-grown into maturity. Before July he may have felt that owing to the press of time he had no alternative save to rule the colony directly and personally. He should have had the foresight to realize that when he quitted Georgia he would leave the colony with an insecure civil structure. Into this power vacuum it was unrealistic to expect a handful of inexperienced officials to move and govern effectively. But by keeping matters in his own hands and by waiting five months to form a government, Oglethorpe established a precedent for his colonists to look to him rather than to their own officials for redress and direction. Even after the civil government had been created but before Oglethorpe sailed home in May 1734, there was no question whom one turned to for decisions. Oglethorpe was the man; the magistrates and the court were as nothing. Even the dimmest witted of the settlers realized where the real power and authority lay in such a frontier society as Savannah's.[62]

Oglethorpe's shortsightedness and reluctance to share power contributed to the chaos that engulfed Savannah and the settlements around it once the leader's strong hand was withdrawn. The colonists split into factions and the magistrates fell out bitterly, each man contending with the other for popularity. When he returned in 1736 Oglethorpe was shocked by the situation, but he need not have been. He had been largely to blame for it.

2   Frederica and Defense Considerations

Well before leaving America for the first time Oglethorpe was in the process of making up his mind on several points—all essential to an understanding of what Trusteeship Georgia was to become. In May 1733, from Charles Town, he wrote the Trustees that certain eminent Carolina merchants were eager "to hire the Liberty of trading with the Indians in our province." In Oglethorpe's opinion the right to the Indian trade in Georgia was worth about twice as much as the £1,000 sterling suggested by the Carolinians. But he doubted that this right should be sold to just anyone, least of all to non-Georgians. Oglethorpe was hopeful that permanent contacts between the Indians and Georgia traders would bring about a flow of goods that would establish the new colony on a firm financial foundation. With its superior location in relation to Indian country Savannah could develop into a busy trading center and someday outstrip Charles Town. He was not quite sure how to bring all this about, but he concluded that he would not act on the Carolinians' request until he had been home and discussed it with the Trustees.[1]

After observing the Indian trade and colonial society for three months, Oglethorpe became convinced that for his dream of Georgia to be brought to reality, there must be a prohibition on both Negroes and strong drink. Rum would be taboo not only for the average inhabitant, but for all traders who might be tempted to use it in their dealings with the Georgia Indians. Allow rum or Negroes, predicted Oglethorpe, and "our whole design will be ruined."[2] Speculation, debt, and idleness would destroy the ideal of a province of shopkeepers, traders, and yeoman farmers. In Charles Town Oglethorpe had been so importuned by speculators and hangers-on that he was thoroughly sick of them. He revealed to the Trustees that some had

John Lord Viscount Percival, the First Earl of Egmont, as a young man. (Courtesy of the University of Georgia Library.)

Johann Martin Boltzius, minister to the Salzburgers at Ebenezer. From a portrait by Jeremiah Theus. (Courtesy of the University of Georgia Library.)

The Trustees receiving Tomochichi and the Yamacraws at the Georgia Office in London, 1734. Oglethorpe in center, taking message from a page. From a painting by Willem Verelst. (Courtesy of The Henry Francis du Pont Winterthur Museum.)

asked for Georgia lands to bring Negroes onto them; he treated such overtures with the contempt they deserved. Had it not been absolutely necessary to maintain decorum, Oglethorpe darkly remarked, "I should [have] kicked the proposers into the Bargain."[3] If the description of how he handled troublemakers on the *Anne* is accurate, he was capable of doing precisely that, but discretion tempered his ire. He must not jeopardize Georgia's existence by alienating Carolina and, more particularly, her Assembly and governor. With his departure not far off he knew he must rely on Johnson's good will to look after Georgia while he was in London. So he held his tongue and controlled his annoyance. In fact, he worked with the Assembly, entertained the legislators and their wives at a dance and buffet, and helped secure passage of an act to raise £8,000 currency for Georgia from a fund to be collected after 1 December 1733 by a duty of three pence on each gallon of rum imported into South Carolina.[4] For his part, Oglethorpe apparently agreed to take a Carolina representation to England and point out to British officials the problems the older colony faced.[5]

Though outwardly calm, and with the compliments of Charles Town ringing in his ears, Oglethorpe returned to Savannah in June with serious misgivings about the Carolinians. He was also troubled about the future of his own colony, and what he found in Georgia confirmed his belief that his colonists were not wholly to be trusted to determine their own fates. His correspondence began to take on an autocratic tone. A new regimen must be imposed in Savannah, and he, of course, was the one who would make his will felt. The settlers must see that their weak ways could lead to the demise of the colony.

In Oglethorpe's own words, he discovered his people "very mutinous and impatient of Labour and Discipline." They were idle and slovenly because of the presence of Negroes on Georgia soil. To cure that problem he sent the blacks to Carolina from whence they came. As for the lack of discipline, it developed because of the ready availability of rum. In fact "Some of the Silly People" tried to sell their food, provided by the Trustees' store, "for a little Rum Punch." To solve the rum issue he simply forbade it to the settlers and "Staved such as I could find in the Town." Ruefully he noted that rum was available at the

Indian settlement, where he dared not interfere lest he disoblige Tomochichi and his tribe. (Oglethorpe was willing to make the colonists "a moderate Allowance of Wine" to be drawn from the Trustees' supply to divert Savannah's absorption with the stronger drink.)

Oglethorpe honestly believed that the presence of rum in Savannah had caused more than twenty persons to die in less than a month. Before that time only one had died in five months—but that had been when Oglethorpe was there "and kept the People from excessive Drinking." The various "burning Feavers," "bloody Fluxes," convulsions, and other horrors were conquered only with the greatest difficulty. The ministrations of a doctor were essential, but Oglethorpe was convinced his own hawklike antirum crusade played the major role in the decline of Savannah's summer sickness.[6]

Apart from his growing obsession with liquor and blacks, Oglethorpe went about his other chores with undiminished enthusiasm. He was kept so busy "tending the Sick," inspecting the nearby country, "marking out Lands, getting Provisions and Treating with the Indians" that again he complained of not having time to report fully to the Trustees.[7]

Somehow he and his colony made it through the summer and fall of 1733. New settlers came to Georgia, including a group of Jews who were permitted to debark at Savannah only with Oglethorpe's express approval. That they arrived with a doctor on board during the height of the summer illness may have been the determining factor in Oglethorpe's decision to let them land and live in Savannah, for he was aware that Trustee sentiment ran strongly against Jews in Georgia. By the end of the year Savannah seemed if not exactly burgeoning to have recovered from its first setback and to be steadily progressing. As Oglethorpe boasted to the Trustees, "We feed 259 Souls in Town."[8] Savannah reached this degree of development in less than a year "by the manifest Interposition of God." Although the illness in the summer had been severe, the numbers of people who flocked to the town more than offset the losses suffered. To protect his colony militarily, Oglethorpe had located Fort Argyle on the Ogeechee River; had planted

Thunderbolt on the inland waterway; had built roads linking Georgia with the Carolina garrison at Palachuckola; and had established the town of Abercorn at a strategic spot on the river to the north of Savannah. Hampstead and Highgate, on high ground three miles south and inland from Savannah, had been founded with ten families each.[9] Fifty houses stood in Savannah, with others under construction, and a ninety-foot beacon, expected to be the pride of the colony, was being built on Tybee Island to mark the entrance to Savannah harbor. Well might Oglethorpe have bragged. His long December letter to the Trustees may, in fact, mark the apex of his career as colonizer. Georgia was no longer Savannah only, and it seemed to the fond eyes of the founder that the new towns and forts were already successful.

Obviously Oglethorpe and the Georgia leaders intended these galaxy towns to become permanent, but most of them did not survive, for their sites were chosen not because of healthful location or fertility of soil but primarily for military and tactical considerations. In addition, much of the land granted proved to be pine barren or marsh, and it was generally held in those days that where the pine tree did well nothing of real value could be grown.[10] This suspicion seemed confirmed by the discovery that where pines flourished the soil was usually sandy and the Georgia colonists, with little farming experience and lacking appropriate agricultural tools, declined the challenge of the earth.[11]

In any consideration of why so many of these little hamlets failed, Oglethorpe, who would have received the credit had they survived, should also bear the blame. It was he who could not be moved by appeals from the desperate settlers for new land when their original grants proved inhospitable. He claimed that if the Trust once allowed such changes then everyone who was for any reason dissatisfied would be found at the Georgia Board's doorstep. In 1738, for example, in answer to appeals from Highgate, he frankly reported to the Trustees that it was true the settlement there was in an area of pine barren. Still, he said, this land could be "rendered very fruitfull." His arguments against change proved so persuasive that the Common

Council of the Trustees, originally unanimous in favor of new grants, reversed itself completely and voted, with the exception of an exasperated Egmont, to refuse the land request.[12] In retrospect there would seem no better way to sign a death warrant for the village.

The vision of the stern but just founding father meting out justice, establishing towns and forts, and expressing interest in every aspect of his settlers' lives is an attractive one. And all things considered, Georgia seemed to prosper—witness various reports from Charles Town at this time indicating Carolina's fear that a competitor was in the making.[13]

Just as Oglethorpe was about to sail for England in March 1734, he unhesitatingly delayed his departure in order to smooth the way for the first debarkation of Lutheran Salzburgers in Georgia.[14] Henry Newman, secretary to the Society for the Promotion of Christian Knowledge (SPCK) in London, had hoped Oglethorpe would still be in America when the Germans arrived. He was pleased to have the report that Oglethorpe had greeted the exiles in Charles Town and had then "return'd to Georgia to give directions for their better Settlemt."[15]

Oglethorpe helped the Germans reach the chosen location for their settlement, laid out the town of Ebenezer for them, and provided each head of family with "a Sow, a Cow, two Fowls, Ducks and Geese" at the Trustees' expense.[16] His personal concern and involvement in their colony was never forgotten by the Salzburgers. In their rather cloying letters and journals Oglethorpe appears supreme. His "fatherly care," alluded to by Reverend John Martin Boltzius, became a phrase repeated over and over by most of the Salzburgers, though Boltzius soon discovered that he and Oglethorpe had their differences.[17] Oriented toward a paternalistic society, Boltzius and his flock perhaps naturally looked to Oglethorpe for leadership and help when faced with the harsh realities of the New World. In his turn, Oglethorpe valued the support of the frugal, well-organized Germans.

With the end of Oglethorpe's first sojourn in the New World in early May 1734[18] his main work as a colonizer of a nonmilitary province drew to a close. Even the settlement at Augusta, established in 1736, was primarily defensive in nature. The fort there was to protect the Indian trade at the spot inland on the Savannah River where the paths to the Creeks converged. Although he made the original grants himself and hoped Augusta would prove to be the key to the Indian country,[19] Oglethorpe did not visit the settlement until he was returning from his conference with the Indians at Coweta in September 1739, and he may have stopped then only because he was exhausted and ill. He appears to have had complete confidence in Roger Lacy, the soldier he placed in charge of the settlement, but Augusta never captured Oglethorpe's fancy as Savannah did. Augusta seemed, however, to thrive in its obscurity; neglect and virtual autonomy may have been the secret of success on the Georgia frontier. If so, other settlements might have benefited from the same treatment.

Perhaps the most objective and detailed account of the early days of Georgia was given by Peter Gordon before the eager Trustees in London on 27 February 1734. The picture Gordon drew was a favorable one, almost as favorable as the résumé made by Oglethorpe in his December letter.

There were, estimated Gordon, about five hundred people in Savannah of whom one hundred were able to bear arms. Forty houses "were already built of Timber & Clap board, with Shingled roofs," but although Oglethorpe was in charge and by every right should have been living in the best of the houses, he "Still lay in his Tent" on the edge of the bluff. An effective battery had been mounted on the river, a guard house had been built, and there were two strongholds "at the Angles of the town" containing four guns apiece. Oglethorpe was untiring in "building the Town, Keeping peace, laying out land, Supplying the Stores with provision, encouraging the faint hearted &c."[20]

In the physical sense, Oglethorpe found it easy to equate with his settlers. His quarters in Savannah never rose in quality much above the tent he stayed in for so long. Francis Moore described the house Oglethorpe used in 1736 as being the same as the "common Freeholders Houses are, a Frame of sawed Timber, 24 by 16 Foot, floored with rough Deals, the Sides with feather-edged Boards unplained, and the Roof shingled.'' Presumably this house is the one described just over ten years later as "a ruinous Heap" with the chimney recently collapsed. When Oglethorpe occupied it, he had in it "a neat Field Bed," but in 1747 the only items left of the cottage's furniture were "an Old broken Table, & 2 Rush-bottom'd Chairs of no value.'' Rather out of keeping with the modesty of the rest of the appointments were the "yellow damask silk Curtains," which had long since disappeared by 1747.[21]

Oglethorpe had never cared for luxury and show. His home at Godalming, Surrey, was large, but plain. After his marriage in 1744 Oglethorpe spent a good part of the year at his wife's home, Cranham Hall, in Essex, another large but essentially simple country house. Basically a man of austere tastes, he found it no hardship to live as his colonists did or even to sleep out of doors in his cloak. Taking this as an effort by Oglethorpe to share the colonial experience with them, his settlers reacted with approval.

On his return to England, Oglethorpe was at some pains to withdraw his earlier comments that might lead prospective colonists to think that Georgia was the biblical land of milk and honey. He and the Trustees made an honest effort in 1735 to prepare new settlers for some of the nastier realities of life on the southern frontier. Although the new colonists would receive land and a year's provisions free, there might be "great Hardships in the Beginning." The land was uncleared and there would be no adequate shelter until the new settlers could provide their own housing. Each man must take his turn standing guard, and coastal Georgia was accurately described as "hot in *Summer*," with "Flies in Abundance.'' Probably at Oglethorpe's urging a warning was issued that various "Sicknesses were dangerous to those who drank distilled Liquors," and so "Temperance" was necessary for the sake of health as well as prosperity. If moderate, "industrious," and faithful, the settler in Georgia could succeed "in a comfortable Way," but the timid who lacked stamina or stomach were warned "by no means to undertake the Voyage." Some of the faint-hearted backed out, but their places were easily filled by other applicants.[22]

Oglethorpe, in two frank letters to Samuel Wesley, admitted there were problems in Georgia which would delay its maturity. For one thing, the sheer amount of timber made clearing the land laborious and so bringing fields into cultivation would be a slow process.[23] He spoke earnestly when he said that a decision to go to Georgia must be pondered long and hard. The climate, the crossing, "and the want of all Luxuries, and now and then of some necessity," was a consideration that should make men think twice. The "Gnats and Flies which are troublesome to the face" were bad enough, but the worst were the "little red Vermin called Potatoe Lice which in Summer time crawl up the Legs of those that lie in the Woods, and if scratched raise Blisters."[24] The second group of settlers would not cross to America unwarned.

Once more Oglethorpe's leadership on the voyage mixed the best aspects of compassionate concern with determination and authority. At one moment, while the new expedition awaited favorable winds, he wrote the harried accountant of the Trust to procure him a quart of "Daffy's Elixir," a well-known tonic of the day, as medicine was in short supply; at another, a broken "Thernomiter" was forwarded for repair, after which it should be sent on to the colony.[25] In December 1735, when tempers and clean clothes grew short as a result of extended foul weather that continued to delay their departure, Oglethorpe spent fifteen shillings to bring fresh water for the people "to wash up the Linnen they had dirtied during our stay in Harbour." Additionally, Oglethorpe "furnished Flour & Plumbs to make Puddens" in order to vary the monotonous diet.[26] He was offered passage on Captain James Gascoigne's man-of-war, ordered to escort the colonists to America, but he declined by saying he preferred going on the crowded and noisy *Symond* so that he could better "take care of the People" in the crossing.[27] After they finally got under way on 10 December 1735, Oglethorpe showed proper deference to religion by ordering twice daily prayers and by having various ministers (including the brothers Wesley, Benjamin Ingham, and August Gottlieb Spangenberg, minister to a Moravian group on board) dine with him.[28]

The trip, an unusually rough one according to some accounts, passed without serious incident. The landlubber Wesleys and others who left a record of this passage were at least as impressed by Oglethorpe's fairness and effectiveness as they were by the monstrous waves which seemed to threaten immediate destruction for all.[29] Ingham provided the best picture of Oglethorpe, as he constantly encouraged the ill and usually himself ate only "salt provisions, (though not so agreeable to his health)," so that he could "give the fresh to the sick." He was generous with his time as well as his food and often called heads of families together to discuss the subject of "living in Georgia." When a giant wave crashed across the ship and drenched crew and passengers, it was Oglethorpe who gave his cabin, which had remained dry, to the sick while he slept in a hammock.[30] It was considered a good omen that the number of settlers at landing on 5 February 1736, was four higher than the 257 who had originally sailed from England.[31]

When the *Symond* arrived at the mouth of the Savannah River, it was decided that the settlers should remain aboard until Oglethorpe could transport them to the site of Frederica, their new home.[32] Before doing so, however, he had to pay a brief visit to Savannah to see the officials and promulgate the Trustees' laws. From there he sent fresh meat and provisions to the new settlers and even returned himself for three hours to quiet the fears of those who were becoming restless.[33] The embarkation slept on the ship, but during the day the new colonists spent their time recuperating on Peeper (now Cockspur) Island.[34]

Again Oglethorpe had to leave the group, this time to hear the complaints of the first group of Salzburgers, whom he had helped to settle at Ebenezer in 1734. Boltzius, their leader, had found the ground there to be pine barren and earnestly sought permission to move to a better and more promising location. He had written Oglethorpe that the soil at Ebenezer was fit for nothing but "peese and potatoes,"[35] but Oglethorpe strongly advised them to stay where they were—"a sweet place"—rather than run the risk of fevers and illnesses contracted while clearing a new area for settlement. Oglethorpe, Boltzius sarcastically noted, saw the "cows come home" at Old Ebenezer and concluded they should not depart, but the Salzburgers, who had done their best and who could be just as stubborn as Oglethorpe, had made up their minds. In some pique Oglethorpe concluded that they were "only ignorant & obstinate," and so he ungraciously granted permission for the removal to Red Bluff, at the confluence of the Ebenezer River and the Savannah, a location which proved far more suitable than the old site. The confidence in them, though slight and grudging on Oglethorpe's part, was paid off by these diligent workers, who promptly turned New Ebenezer into the most prosperous town in Georgia.[36]

These pressures meant that it was almost a fortnight after their arrival at the mouth of the Savannah that Oglethorpe and the vanguard of his settlers finally landed on St. Simons Island and sketched out the fortified town of Frederica.[37] He marked out a fortress and demonstrated how the ramparts were to be sloped and how the moat was to be dug. Temporary huts or sheds, covered with palmetto fronds, were erected for the main group of settlers, still patiently waiting to be led to the island.

But again Oglethorpe could not give undivided attention to Frederica. He found it expedient on 22 February to leave St. Simons for a hurried visit to the Scots at Darien, and he was delighted by what he found. Hugh Mackay's leadership was exemplary, the fort at Darien was in ready repair, and the Scots themselves presented "a most manly appearance with their Plads, broad Swords, Targets & Fire Arms."[38] Mackay offered Oglethorpe "a very good Bed," but he refused the courtesy, choosing instead to sleep in the open "under a great Tree."[39] His precedent was followed by Mackay "and the other Gentlemen ... tho' the Night was very cold." Apparently as a compliment to the Scots, with whom he got along famously, he had worn a "*Highland* Habit." As he lay "at the Guard Fire, wrapt in his Plad,"[40] Oglethorpe could well take pride in his growing colony. Even before he left Darien a contingent of Rangers arrived from Savannah thereby opening overland communications "for Horsemen between the two Towns."[41] The triangular section of Georgia stretching from Savannah to Darien, bounded by the overland road now being cut and by the settlements along the coast, was now being made secure and strong.

Meanwhile the main body of the 1735-36 embarkation had been in Georgia waters for three weeks, but it must have seemed to the colonists that they were no closer to settlement than ever. Unable to secure a ship large enough with a captain willing to undertake the task of moving them, Oglethorpe returned, on the evening of 25 February, to explain matters to his people. They must, he said, go to St. Simons Island in a number of small boats. He warned that the trip might take up to fourteen days and could be most uncomfortable, and so he offered them an alternative: those who so desired could go to Savannah rather than brave the unknown. He gave the freeholders two hours to make up their minds. It should be considered a vote of confidence in Oglethorpe that Frederica was the unanimous choice.

The little flotilla, with Oglethorpe bringing up the rear in a scoutboat, set off down the inland waterways to St. Simons. He ordered all the ''strong Beer'' to be put on the lead boat and instructed the remaining piraguas to stay as close together as possible. There were no serious problems encountered and the journey was accomplished with dispatch in only five days. After landing on St. Simons and reuniting the settlers, Oglethorpe saw to it that Frederica's streets were marked off, shelters provided, and the fort well under way. He divided the new-comers into parties each with a specific job.[42]

No sooner had the town been laid out than Oglethorpe had to turn his attention to the Spanish menace. Enraged by the Scots' intrusion and then by Frederica, the Spaniards had begun to lay plans to destroy the English position.

Oglethorpe knew that Georgia's southern settlements were too weak to withstand a concerted frontier war. Hence he set out to play for time. The Spanish threat and how to foil it began to absorb most of his waking hours. His career as a colonizer, which seemed at its zenith on St. Simons Island in 1736, was in actuality at its close.

As a colonizer of nonmilitary settlements, Oglethorpe's role during his second sojourn was highly restricted; he often found himself simply encouraging others in work they had begun largely or wholly independently of him. New Inverness, or Darien, for example, had already got its start on the north bank of the Altamaha by the time Oglethorpe returned. It was to prove one of the few lasting towns to be placed on Georgia's soil during the decade when Oglethorpe dominated the colonial picture, but there is no evidence that he alone was responsible for the choice of locations. Indeed, the spot was the one suggested by Governor Johnson for Georgia's original settlement and had been the location of Carolina's Fort King George back in 1721.

Oglethorpe may have finished making new settlements but his ideas of how to establish a permanent colony did not remain static. As domestic strife built up in Georgia, he began to alter his notions of the kind of person who would be the best settler for his colony. After Spain assumed an aggressive posture in 1736, he was strongly influenced by the necessity of defense considerations. A community must first of all be able to ward off attack. The fortified towns of Frederica and Darien, and the little forts being established on the sea islands to the south of St. Simons began to absorb much of his attention. As the international crisis deepened and war with Spain impended, Oglethorpe, who after 1738 had his own regiment with him in America, placed more reliance upon and more confidence in those areas of Georgia best able to defend themselves. This meant an emphasis upon warlike preparedness rather than upon the rough sort of agrarian equality that had been his earlier aim.

Egmont and the Trustees had hoped that each Georgia settlement would become self-contained and self-defending, but it was fairly obvious by 1739 that this aspect of the Georgia experiment had failed. The idea that the inhabitants of Savannah, for example, would leave town in the morning in order to till their forty-five-acre plots in the countryside, return cheerfully at night, and help stand watch in order to keep the community secure may have been feasible in feudal days, but on an eighteenth-century American frontier it was unthinkable. In Georgia the notion died from a whole series of ailments. Much of the nonmarshy land granted along the coast had

proved infertile, Oglethorpe had been reluctant to allow trans-
fers, and there was a shortage of both capital and markets which
might encourage the kind of agriculture that could bring success
to the Trust's ideas—ideas not always thought out to their
logical conclusions.

The threat of invasion and war, however, played the largest
single role in bringing about the demise of many of Georgia's
settlements. The Spanish ultimately failed to destroy Oglethorpe's province, but they might have taken some satisfaction
in the fact that they wrecked his dreams for the creation of a
yeoman-farmer colony on the southern frontier. His ideas of
whom to utilize as new colonists had changed substantially by
1739. German servants, because they were docile, hard-working,
and would not run away, were most desirable. To his colleagues in 1741 he wrote, "send the Germans from Rotter-
dam hither as they do to Pensilvania."[43]

Soldiers were needed too as settlers, especially married ones.
Presumably men with families would have a larger stake in the
colony and would be more willing to fight to save it. Also,
married men did not get into as much trouble as single men.
Oglethorpe, a bachelor himself, asked the Trustees to send over
the wives of the men being recruited for Georgia in 1740.
Leaving their mates behind "plunges them into great difficulties."[44] At a later date, as he awaited the Spanish counter-
thrust following the unsuccessful siege of St. Augustine, he
plaintively repeated his plea: "as I have already mentioned the
greatest services that can be done is to send over married recruits
with industrious wives."[45]

When he began to lean more heavily upon the military to
people and support Georgia, he found himself drifting farther
from the thinking of the Trustees. Oglethorpe's policies,
because of their scope and their cost, were predicated upon the
assumption of large infusions of public money into Georgia.
The Trustees feared that too much reliance upon Parliament
would effectually put them out of business as directors of their
province's destiny. Basically they were correct. As the years
rolled by the government, with its power over appropriations,
wielded more and more influence on the Georgia Board.[46]

In the broad area of colonial theory Oglethorpe offered little new. His concept of a colony and how it should be peopled was first conditioned by his limited experiences in London and by his reading. After going to America and facing the grim possibility that Georgia might not survive, he abandoned his earlier theoretical stance and looked reality in the face. Defense assumed the utmost importance in his mind, and because effective defense implied effective discipline, his attention settled upon those residents of his colony who had proved most reliable: the Germans and the Highland Scots. Both were oriented toward authority—the Scot to his clan and chieftain, the German to his minister.

More than a dozen years after his final return from Georgia, Oglethorpe composed a long and rambling letter to an old friend, Field Marshal James Keith, in which he returned almost nostalgically to his earlier position on colonization. Time had permitted him to forget or his memory to blur some of the miscalculations both he and the Trustees had made. Although he wrote in generalities, it is apparent that his early Georgia enthusiasm had returned. He spoke mysteriously of a colonization scheme he had formulated before Walpole's fall from power, a scheme that would have been "carried into execution," had Walpole survived politically. Oglethorpe's projections "would have established a plantation more advantageous than any England yet has, and which neither France nor any other European power had the least clame to pretence to apose." The area he had in mind was even in 1756 "vacant from Europeans," but Britain had wasted her strength and money on unsatisfactory settlements and had been rewarded by "a ruinous war."[47] He failed to pinpoint the site he had in mind, but it is the revival of his interest that is worth noting. His involvement with Georgia during the last years of Trusteeship control had been minimal and it is difficult to imagine him as anything but disgusted by the Trustees' 1752 memorial defending their position and recommending Georgia to the care of the government just before they surrendered the charter. In this memorial there was not even a passing reference to Oglethorpe and his decade of labor.[48] Four years later this slight had been forgotten; Oglethorpe's confidence had returned.

What can be said of Oglethorpe's career as colonizer and

settler? Measured by most reasonably objective standards Oglethorpe must be accounted successful. His astonishing energy was essential for the Georgia movement to spring to life in Great Britain, and his immense dedication was a quality the colony needed and relied on to meet its various challenges.

Oglethorpe's highest achievement as settler was permanency for Georgia. It may sound simple but this was no mean feat when the conditions under which settlement took place are borne in mind. With the exception of the border with Carolina, Georgia's chartered limits were surrounded by potential enemies. The Indians, Spanish, and French waited for the province to collapse, but though Georgia faltered, she never fell.

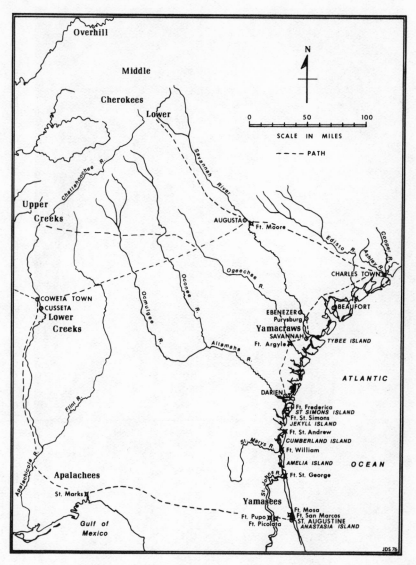

The Georgia frontier during the Oglethorpe years.

1734 View of Savannah, by Peter Gordon, showing the layout of the town, the bluff, and Oglethorpe's tent. (Courtesy of the Georgia Historical Society.)

3   Correspondence and Finances

That Georgia was to pose complex problems for Oglethorpe and the Trustees was not immediately apparent. It is surprising that the originators of the project did not foresee many of the difficulties that were to plague their colony, but even had Oglethorpe known the trials Georgia was to cause him it is doubtful he would have acted differently. He liked a challenge. In Georgia he got one.

When Oglethorpe sailed with Georgia's first settlers, he was praised by all concerned. The Trustees particularly were pleased that he, the leader of the movement, had volunteered to head the first shipload of colonists across the troublesome Atlantic. Britain had been deluged by a wave of Georgia literature, termed by a recent author "the rhetoric of allurement."[1] The number of applicants for Georgia far exceeded the Trustees' expectations, and contributions came to the Georgia Office from all parts of the country. The Trust rode a flood tide of popular approbation. Small wonder the Trustees themselves were so enthusiastic. They had confidence that Oglethorpe would handle with ease any problems that came up.

The Trustees constituted a highly individualistic body. The Common Council, made up of fifteen Trustees, was expected to be a kind of executive committee for the Trust. Each man was keenly aware of his position on the Georgia Board and in the public eye. Percival, newly created Earl of Egmont, Thomas Coram, James Vernon, and a number of others had involved themselves in a prominent and distinguished way in London's and the country's affairs for years. Each had a strong personality and a number of them shared a deep suspicion of Robert Walpole and the Board of Trade. They were determined the Georgia scheme was not to be like so many earlier colonial ventures. With such a group of dedicated workers failure was not to be expected. When the charter expired in 1753 the Trustees would deliver to the king a province fit to be accepted as an equal with Virginia or Massachusetts.

The Trustees did not give Oglethorpe the full power he needed. As an executive in Georgia he was hampered from the start by the fact that he held no official position. He was expected to found, settle, order, protect, and otherwise administer the colony, but without the perquisites of power deemed so important by the eighteenth century. Oglethorpe, as a Trustee, was forbidden, under the charter, to hold office in Georgia, and it is clear that the Board had no intention of letting him completely dominate policy. Georgia belonged to the entire Board and they would exercise the final power.

The Trust quite naturally expected to be kept well informed of the happenings in their province. Considering that the Trustees were men experienced in the ways of the world, it is a mystery why the necessity for a full-time secretary in the colony was not clear from the start. Writing frequent and lengthy letters home was but one more duty expected of Oglethorpe himself.

In the early stages of the colony Oglethorpe was all that could be expected; his letters to the Trustees are clear, detailed, and incisive. But he soon found, to his own irritation and to the increasing dismay of the Georgia Board, that with the growing complexity of his duties there were not enough hours in the day to do all that was expected of him. Less than ten days after Savannah was founded Oglethorpe complained that he was so involved that he could hardly spare the time to write the Trustees at all, but perhaps he would do better once the original problems had been handled.[2] After a hectic summer the situation had not improved, however. He found himself apologizing to the collector and naturalist, Sir Hans Sloane, for failing to send a collection of Americana to him—a sampling from Georgia "agreeable to one of your curiosity." He had waited for the luxury of leisure time, "but Business Still increasing rendered my Attempts the more impossible: therefore I thought it better to write a short Letter than not at all."[3]

Even before 1733 was out Oglethorpe found himself making excuses for not writing Peter Gordon a letter of recommendation to the Trustees. Oglethorpe was "so much hurryed," Gordon reported, "that he hade scarce a moments time to spare." He could not write the Trust on Gordon's behalf, Oglethorpe explained, as he had written no official word "for some months" and if he wrote a letter for Gordon he must obviously report to the Trustees as well. To cover the full spectrum of Georgia affairs would take "more time thane he could possibly spare thene."[4] Even in 1733, with the colony barely underway, Oglethorpe was worried about what the Trust thought of his relative silence—and with justification, for the Trustees were indignant. James Vernon, who expected affairs on the Board to go his way and who, therefore, had frequent clashes with Oglethorpe, took Egmont aside in March 1734 to complain of Oglethorpe's "neglect." As a result of this— Oglethorpe had not written from Georgia since December 1733, and "never once in any full and satisfactory" fashion. The Trustees were "in great ignorance."[5]

Ten days after the Egmont-Vernon meeting, the committee of correspondence of the Trustees drew up a letter to Oglethorpe expressing the group's displeasure. They found themselves "not in a condition" to keep Parliament and interested parties fully informed. If Oglethorpe had not the time to write he was instructed to find a person who did.[6]

Further objections of this nature were successfully stopped by Oglethorpe himself upon his return to England in 1734. His appearances before the Trustees were personal triumphs, and he fielded with authority all questions put to him. The fact that he had brought with him Tomochichi and other friendly Indians probably tended to distract the attention of some Trustees from more searching questions at the time. But they did not entirely lose sight of the desired end of securing a punctual and dependable source of information. Francis Moore was named recorder and storekeeper for the new settlement planned in the southern part of the colony, and he was expected to write the Trustees periodically.

The 1735–36 sailing of Georgia's "great migration" of

Salzburgers, Moravians, John and Charles Wesley, and others was delayed by bad weather and contrary winds. Oglethorpe, who wanted to make sure of arriving in Georgia before it was too late for spring planting, showed his impatience. After waiting for weeks to put to sea, on 20 November 1735 they made a premature effort to sail and were forced back into harbor. The fretful Oglethorpe vowed that he would rather risk destruction at sea than to lose "the season of the year in Georgia."[7] Such rashness hardly speaks well of his judgment. He was, after all, responsible for the entire embarkation, but when one considers how much work awaited him in Georgia it may be easier to comprehend his irritation.

Upon his return to Georgia, in addition to everything else Oglethorpe found himself in the midst of a bitter internecine fight in the Salzburger camp—a fight he was expected to arbitrate.[8] He sent the Trustees an apologetic letter on 28 March saying that since he "cannot write long" he would dispatch a copy of the letter he wrote to Carolina's Lieutenant Governor Thomas Broughton on the question of frontier defense and the Spanish threat. He hoped it would satisfy the Trustees' thirst for information. He would have written Vernon "but could not till three days since spare time to undress myself, and have not lain in sheets from leaving the ships till then."[9]

By late spring 1736, the controversy with the Spanish had reached the point where Oglethorpe had to spend most of his time on the southern frontiers. Considering the urgency of the situation it is not surprising to find Oglethorpe writing the Trustees that owing to the press of events he cannot send "particulars."[10] But "particulars" were just what the Trustees wanted.

In June 1736 he dispatched a long and reflective letter to the Trustees outlining for them the magnitude of the job that had faced him since his return. As he saw it, he had three major matters with which to contend. In the first place, he had to settle the question of the frontiers with Spain without jeopardizing the English position. His letter went into considerable detail on how that had been accomplished. Secondly, "some Merchants of Charles Town" had set the Carolina Assembly against Georgia, and he had yet to find a solution to that problem. Finally, Georgia's various domestic affairs had to be faced, justice administered, the frugal encouraged, the prodigal discouraged, and the wicked shown the error of their ways.[11] This was no easy job, but not so hard as the first two tasks that fell to him. The letter is a plea to the Trustees to try to grasp the complexity of the issues, administrative and otherwise, which kept him too busy to report to the Georgia Board.

Not being actually on the scene and not experiencing the realities of colonial life, the Trustees showed little comprehension of Oglethorpe's dilemma. Like the Trustees, the dispassionate observer can only partly appreciate the work load that prompted this cry from Oglethorpe: "The Day and Night together is not long enough to dispatch the number of trifling things that are here necessary."[12] Moore backed him up by writing that Oglethorpe "is so hurried with business that he has scarce time to eat or sleep."[13] Such remarks were lost on the implacable Vernon, who confided to Egmont that it was his opinion Oglethorpe had forbidden any of the Georgia officials to write to the Board, while he himself sent almost nothing; he kept the Trustees in the dark in order to run the colony as he saw fit.[14]

As he had done earlier, Oglethorpe was able to overcome the opposition when he had a chance, in 1737, to meet the Trustees face to face. Still, they determined upon an administrative reform to improve the governing of Georgia and at the same time provide them with accurate reports. A secretary, William Stephens, was named who would represent the Trustees in Georgia and provide them with a regular source of information. A native of the Isle of Wight and son of Sir William Stephens, who had been the island's lieutenant governor, Stephens had bachelor's and master's degrees from King's College, Cambridge. He had served in Parliament from 1702 to 1722, but then had a series of unfortunate business experiences and at one point even had to flee his creditors. While helping with a survey in Carolina Stephens became acquainted with Oglethorpe and later with Egmont. The quality of his writing particularly commended him to the latter, who was one of the most astute diarists of his time.[15] Stephens, it was discovered, would be glad to go to Georgia, and he received his official appointment from the Trustees in April 1737.[16] Fortunately Stephens did not consider it an ill omen when, as he was coming by boat to Savannah in October 1737 "a Buzzard, weary of flying, came and pitched upon our Bolt-Sprit end," whereupon the bird was shot and killed.[17] Had Stephens been superstitious he might have headed back to Charles Town, but accustomed to trouble (and needing a paying job) he persevered.

Oglethorpe found himself under the usual pressures when he went to Georgia with his regiment in 1738. He had to devote his "unwearied Application" to problems in Savannah and insisted upon going into every tiny point in order to comprehend what was at issue.[18] Much to his dismay, he became enmeshed in the affair of Thomas Causton, the Trust's Savannah storekeeper, who had been guilty at the least of inefficiency and arrogance in distributing the Trustees' stores. To Egmont it appeared that Oglethorpe sought popularity at the Trustees' expense by giving the Savannah inhabitants the idea that he protected Causton. Oglethorpe did treat him with unaccustomed mildness, perhaps because he had been Oglethorpe's own choice for the post.[19]

Whatever the case may be, Causton's books have never been clarified to the point that he could be said to be guilty of questionable practices, as many of his opponents claimed, or simply of financial naiveté. If the latter, then small wonder Oglethorpe, who admitted quite frankly that he himself did "not understand Accounts"[20] sympathized with the store-keeper and wanted to see him given every chance to clear his name.

As the southern frontier drifted into war in the summer of 1739, Oglethorpe was still saddled with the necessity of making dozens of inconsequential decisions.[21] After trying again to have the Trustees understand, he cried out in frustration to them in a letter of 4 July: "it is impossible to explain all things at this Distance."[22] Shortly afterwards he stopped in Savannah on his way to parlay with the Creeks in Indian country and was besieged by all kinds of people and problems. There was, Stephens marveled, "Great Crouding and Hurry of Business" as everyone wanted to get in a word before Oglethorpe set off into the wilderness.[23] The fate of the colony hung in the balance while Oglethorpe prolonged his stay in Savannah to make last-minute judgments on local affairs.[24] In Ebenezer on 18 July, and again desperately trying to escape the local decision making, he was "troubled by a great many Groundless Complaints" from the Salzburg schoolmaster, Christopher Ortmann. Oglethorpe unselfishly, but with no eye toward distinguishing the unimportant from the important, devoted "almost half a Day" to Ortmann.[25] With the Spanish attempting to unravel the threads of Anglo-Indian accord, to spend twelve hours on a petty schoolmaster's petty complaints seems at the least a waste. Later, during his busy trip to Indian territory, Oglethorpe took time to write to Savannah on the issue of criminal justice there.[26]

Oglethorpe was not the only one who was so rushed. Thomas Christie, Savannah recorder, reported to the Trustees: "my life has been a whole Scene of Action since I came into this Collony Insomuch that I have not time to procure my Self the necessaries of life much more write."[27] At Port Royal, even before Savannah was established, Causton groaned that after Oglethorpe gave him the office of storekeeper he was kept so busy that he could not escape from his books and stores long enough to see the South Carolina town at first hand.[28]

In the fall of 1739, a half-sick Oglethorpe returned to Savannah from his talks with the Creeks. Here, in addition to coordinating military measures now that there was war with Spain, Oglethorpe had to review "the publick Proceedings" in his absence. This involved him in investigations centering on two accused murderers, in how to guard against correspondence with the Spanish, and in a dozen minor affairs including organizing a weed-pulling expedition in town (in which he himself helped clear the Savannah Common and "publick Squares").[29] Oglethorpe's "continual Application to regulate every Thing that he thought Expedient" took up almost all of the usually uncomplaining William Stephens's time too.[30] In order to take pressure off himself, Oglethorpe asked Stephens and Thomas Jones, Causton's successor, to substitute for him and write "very full answers" to the Trustees. As he expected hostilities momentarily, he pleaded his inability to write London detailed reports on any subject. He said, with some justification, that he barely had time to compose "the different necessary orders for the Indian Nation, the Rangers, the Garrisons, the Boats and Letters to Carolina, Virginia, the Northern Colonies and Men of War. As the safety and lives of the People and honour of the English Arms" depended upon using every available moment, he hoped the Trust would not be annoyed.[31]

As events moved toward a climax with the Spanish in Florida, Oglethorpe was "so thronged with Affairs of various Kinds" that Stephens could not get proper instructions "how to conduct myself hereafter." Oglethorpe did manage to deliver to Stephens an old packet from the Trustees, dated almost a year earlier, but he failed to bring a box of papers which had lain unread somewhere in Frederica for months.[32] By this time Oglethorpe, who more and more resented Stephens's popularity among the Trustees, had begun to treat the older man, later to become the administrative head of Georgia, rather disgracefully. For example, Stephens noted to the Trustees in August 1740 that he would not presume to report on the fate of the St. Augustine expedition as rumor had been his only informant. From Oglethorpe he had heard nothing.[33] It was well over a month after the withdrawal from Florida that Oglethorpe finally sent Stephens word of his return to Georgia. Upon receipt of the letter Stephens, in his Journal, ironically feigned "much Pleasure, having not had the Honour of any from his Excellency for several Months past."[34]

It is understandable that Oglethorpe could not for lack of time satisfy all the demands made by the Trustees, but to keep the officials of the most important nonmilitary section of his colony in the dark as to his whereabouts was plain negligence, and the situation grew worse rather than better. For over four months during fall and winter, 1740–41, Oglethorpe refused to tell Stephens all that he needed to know.[35] Thomas Jones thought Oglethorpe disliked the secretary because Stephens had a poor opinion of some of Oglethorpe's Savannah friends.[36]

This may have been the case (although Jones himself was a notorious gossip), but the fact still remains that it was unlike Oglethorpe to act in such a fashion.

Similarly Oglethorpe failed to keep Stephens posted on events at St. Simons during the Spanish invasion of July 1742. The Savannah officials too, along with Stephens, expressed amazement at being kept in the dark. Stephens wrote in his Journal that he hoped Oglethorpe had been able to finish off the Spaniards but that owing to the lack of information he had used "Imagination only" to predict victory.[37]

Oglethorpe's behavior in these cases, particularly when he must have known how desperately Savannah wanted reliable news, cannot be defended. Savannah was in a state bordering on panic during the invasion of Georgia. A fever was afflicting the people; a frightening disease was striking and killing the cattle. Some citizens had fled, and the women and children had been evacuated to Ebenezer where they would be out of harm's way.[38] Still Oglethorpe failed to send a reassuring word to his once-favored town.

By March 1743, Stephens was at his wit's end. Apparently he made an overture to one of Oglethorpe's German servants suggesting they correspond so that Stephens could get an inkling of what was taking place in Frederica. When Oglethorpe heard of this he lost no time, for once, in writing Stephens to let him know that he resented the intrusion into his affairs. His specific permission must first be granted before any such correspondence could be initiated, he said, and he made it plain that what he did was none of Stephens's business. He darkly included "other Cautions" and let Stephens know that he considered the effort to look into Frederica affairs little short of meddling.[39]

Oglethorpe's chronic weaknesses as a correspondent, however, were not primarily the result of such whims or jealousies. More important was his inability to do everything he thought he could in the time allotted. He tried and failed, and proved to be so victimized by overconfidence and so jealous of his authority that he was unable to admit defeat. The problem was one of personality, but it also highlighted a major administrative fault:

Oglethorpe did not know how to delegate authority. And the Trustees in general exhibited the same weakness.

Oglethorpe's handling of the financial aspect of his administrative duties in Georgia was, as far as the Trustees were concerned, nearly disastrous. It had been anticipated that he would incur certain unforeseen expenses in America; after all, the Board could not think of *every* contingency. But the more the perplexing world of credits, drafts, and bills of exchange is examined, the more it becomes apparent that Oglethorpe knew little of finances and learned to care less. He spent Georgia's money liberally, and although he was constantly lectured by the Trustees, many of them experienced businessmen, he paid them little heed. Finally, when both the Trust's credit and its patience seemed exhausted and the government appeared reluctant to underwrite the Georgia experiment further, Oglethorpe in a grand gesture put up his own personal assets as security against expenses. He spent money as though, contrary to fact, he had enjoyed unlimited quantities of it all his life. (His basic generosity as well as his lack of understanding of finance helps explain why his wife, the heiress Elizabeth Wright, with whom he made a fortunate alliance in 1744, handled the family financial affairs.)[40]

An indicator of how vague the Trustees were when it came to the expenditure of money in their colony was the fact, hard to believe, that Oglethorpe was not specifically empowered to fall back on the Trust should the financial situation in Georgia make it necessary. Lacking directives or, for that matter, even power over finances in Georgia, he was thrown upon his own resources to handle unforeseen expenses as best he knew how. Not having the necessary cash, Oglethorpe began to draw on the Trustees for bills of exchange. When these bills were first presented, the Common Council accepted them without demur,[41] but it was Oglethorpe's failure to return vouchers along with the drafts that began to bother the Trustees and, finally, played a large role in bringing about his return to England in 1734.[42]

In addition to his ominous remark to the Trust early in 1733 that he was "obliged to make many expences" of an unexpected nature in Savannah,[43] his free-spending proclivities seemed to grow with the colony. As one early example, Oglethorpe contracted with Captain James McPherson of the South Carolina Rangers to construct for £200 currency a stronghold to be called Fort Argyle on the Ogeechee River. When the fort was half finished it was discovered that fallen trees had blocked passage of the river below the fort's location, whereupon Oglethorpe ordered the structure abandoned and picked another site ten miles downriver. He generously credited McPherson with £50 currency "for the Work already done" and proudly proclaimed in September to the Trustees that the fort was completed and ready against all comers.[44]

Less than two months later he wrote the Trustees saying he realized they would be appalled to hear of significant new disbursements, but prices in South Carolina had skyrocketed, the Georgia crops had failed, and he had found it necessary to issue more drafts to pay for the labor of Negro sawyers who had been in Savannah earlier. Expenses in Charles Town for the Trustees' garden were unavoidable, as was the additional money paid out for the encouragement of silk production. Finally, he said he had thought it wise to set up a system of prizes and awards to give the people of Savannah a lift in spirits.[45]

While Oglethorpe was in England, Vernon and his friends made an effort to clarify the financial situation by securing the right for the Trust to issue £4,000 in bills of exchange. Called sola bills, they were to be used by Oglethorpe in America for expenses he would incur after he returned there. If properly handled these bills, when presented to the Trustees in London, would be made good. Supposedly Oglethorpe would no longer need to make other drafts on the Trustees.[46] But he did, and his expenses were particularly heavy in 1736–37 when it was feared that war with Spain would break out at any minute. The economy-minded Trustees were dismayed.[47]

Although Oglethorpe promised to mend his financial ways, he resorted to the same scatter-gun spending that had been typical of his first stay in Georgia. Since he had a total of about £5,000 in cash and bills with him, it is understandable that Egmont and the others were "extremely displeased" when, instead of utilizing what he had at his disposal, Oglethorpe began once again to "draw upon us."[48] The Trustees decided on a strong step: it must be publicized in London and Carolina that Oglethorpe's unauthorized bills would no longer be accepted by the Georgia Office. It was a necessary move, Egmont rationalized, for without it, there might be no end to the financial drain. It was clear that neither Oglethorpe nor Causton understood the reality of the situation.[49]

In the summer of 1736 the Trustees refused to accept a £500 bill of exchange drawn on them by Oglethorpe. Egmont thought it exorbitant when he found the money would ultimately be used at military positions beyond Georgia's chartered limits. Bills for such expenses should be sent to the government. It was too bad the protest charge of 30 percent would fall on Oglethorpe, but he had brought the difficulty on himself by "going too near the Spaniards."[50] When Samuel Eveleigh, the merchant to whom the money was owed, discovered that the Trustees had refused the bill, he was incredulous. Oglethorpe had simply picked up a store of guns and cloth to thwart the Spaniards, who had been angling to get them. Had Oglethorpe sat by idly and let the enemy make the purchase, he would have enabled Spain to take an important step in implementing plans to invade and destroy Georgia.[51] The gossip in London had it that the Trust, by refusing Oglethorpe's bills drawn in America, "will blast his credit in Carolina, where they are already sufficiently exasperated." If the Spaniards now "fall upon and Swallow up Georgia," Oglethorpe will have good reason to resent the Trustees' actions and "reflect upon poor Sir Walter Raleigh's unhappy case when he was betrayed and given up to the Spaniards."[52] Even his colleagues and associates on the Board, wrote John Wesley, refused Oglethorpe's bills and accused him of mismanagement of funds. Have strength, he counseled, God will protect the just![53]

Although Oglethorpe was ultimately able to have Eveleigh's bills accepted by the Trustees, they had even less confidence in his financial abilities after this episode. And their faith was hardly strengthened by the receipt in July 1737 of a bill for £915 for Madeira wine—called by Egmont, with some justice, "a prodigious article."[54]

By 1738 it was apparent that a reorganization of Trustee finances was in order. Causton must be dismissed and expenditures must be cut to the bone with all "expenses of a military nature" eliminated. The colony was coming under increasing criticism in Parliament; appropriations for warlike purposes would have to come from the government with the Trustees in no wise being responsible for the pay and upkeep of Oglethorpe's regiment, then being raised in England to defend Georgia from the Spanish. Indian gifts had to be slashed, amicable relations must be restored with Carolina, and no more bills were to be drawn on the Trustees. Oglethorpe, in London when these decisions were made, apparently boycotted the meetings of the Trust, saying to Harman Verelst, the Trust's accountant, that he wanted no part in cutting the expenses of the colony.[55]

Although Oglethorpe and Vernon, friendly antagonists through much of the period, had "some warm words," with Vernon suggesting that Oglethorpe look to the military situation while the Trustees handled all the rest,[56] Oglethorpe made a sincere effort to keep civil expenditures in line on his return to Georgia. He emphasized, however, how hard a job it would be. "I shall strive," he wrote Trustee Thomas Tower, "to do all I can to prevent the people from starving, without giving any demand upon the Trust, till their farther Orders."[57] He complained of the "great difficulties" he met in Georgia, particularly the "mouths to feed, empty Magazines and no Money."[58] The colony was in a deplorable state, threatened with collapse and ruin. Perhaps to shame some of the more niggardly of the Trustees, Oglethorpe mentioned that he had used a good deal of his own money in Georgia but that this did not matter for he would rather "lay it out in supporting the Colony . . . than in any other Diversion."[59] By spring 1739, Oglethorpe had already spent about £2,000 of his personal capital, had drawn numerous bills on Verelst for his own account, and "ordered all my Cash, Pay and Salary & appointments . . . to answer those Bills" that had accumulated in the five months since his arrival.[60] The "delightfull Situation" in which he had earlier found Georgia—in debt, defenseless, without supplies, devoid of money or credit, and with "muti-

nous Soldiers to command"—had been alleviated temporarily.[61] His own fortune, however, could only be a stopgap; the
expenses of a hotly contested frontier must be borne by the
government.

The government did just that. During the Trusteeship period
Parliament granted in the neighborhood of £136,000 to be
expended in Georgia, a move that had "no precedent in British
imperial history." Because of its charitable overtones and
exposed position, the colony was considered unique and was,
therefore, supported by public as well as private monies. The
Trustees found themselves relying upon these parliamentary
grants and becoming progressively more dependent upon that
body. The yearly requests for funds, which always proved the
occasion for questions in Commons, came to seem demeaning,
but a motion to have an automatic annual grant made to the
Trustees was unsuccessful.[62]

By fall 1739 the financial status of the colony was in doubt,
and the Trustees' stores were closed because of the bind in
which the Trust found itself. More important in creating general
confusion was the reality of war with Spain and the continuing
divergence of the ideas of the Trust from those of its representative in America. To the former it seemed irresponsible to spend
money at the rate Oglethorpe did, whereas to Oglethorpe it
seemed foolhardy to pinch pennies when the future of the
colony was at stake. As the Trust continued to urge economy,[63]
Oglethorpe did what he felt had to be done to keep Georgia
secure.

His attitude, as usual, was difficult to predict. In the very
midst of the war and the excitement attendant thereon, he
wrote that because of the "great damp upon Planting," he
thought it best to encourage crop production by placing "a
bounty of two shillings per Bushell upon Indian Corn and
pease, and one shilling for Potatoes" in the Savannah district.
He frankly admitted he had no idea what such a bounty would
cost the Trustees, but he supposed some of the cost would be
balanced against the grower's debts to the Trustees' store. In the
administration of the bounty fraud would be impossible as the
crop must first be observed growing in the fields, and once

harvested it would be properly measured.[64] Apparently he was wholly oblivious to the administrative detail and incredible complexity, not to mention the expense, that such a plan would cause if it was to be thoroughly implemented. Such muddle-headedness must have been maddening for some of the Trustees; the looks of dismay as they read this news can only be imagined.[65]

The Trustees indeed had reached the end of their patience. With Egmont trying vainly to moderate, Oglethorpe was told that the Trust was highly displeased. He spent too much money; his estimates were often too low; "some of his schemes and dispositions" he had been "too tenaceous to abandon"; and he had overrated Georgia's ability to get money from Walpole. In anguish Egmont wrote, "God knows, we were now almost entirely sunk in our credit."[66]

The next step, taken in January 1740, which "totally excluded Genl Oglethorpe from handling our money," was a logical outgrowth of the dissatisfaction that had been building since 1733.[67] The Savannah officers, Stephens, Christie, and Thomas Jones, were now empowered to look to "defraying the estimated expenses of Georgia."[68] The Georgia magistrates were sent "peremptory orders" to follow the Trust's instructions without waiting, hat in hand, for Oglethorpe's "pleasure."[69]

After January 1740 Oglethorpe's civil and fiscal powers were restricted on paper to a relatively narrow sphere. His pride was hurt by this slap from his peers in London. As Stephens, who had felt the whiplash of the founder's anger, explained to the Trustees, Oglethorpe's "Honour will admit of no Stain."[70] But he had largely himself to blame. His slipshod administrative procedures and his tendency to ignore the orders of the Trustees or to interpret them to suit his purpose were traits that could bring no credit in either the civilian or the military establishment.

4   Rum and the Indian Trade

Part of the duty of a colonial administrator was to introduce regulations or laws and see to their enforcement. Not instructed by the Trust and lacking experience, Oglethorpe did what he thought best in this administrative category. Owing to his restricted powers, the legitimacy of his actions during his first stay in the colony might have been questioned. His policies, however, went unchallenged. In Egmont's words, when Georgia's government was being set up the Trustees "were not particular in establishing the constitution, because up till we come to that the laws of England take place."[1]

As the colony grew more complex, and as new villages were created, it became obvious that in addition to local ordinances and restrictions, Georgia as a province needed laws applicable to all her settlers. An elected colonial assembly was out of the question as far as the Trustees were concerned, but Georgia must have regulations and it was up to Oglethorpe and the Georgia Board to frame them. But the Trustees, jealous of their power, feared that if they passed many "laws" in the traditional manner the Privy Council and Board of Trade would utilize their right of legislative review. If Georgia as a white, yeoman-farmer-oriented colony was ever to evolve, however, this desired ideal must be expressed on the statute books. On Oglethorpe's recommendation, three acts were passed by the Trustees and given final approval by the crown in April 1735.[2] It was hoped these measures would bring Georgia into being as the sort of colonial outpost the philanthropists, imperialists, and reformers at the Georgia Office most wanted. No more acts were passed by the Trustees during their tenure. They relied upon ordinances and regulations to make their feelings felt.

As Oglethorpe saw the situation, a series of interrelated threats seriously menaced the creation of the kind of Georgia he envisioned. These were Negroes, strong drink, Spaniards and Frenchmen, and Indians—in this or any order. If Negroes were prevented from entering the colony, the limited size of the land grants would be more palatable. Each head of family would till his own soil, perhaps with his own labor bolstered by a white servant or two. The Spaniards would thus be deprived of a deadly weapon, for the Negro was viewed as a willing insurrectionist. If slavery and black labor were prohibited in Georgia, the preconceived idea of what the colony *should* be would come one step nearer realization.

Rum was another danger to which Oglethorpe wanted everyone alerted. This vicious liquid could drain Georgia to the point where she might be unable to resist incursions by even the weakest of her enemies. It was rum, Oglethorpe reported, that had been responsible for the disaster he had found in Savannah in the summer of 1733 upon his return from Charles Town. Many settlers died during this first seasoning period, and he laid the blame on the colonists' easy access to rum.

This baneful drink was not only a scourge for the white man, it was debilitating to the red man as well. Over and above any theoretical objection to strong drink lay a very practical point: Georgia was not only the newest of the English colonies, she was also the most exposed. She was at the mercy of the natives by whom she was surrounded, and the point had been made to the Trust that the abuse of rum as an item in the Indian trade caused "great disorders" among the red men.[3] This was just the sort of thing the Georgia Board wanted to avoid.

The result of Oglethorpe's effective campaign in London during the early months of 1735 was the passage of acts prohibiting the entry into Georgia of Negroes, forbidding the use of "Rum or Brandys nor any other kind of Spirits or Strong Waters" in the confines of the colony of Georgia,[4] and, perhaps the most important bit of Trustee legislation, regulating the Indian trade.[5] In their determination that Georgia should not develop into another South Carolina, the Trustees tried to profit from the mistakes made by the older colony. It was generally understood not only that slavery and the large numbers of Negroes had led to dire problems there but that speculation and the haphazard system of land development had retarded Carolina's growth and made it hard for her to defend herself. By forbidding Negroes' entry to Georgia, in addition to the already restricted amount of property the average man might own there, the Trustees hoped to avoid these flaws in their colony.

The legislation concerning rum and the administration of the Indian trade also bore directly on the settlement and defensibility of the colony, for Oglethorpe knew that the key to Georgia's immediate future lay with the Indians. If they could be firmly allied to the British interest Georgia would be safe. The best way to assure the colony of the natives' friendship was to make certain they were treated fairly, and the only way to do this was for the colony to control and police the Indian trade responsibly and firmly. Georgia could not afford to have Indian affairs go against her.

The legislation passed by the Georgia group in London also indicated the mild reform interests of the Trustees. The antirum sentiment, for instance, was at least partly a reflection of the horror with which most Londoners looked upon public drunkenness. William Hogarth's etchings of contemporary London, such as the graphic *Gin Lane*, say more than words can express, and even Parliament, under Sir Joseph Jekyll's leadership, had stepped into the picture by passing the Gin Act.[6] The Negro prohibition, aside from the practical motivations that recommended it, was an example of the benign and limited antislavery feelings of the day, and no one in public life epitomized this sort of philanthropy better than James Oglethorpe, even at this time the patron of the freed slave Job Ben Solomon.[7] In an eloquent letter Oglethorpe later implored his associates on the Board to resist proslavery pressures: "if We allow Slaves, we act against the very Principles by which we associated together, which was to relieve the distressed." Give in, he continued, and we shall "occasion the misery of thousands in Africa" by enslaving thousands who live free there now.[8]

In spite of the contentions of numerous historians that the slave prohibition was dictated by economic considerations,[9] there was a strong element of humanitarianism apparent among the Trustees. This sentiment, relatively powerful at first but waning toward the end of the Trusteeship period, was the legacy of the Associates of Thomas Bray to the Georgia Board and is most clearly reflected in the anniversary sermons preached yearly before a combined meeting of the Trustees and the Bray Associates. As the years rolled by, the charitable and humanitarian purposes of the colony became sublimated and the positions of the ministers and reformers were filled by merchants and members of Parliament who were more interested in the pound sterling than in social issues. Ultimately, though not without a fight of significant proportions, Georgia's Negro ban was revoked.

As for the Georgia Indian Act, it too can be viewed as attempted reform, again reflected best in Oglethorpe. His admiration and respect for the natives were not just for show; his rather patrician and fatherly approach to their problems mirrored a sincere desire to treat them fairly. On the other hand, his policy toward them was predicated upon the practical realization that the Indian trade must be carefully watched and controlled.

As for the specifics of the legislation, the Rum Act forbade importation into the colony of any strong drink. When barrels of liquor were seized, they were to be "Staved and Spilt," and the offending importer proceeded against accordingly. Colonial voices such as Governor Thomas Penn's, who said rum added to water, especially during the American summertime, was absolutely indispensable,[10] went unheeded.

The Indian Act, complementary to the Rum Act and passed at the same time, was a detailed piece of legislation. Its main burden was to secure authority for Georgia over the trade carried on between British subjects and the Indians in the province. The act stipulated that those who wished to trade must go yearly to Savannah, pay a fee to the appropriate official for a license, and post bond that they would observe the rules and regulations of the colony. Rum was, naturally, to be taboo in the Indian trade, with violators running the risk of losing not only their bonds but their licenses as well. The act provided for a Georgia

Indian commissioner who was to supervise the trade in the colony. He was to have an agent to go out among the tribes to oversee the general situation of each, expel wrongdoers, and report to the commissioner on his findings.[11] Oglethorpe, to no one's surprise, was designated the first commissioner.[12]

Curiously, the Trustees used the Carolina Indian Acts of 1731 and 1733 as their models when framing the Georgia legislation.[13] Charles Town was not flattered, however, for the Carolinians feared that Georgia, a colony they had fostered, would try to dominate the Indian trade of the southern frontier.

As for the Negro Act, after 24 June 1735 entry into Georgia of "any Black or Blacks Negroe or Negroes," was forbidden. An offender could be fined £50 "Sterling Money," and if blacks were discovered in Georgia after the above date, they were to be seized by the Trustees' agents "and disposed of" as the Trust thought fit. Provision was made for return of runaway slaves to Carolina or to any other plantations.[14]

As though in 1736 Oglethorpe were not laden with enough responsibility in settling Frederica, soothing Salzburgers, calming Savannahians, and reassuring the skeptical Spanish, he now had the additional burden of introducing the Trustees' Rum, Negro, and Indian Acts and making them work. In many ways these regulations were the quintessence of Trusteeship Georgia. If they failed, then Georgia did too.

Even before Oglethorpe returned to America in February 1736, the controversy with Carolina over the Indian trade and the rum prohibition waxed hot. Thomas Causton, left in charge when Oglethorpe returned to England in 1734, had taken it upon himself to see to it that Carolina rum would no longer be unloaded at Savannah. He and the colony's recorder, Thomas Christie, seized and themselves staved two barrels of the liquor belonging to a Carolinian by the name of Morgan. The latter said that the content of the barrels was "Cyder" only, but inspection proved otherwise. So Causton and Christie acted. They tempered discipline with mercy, however, for when Morgan pleaded "his Poverty" he was permitted to carry his remaining four barrels back to Charles Town.[15] This burst of energy on the part of Causton and Christie may have been the result of a letter to the Trust from a critic of the two magistrates who pointed out that those responsible for enforcement of the rum prohibition in Savannah were actually "the furthest from it." In fact it was claimed that "their is hardley twenty Houses in the town but what doth Sell Rum and allso other Liquors." Causton winked at violations; Christie dispensed not only rum but also "other Liquors by Retail Even by Qrts."[16] With Oglethorpe expected to return at any time, bringing with him the official Rum Act and a stern countenance to match, Causton and Christie might have felt it wise to crack down lest they run the risk of incurring Oglethorpe's famous temper.

The rum-staving episode ruffled Carolina-Georgia relations, but it was rivalry over the trade of the Indians in the back-country that caused a serious confrontation between the two colonies. Hardly had Oglethorpe left for England in 1734 than Patrick Mackay, who had been designated both Georgia's and South Carolina's agent with the Creeks, began to be a cause of controversy.[17] Mackay had received his post with the older colony as a gesture of harmony by Governor Johnson, but incident piled upon incident to the point where finally Mackay was forced out.

The issue centered on the licensing of traders to the Creeks and the Choctaws. Carolina trading interests were especially alarmed by the Choctaw question. For years unsuccessful efforts had been made to lure that tribe to parlay in Charles Town. But now Thomas Jones, sent by Oglethorpe to Choctaw territory, per-suaded these Indians to treat with the British in Savannah. The Choctaws showed interest in having a trading path opened between them and Georgia. Mary Musgrove jubilantly wrote Oglethorpe that all this was "more than ever Carolina could do."[18] Mackay thereupon claimed for Oglethorpe and Georgia the right to license traders, including those from Charles Town or elsewhere, to the Choctaws.[19]

In November 1734 the Carolina Assembly, over the violent objection of Sam Eveleigh, passed a new Indian Act. Not only was the fee for trade licenses increased, but an extraordinarily heavy duty was levied on "every skin and furr" handled.[20] Eveleigh predicted that such discriminatory tactics would drive the South Carolina traders into the waiting arms of the North Carolinians or the Georgians. Palpably, Eveleigh said, the act was aimed at himself and a few others who would now refuse to take out their licenses in South Carolina and would turn instead to Georgia.[21] It is not clear what was happening in South Carolina during this affair, but apparently Eveleigh's enemies were ganging up on him. It may be that he had been too pro-Georgia for some of his rivals and they were using this measure to enter areas of the trade where he had previously been dominant.

Meanwhile, Mackay had problems with the Carolina traders in the Creek country. He noted that because Carolina felt the trade slipping away, she was "Indifferent" to its regulation. Consequently anyone who wanted a license in Charles Town was given one, the result leading to bitter competition, cheating, loss of trade, and a possible "Rupture" in Indian relations. Furthermore, large amounts of rum were being introduced among the Indians. Mackay hoped the Trust would consider and clarify the situation which, if left to drift along, could only become more chaotic and dangerous.[22]

Governor Johnson, sympathetic all along to Georgia and to Oglethorpe, had cooperated in every way he could concerning the handling of the Indian trade.[23] He "regarded unified trade regulation as a necessity" and was no special friend to the vested Carolina trading interests. But Johnson died in May 1735 and was succeeded by his harsh and undiplomatic brother-in-law, Thomas Broughton.[24] The new governor was in favor of a confrontation with Georgia over the trade and, in retrospect, it seems as though he set out deliberately to worsen relations between the two colonies. His friends and allies, the merchants, cheered him as he determined to thwart Georgia's bid to control trade once dominated by the Carolinians.

During the summer of 1735, Mackay began to proceed against traders in the Creek country who did not possess licenses taken out in Savannah. Not unexpectedly, important Carolinians such as John Fenwicke of the Council feared Mackay might be too inexperienced to deal with the Creeks or with French influence in the area.[25] But it was Broughton who finally took the offensive in efforts to secure Mackay's downfall and, by so doing, to topple the Georgia Indian Act as well. Memorials and affidavits of Carolina traders who had been evicted from Indian country piled up before the Carolina Council, and in June Fenwicke sent a strong letter full of objections to Mackay.[26] In the following month, Mackay was in Savannah, where he rejected some license applications from Carolinians but accepted others. Those who were turned down went to Charles Town to secure South Carolina permits, but Mackay promised to expel them from the Georgia Indian territory if he discovered them there without the necessary authorizations.[27]

Once they saw how the wind blew from America, the Trustees concluded that in the interests of harmony Mackay must be replaced,[28] but the dismissal of the agent did not satisfy Broughton, whose aim all along had really been to have the Georgia Indian Act completely voided. In the end South Carolina sent a remonstrance to the Board of Trade in London.[29]

Oglethorpe returned to America early in 1736 and on 14 February sent copies of the Georgia Indian Act to Savannah Town, a Carolina trading post up the Savannah River across from the future site of Augusta. From that point the news of the specifics of the Georgia act was to be sent into Indian country; all traders there "must give Security for their good Behaviour."[30] Oglethorpe determined that the Indian and Rum Acts, interrelated as they were, must both be enforced. The decision precipitated a crisis with Carolina that did not cool off until after Broughton's death in 1737. But before that time and with his encouragement South Carolina passed an ordinance indemnifying any Carolina trader who might have suffered seizure of property at the hands of Georgia officials.[31] A committee from the South Carolina Assembly met with Oglethorpe in Savannah on the question of Indian trade and allied problems between the colonies.[32] They reached a compromise,[33] but the terms seemed to give Oglethorpe too much influence and discretionary power to suit the Carolinians. On 18 September 1736, anti-Georgia feelings were given a boost when the latest Indian-trader atrocity story was trumpeted by the *South Carolina Gazette*. A man licensed from Carolina, who was doing business more than one hundred miles from Georgia, had his store broken open and his "Goods and Skinns ransackt, seiz'd and taken" by the Georgia agent to the Cherokees, Roger Lacy. The Carolina trader was ordered to leave Cherokee country in four days or be carried off to Georgia and imprisoned.[34] Or so said the *Gazette*.

Ultimately the Carolinians, who feared that Georgia's superior location in relation to Indian country might have an effect, published separately the findings of the committee that had met with Oglethorpe in the summer of 1736.[35] Georgia's Indian Act was branded unconstitutional and Oglethorpe was denounced as having gone back on his word by meddling in Indian territory—something he said he would not do, at least until Georgia's limits were positively determined.[36]

Sirmans's work on colonial South Carolina concludes that relations between Georgia and Carolina had sunk to this low point because "Broughton's actions must be regarded as a deliberate attempt to sabotage the negotiations with Oglethorpe." Broughton was motivated, perhaps, by the fear that Oglethorpe had many friends, especially among the planter element, in the South Carolina Assembly. The compromise reached between Oglethorpe and the Assembly as a result of their meeting in Savannah, then, might prove "unacceptable to the merchants" whose spokesman Broughton was.[37] There is no doubt that Carolina feared a loss of trade revenues should Oglethorpe succeed in establishing Georgia's control in Indian territory. As Joseph Wragg, prominent Charles Town merchant, frankly stated, he was "very apprehensive of looseing our trade, with the Indians for deer skins, which is the most valuable." Already a number of traders had taken out licenses in Savannah "for fear of Ruin by haveing all their effects in the Indian nations seized, and forfeited, their persons imprisoned, and fined."[38] Speeches were made and appeals sent to the Board of Trade.

Appeals before various government bodies in England provided something of an anticlimax to a struggle that threatened more than once to break into violence between advocates of the two colonies in the disputed Indian country. The Board of

Trade heard South Carolina's petition in September 1737 and reported in favor of the Carolinians. The colony should be permitted to trade with Georgia Indians by licenses granted in Charles Town under terms of Carolina's Indian Act, and there should be no interference with trade and navigation on the Savannah River unless there was certain knowledge that rum was to be landed where it was forbidden.[39] Fearing emasculation of their act, the Trustees appealed to the Privy Council against Broughton and his Assembly for obstructing Georgia's legislation. To the satisfaction of the Georgia partisans, the earlier South Carolina ordinance of indemnity, a sort of insurance policy for Carolina traders should they suffer damages in the backcountry at the hands of Georgia officials, was disallowed. The Council suggested, however, that both provinces construct new Indian acts. In the interim Georgia was to grant licenses to all Carolinians who applied, with the Charles Town officials bearing the responsibility that such men be honest and law abiding.[40]

By its March 1738 decision the Privy Council thus strongly recommended compromise, and after this the controversy over the Georgia Indian Act cooled off noticeably. For one thing, Broughton died and Samuel Horsey, who owed his appointment to the patronage of Oglethorpe and the Trustees, was named his successor.[41] Georgia's plans to reconstruct amicable relations with Carolina based upon the proper enforcement of the Georgia Indian Act were then frustrated by Horsey's sudden death in August 1738.[42] James Glen, who followed Horsey, proved to be refractory, but he did not go to his post until 1743. Consequently Oglethorpe was left to conduct Georgia–South Carolina Indian affairs with the new lieutenant governor, William Bull. The two men had been friends since Oglethorpe's first arrival in America and agreed on most questions. Bull let Oglethorpe handle Indian as well as military affairs, and when war with Spain loomed, the situation had moderated to the point that the provinces could cooperate wholeheartedly against the mutual enemy.

War disrupted the peaceful flow of trade to and from the English colonies and the Indian country. The competition between Georgia and Carolina over that trade was all but over by that time. Although Oglethorpe had won the admission from Bull that he was "best able" to handle Indian affairs,[43] it was apparent that Georgia as a colony had not lured the Indian trade from Charles Town.

It would appear in retrospect that prosperity, if it was to come quickly to Georgia, must be based on a large and lucrative Indian trade. Oglethorpe must have known that the various restrictions—such as the prohibition of rum, a prime commodity in trade with the Indians—would keep Georgia from becoming an economic rival to South Carolina, but if he *did* understand this, he kept his comprehension disguised. Eveleigh, who had a reasonable plan to make Georgia strong through trade, was rebuffed at every turn. Ironically, at almost the same time that the Trustees were trying to repeal their ill-conceived Rum Act, Oglethorpe was imploring them to keep it in force.[44] Ten years had gone by since his first colonial experience, and his notion of that old devil rum had changed not at all. Instead of viewing controlled rum imports—or even production of the liquor—as having possibilities for the Georgia economy, he stressed the colony's image. To permit rum "would destroy the Troops and labouring people" just as it was doing in Jamaica and Cuba. Rum would give Georgia "a reputation of unhealthiness."[45] It is hard to say what sort of reputation Oglethorpe thought Georgia already possessed.

A complete repeal of the Rum Act just might have breathed life into the Georgia economy and made her eventually a rival of South Carolina. Several factors militated against this, however. The Trustees and the Board of Trade were at loggerheads concerning repeal and jurisdiction, but more important is the fact that the dominant figure of Oglethorpe was to leave the American scene shortly. No one of his stature remained in the colony or among the Trustees who might mold the situation into a favorable one for Georgia.

It is clear that Oglethorpe knew pathetically little about trade, as well as about economics and finances in general. Even lumber in the form of clapboards, shingles, staves, and the like, used by most new colonies in their earliest days to get on their economic feet, was ignored as somehow an unacceptable product upon which to build trade. Pine, oak, bay, ash, and all the others were, to Oglethorpe, simply obstacles to be cleared before his settlers could begin growing their vines and cultivating their silkworms. When the colonists had been in America for some time and could "live comfortably," then would be the time "to think of Exports."[46] He stressed the importance of olive oil, silk, and wine, but on the question of where the goods and capital were to come from to make everyone comfortable Oglethorpe was mute.

Charles Town's advantages in the Indian trade finally proved decisive. She had the credit, she had the warehouse facilities, she had the group of vocal and independent merchants and traders, she had the commodities the Indians wanted, she had the experience, and she had the port that offered all these things together. As John Brownfield, probably the first man in Savannah to try to set up a proper mercantile establishment in a professional way, said, Savannah's trade would never flourish "till some product is raised" or until her inhabitants became self-sufficient. "Savannah could," Brownfield wrote, "produce lumber, but what good would that do until a West Indian trade had been initiated?" Furthermore because Savannah lacked basic supplies, "a Wharf & landing Place," and a crane, the Indian traders went to Charles Town for their goods.[47] Although Georgia continued to grant Indian trading licenses, the boats loaded with goods from the backcountry glided silently by Savannah on their way to or from Charles Town.

Oglethorpe stood solidly and unmovingly behind the Trustees' Rum and Indian Acts because he felt that they were each essential to the creation of the kind of Georgia the Trust wanted to see rise between the Savannah and the Altamaha. When the restrictions ultimately were withdrawn, it was not so much in defiance of Oglethorpe's intransigence as because of basic human nature.

5　Land Grants, Negroes, and Slavery

Just as the rum prohibition and the attempt to control Indian affairs in Georgia's immediate vicinity seemed to fit together, so it was with the land and Negro restrictions adopted by the Trustees for the Georgia settlers. To bring about a yeoman-farmer, free labor, defensively sound province, it was soon determined that all individuals crossing to Georgia at the expense of the Trust would be eligible for a maximum land grant of fifty acres. This property was not to be held in fee simple but on a tail-male basis and could be alienated during the owner's lifetime only with the specific permission of the Trustees. If there was no male descendant the land reverted to the Trust. There were other restrictions tied to the grant, including provisions concerning clearing the soil, raising a certain number of mulberry trees, quit rent payments, not committing a felony, and so on,[1] but the most irritating restrictions seemed to be the inalienability of the grant and the fact that the property could not be leased, mortgaged, or rented. Most of the grants were expected to be for fifty acres—a size too small to breed aristocracy and the plantation system and yet generous enough to provide the basic comforts for which any respectable yeoman farmer yearned.

When a person who could pay for his own passage applied to the Georgia Office, he was eligible for a larger grant if he agreed to certain restrictions concerning land usage and rents, but he also must contract to take a number of white servants with him. Under no circumstances were such grants to exceed five hundred acres. Another guard against land speculation specified that no Trustee was to own as much as an acre of Georgia's soil—a provision that meant Oglethorpe became a landowner in Carolina rather than in Georgia.[2] He thoroughly approved, however, of the limited grants idea in his colony. Owing to their ingrained suspicion of the government the Trustees' land policy was set forth by "rules" and never took the form of official acts requiring the Trust's seal and the approval of the king and Council. Furthermore, these rules were apparently considered so controversial that they were not included in the minutes of the Common Council or the Journal of the Trustees. Whether such action was taken as a result of fear of government interference is not known for certain, but is likely.

Prospective settlers as well as more objective observers were skeptical about the land restrictions from the start. To Jonathan Belcher, the inheritance provisions on land would make younger sons and daughters who might be ignored by their father "appear they have been only slaves to the designated heir." He also thought the reversion idea was unfortunate and would retard the colony's development "by the inhabitants strolling to other parts of America to get lands on much better terms." It was true, Belcher said, that it had been done that way—at least insofar as female inheritance was concerned—in England, but English lands had been under cultivation for "some thousands of years." It would take centuries before such a practice would be established in America's wildernesses. But Belcher's experienced voice fell on deaf ears.[3]

Belcher was perfectly right. Oglethorpe has left no evidence of his reactions to the governor's frank observations, but to judge by his deeds it is clear he ignored the advice. Once Oglethorpe had his mind made up on a particular subject he was all but immovable—fifty inalienable acres on a tail-male basis it would be. And since Oglethorpe was originally empowered by the Trustees "To Set out limit and devide" the land upon his arrival,[4] he could keep fairly close touch on the enforcement of the property restrictions.

While Oglethorpe's stance on land grants was clear from the start, his position on the Negro's role in Georgia evolved more gradually. Negroes were apparently present in Savannah's earliest days, helping to clear the bluff and build the huts and shelters and performing other chores while Oglethorpe laid out the town.⁵ Evidently Oglethorpe did not then look upon black labor as necessarily detrimental to the spirit of Georgia. But Samuel Eveleigh (whose frank letters are good reading as well as a source of considerable information) immediately perceived that Georgia would not succeed without such labor. He begged the Trustees' pardon for saying something he feared they would dislike, but it was his opinion that forbidding blacks to enter the province would be "a great prejudice if not a means to Overset your Noble design." There was good land near Savannah, he noted during his visit in March 1733, but it must be cleared and, Eveleigh maintained, white labor would not be adequate. It was even harmful, said he, for whites "to hoe and tend theyr corn." Negroes must be permitted on a permanent basis to do work for which Englishmen were unsuited.⁶

It was after his experiences in Charles Town during the early summer of 1733, when he was importuned to permit Negroes, rum, and the plantation system, that Oglethorpe's attitudes hardened. He returned to Savannah burning with indignation at the Carolinians who tried to tell him how to run Georgia. His astonishment at what he found on the bluff convinced him that blacks as well as rum must be eliminated from the Georgia scene. Where the latter was unhealthy for the body, the former were just as damaging to mental attitudes. The Negro laborers then present in Savannah, who, if Oglethorpe is accurate, caused considerable dissatisfaction in the new province, were forthwith sent back to Carolina.⁷

In spring 1734, as Oglethorpe was on the high seas, James Vernon expressed his thoughts on the subject of land tenure. Possibly influenced by Belcher's sentiments, Vernon felt that the other American colonies had superior systems. If Georgia persisted in its own peculiar plan it would "breed Discontent" and the colonists would go elsewhere.⁸ Even while Oglethorpe was in England Eveleigh repeatedly suggested to the Trustees a change in land tenure and toleration of Negroes. There was, he reported, a clique in Savannah that met at brickmaker John West's house, and West and his friends were annoyed "That they have not Liberty of getting Negroes." Eveleigh said the Trust should permit each family to own at most two slaves if they so desired. As for the soil, the people on Skidaway Island "were discouraged from makeing Improvements, because they had no Title to their Lands."[9] About the same time, Thomas Christie gloomily wrote Oglethorpe that the Carolinians, Georgia's former friends, were no longer as cordial as they once were. Their praise of Georgia had, in fact, turned to "many Aspersions," and to make matters worse, they bragged that with Negroes to raise Carolina's crops the Georgians "need not sow any Corn or Rice for they will always undersell us."[10]

Eveleigh continued to complain to the Trustees throughout the winter and spring of 1735. In his one-man campaign to change the plans of the Georgia Office he said it was generally concluded on the southern frontier that "Georgia can never be a place of any great Consequence without Negroes."[11] Georgia's enemies in Carolina "rejoyce" in the prohibition, and though the older colony had too many slaves Georgia could set "The Golden Mein" with proper Trustee leadership.[12] Also to assure prosperity, a bounty should be put upon lumber, "which would be of great Advantage to Georgia."[13]

Eveleigh's advice, like that of other protesters, had no effect. The Charles Town merchant was given a lesson in the economics of labor and informed that German servants were preferable to Negro slaves.[14] Female inheritance of lands in Georgia was, for the time, scotched also.[15] Oglethorpe, riding a wave of popularity, was clearly in control of the situation and could defeat any Trustee opposition.[16] And when he told the Trustees, toward the end of July, that he would go to Georgia again with the next embarkation,[17] his colleagues could only have been pleased.

When Oglethorpe returned to Georgia, his strong presence in the colony calmed the internal bickering for a time. Furthermore, taking into account his single-mindedness of purpose and his authority over granting lands, it seems safe to conclude that while Oglethorpe was in Georgia the Trustees' land and labor regulations would remain essentially intact. Although reports exist of Negroes being smuggled into the province, most of these stories cannot be substantiated. Apparently some Negroes were present in Georgia's northern reaches near Augusta, but Oglethorpe was there only once and if he actually saw blacks in the neighborhood he failed to mention it. Not to face an issue would have been unlike him.

Contemporary complaints against Oglethorpe are not that he was lax but that he was too harsh in enforcing the regulations. As opposition mounted to the Negro, land, and rum restrictions Oglethorpe, instead of compromising, became more adamant in his position that change might ruin Georgia. Those who desired to see the Trustees' experimentation altered or abandoned therefore experienced a growing sense of frustration.

At first, an articulate opposition, headed by a Scottish doctor named Patrick Tailfer, did all it could by letter and memorial to bring changes, even before Oglethorpe returned to Georgia in 1736,[18] but as early as September 1735 Eveleigh himself was almost ready to admit defeat. He wrote that his effort to develop Savannah into a trade center had been rendered futile by the incredibly high costs in Georgia. The same work whites did in Georgia in cutting and preparing lumber for market could be done by blacks in South Carolina, he estimated, at one-quarter the price. The Negro prohibition looked good on paper, perhaps, and it may have made a favorable impression in England, but those in America who were ''better acquainted'' than the Trust with the reality of the situation felt certain Georgia needed a form of cheap labor to succeed.[19] Rent in Savannah was ''extravagantly dear,'' and the land terms so far-fetched that Eveleigh refused to waste good money on further improvements.[20] He had returned to Charles Town by the time this letter was written, and with him went Savannah's best opportunity to develop a challenge to Charles Town as a port and trading center.

After a stay in Georgia of less than a year Oglethorpe sailed for England in November 1736, this time to help the Trustees appeal to Parliament for funds to ward off the Spanish threat.[21] He had made the Trust's laws operational in Georgia, but he left behind him a province that fell quickly into warring factions. No one else, particularly Thomas Causton, had Oglethorpe's stature, influence, or ability to minimize dissension. Agitation against Causton and the Trustees gathered steam.

In England Oglethorpe, absorbed by the threat of Spain,

campaigned to secure a regiment to take back to Georgia with him. Still he found time to defend the Trustees' laws where necessary. When another move was made on the Georgia Board, with Egmont in the vanguard, to allow female inheritance "under certain restrictions," Oglethorpe bristled. Egmont's supporters said thrift would be encouraged, people would feel more secure, and improvements would be made that would not be made if the tail-male restrictions were retained. During a two-hour debate on the subject, Oglethorpe was "especially" opposed. The Carolinians and the Negro faction in the colony were behind this agitation, he said. Apparently he argued persuasively, for his followers defeated all efforts to alter tail-male. In addition Egmont's suggestion that the Trust's reasons for its actions should be incorporated into a letter and sent to the colony was rejected too. For the Trust to justify itself was "too great a condescencion" to the Georgians, thought Oglethorpe.[22]

Oglethorpe's triumph was only temporary. The criticisms leveled at the Board from England as well as from America did not cease and two weeks later the most active Trustees— Oglethorpe, Egmont, and Vernon among them—met at the Cider House and reached a compromise concerning "some alteration" of tenures in Georgia.[23] About the same time, Oglethorpe, whose voice had been so influential, began to find himself on the losing end of other internal battles on the Georgia Board. He and Vernon had a conflict early in May when several of the Trustees met at Oglethorpe's house to discuss the financial plight of the colony. Vernon blamed storekeeper Causton for placing everything in jeopardy because of his fiscal irresponsibility. Oglethorpe, sensitive to criticism of Causton as an indirect slap at himself, took exception to Vernon's remarks. The latter suggested that Oglethorpe tend to the colony's military side while the rest of the Trustees handled the civil concerns from London.[24] The moment must have been a tense one, but the men apparently parted in a friendly fashion.

Finally, on 10 May 1738, the day Oglethorpe received the king's orders to proceed to Plymouth in preparation for his third voyage to Georgia, the Common Council turned down "several expenses" Oglethorpe considered imperative for the continued success of the colony. Causton's excesses were once again cited. Oglethorpe was obviously exasperated, but the councilors were, Egmont confided to his diary, "unanimous and Mr. Oglethorp yielded, though with reluctance."[25]

Back in America late in 1738, Oglethorpe devoted his time to war preparations. Without his strong presence in London, the most objectionable features of the land regulations were altered in the spring of 1739,[26] and in the summer a resolution was passed all but eliminating the anachronistic tail-male restrictions.[27]

Upon being informed of these developments, Oglethorpe took time out from his military preparations to write one of the longest letters he ever sent from Georgia. There were many things bothering him, and he had much on which to report, but one matter "of great Importance" was the land question. "There are infinite Difficulties," he said, in seeing to the proper execution of the laws already passed for Georgia; so, please, no "new ones" at this time.[28] Land titles were clear; those who agitated most in Georgia were those who had done the least. Oglethorpe carefully pointed out flaws in the Trust's approach, among them, specifically, that the new policy of lowering barriers would lead to amalgamation of lots, thereby "destroying the Agrarian Equality" which was one of the original motivations of the Trustees.[29] Lawyers and additional courts would become necessary for the colony, with all the attendant fraud and dishonesty associated with these institutions in England. Oglethorpe felt confident the Trust would do nothing until the "Affairs of the Colony are settled," but he should not have been so sanguine. Once the first bars fell, the others followed.

In spite of Oglethorpe's admonitions more changes were made during the 1740s. In May 1750 Martyn, the Trust's secretary, was instructed to insert in the London *Gazette* a notice that grants of land in Georgia were to be "extended to an absolute Inheritance; And that all future Grants of Land shall be of an Absolute Inheritance to the Grantees, their Heirs and Assigns." The tenure of land in Georgia was thus changed to fee simple ownership,[30] approximately the same as in any other British continental colony. The ceiling on the number of acres a person could own was lifted as well, and the evolution of another southern colony like the Carolinas began to be a possibility.

The status of Negroes and slavery in the colony was in doubt for years. Given the circumstances under which Georgia was settled and developed, it was inevitable that there should be agitation for the introduction of blacks, but that the proslavery forces would triumph was not preordained by the impersonal laws of economics or by any other factor. Oglethorpe, motivated by both practical and idealistic considerations, fought the fight of his life on this issue. That he ultimately lost is owing principally to a decline of his and the Trustees' interest in the colony. The ramifications of Oglethorpe's defeat have been— and are still today—so widespread and important as to call for a separate volume to be handled properly.

Many were the letters, petitions, and memorials addressed by the advocates of Negroes to Oglethorpe and the Trustees. Where Eveleigh's approach to Oglethorpe on slavery had been practical and pragmatic, Hugh Anderson's articulate letter to the Georgia leader in January 1739 came as close to eloquence on the subject as any writing in Georgia's early period. Himself a gentleman, his wife descended from a member of the nobility, Anderson and his family had met with one misfortune after another in Georgia.[31] As inspector of the Trustees' gardens his duties were not onerous, but his effort at planting and his experiences with white servants showed him beyond question that Negro slavery must be permitted before Georgia could prosper. Before abandoning Georgia for South Carolina, Anderson penned his advice to Oglethorpe and, hence, to the rest of the Trustees as well.

Writing under the name Plain Dealer, Anderson complimented Oglethorpe profusely for his charity, sacrifice, and patronage to the oppressed. All this aside, however, it was clear that Negroes, even in limited number, were essential to Georgia just as were fee simple land grants. "We still Love, honour, and Respect you," wrote Anderson, "and will continue to do so" as long as you follow a path that has "our Prosperity" as its ultimate goal. But "Smiles cannot be expected amidst Disappointments and Wants." Embrace our notions, abandon your impracticable ones, and "restore to us, in Mr. Oglethorpe, our Father and Protector." Then "your Name with Blessings will be perpetuated."[32]

Oglethorpe was not tempted. To him, the Savannah agitation had as its aim a monopoly of the slave trade and of the land by a few designing men. Negroes would be disastrous to Georgia, for they would very likely desert to Florida where they were offered freedom, land, and protection. The local malcontents "pretend" to advocate only a limited number of blacks, but in practice such a limitation would be impossible. Furthermore, Oglethorpe contended, where there are Negroes the whites "grow idle." Savannah, by virtue of its proximity to Carolina, was shiftless, while the southern section of Georgia was orderly and industrious.[33]

Also, still responding to Anderson's letter, Oglethorpe claimed that to permit black labor would "glut the Markets" with the common American crops, ruin recent improvements made in the cultivation of mulberry trees and grapes in Georgia, and weaken American frontiers. His main objection on the slavery issue was, however, a philosophical one: the original design of the Trustees had been to help the oppressed and the unfortunate. This ideal would be dissipated by allowing such an oppressive institution as slavery in Georgia.[34]

Odd words, perhaps, for a former director of the Royal African Company, but what justification is there in the cynical conclusion that Oglethorpe was speaking dishonestly? Oglethorpe had seen little of slavery at first hand until his experiences in the colonies, and what he saw obviously repelled him. He would have agreed with John Tobler when, commenting on the sad plight of the blacks in Charles Town, he concluded that "they live like cattle."[35] In light of his consistent interest in reformist causes it may be that Oglethorpe's American experience with slavery proved decisive in bringing about his revulsion against the institution. His mind and attitudes were being prepared for his later alliance with Granville Sharp in fighting impressment and Negro slavery during the period of the American Revolution.[36]

Just as war broke out with Spain in 1739, South Carolina was swept by a frightening slave insurrection. Oglethorpe was certain not only that the Spanish had been the instigators of the Stono Rebellion but also that it demonstrated what folly it would be for Georgia to repeal its Negro ban.[37] Now that war was declared with Spain each Negro tolerated in Georgia would be a potential enemy of the province.

With the war, Oglethorpe began to associate slavery and treachery, and some of his remarks took on a Negrophobic cast. He linked the institution of slavery with the enemy, but by enemy he came to mean something more than the Spanish. In effect he began to consider those of his own colonists who agitated for slaves to be the foes of Georgia just as plainly as the Spanish. After all, they worked in the Spaniards' interest by calling for slaves, and because the Negroes in Carolina or Virginia were the passive instruments utilized by hostile agents to undermine domestic tranquility, all blacks came to be grouped in his mind with evil and danger. After the Stono uprising he sent an account of the insurrection to the Trustees asking that it be "inserted in some Newspapers," presumably as an object lesson for those who might be wavering on the issue.[38] Not long thereafter a slave who had been shunted "to and fro betwixt" South Carolina and Georgia "in a clandestine Manner" was taken by the Savannah magistrates and held. Oglethorpe, whose theories of abolition at this point were restricted at best, ordered him to be sold.[39] Georgia officials had all along been cooperating by helping to return runaways to Carolina upon presentation of sufficient proof of ownership and payment of a premium,[40] but the peculiar circumstances of this case and the reality of war with Spain probably made Oglethorpe act as he did.

To demonstrate his determination that Negroes would not be allowed in Georgia, Oglethorpe appointed a commission in Savannah to make doubly sure the antislavery regulations were enforced to the letter.[41] Unless new and substantial evidence comes to light, this commission in Savannah and environs and

Oglethorpe in the south seem to have kept Georgia nearly free of Negroes. If it were not so, why the continued complaints of the pro-Negro faction? Unlike rum, the ban on which was almost impossible to implement because the liquor could be kept largely out of sight, blacks were not so easily hidden. And the financial loss, if one were caught disobeying the law, could be ruinous. So, all things considered, it is hard not to conclude that the Negro Act was effectively enforced. There were violations, but the significant numbers of blacks throughout the colony so often cited by those attempting to defeat the Trustees' regulations cannot be documented.

In the delightful mock-heroic dedication to *A True and Historical Narrative of the Colony of Georgia*, the authors predict that it was only a question of time before Trustee Georgia "shall vanish like the Illusion of some *Eastern Magician.*"[42] The same quotation can, perhaps with a twist of irony these talented writers themselves would have appreciated, be turned against the malcontents. The same "Eastern Magician" seemed to be at work causing the elusive blacks who, they maintained, were in Georgia to vanish when observers approached. It must be borne in mind that the authors of this diatribe dealt consciously in hyperbole—one of the stock items used by eighteenth-century pamphleteers for literary and dramatic impact. The figure of one hundred Negroes in Augusta should not be taken at face value. But on the other hand, although the judicious William Stephens felt the authors made "Molehills into Mountains," he did not deny entirely the presence of blacks in remote Augusta. Savannah, however, had not sat idly by but had "discountenanc'd" and "forbidden" Negroes to its inhabitants. As he with considerable effectiveness asked, "is it probable then, that such a Number can lay conceal'd, like Bays's Army at Knights Bridge in Disguise?"[43]

Oglethorpe's imagination, always fervid, began to get the best of him in 1741. Writing to Robert Walpole to dramatize Georgia's importance and his own isolation in America, he projected the Negro and the Spaniard as equal partners who schemed to wreck British settlements in the New World. Georgia was the bulwark to all North America, and if she fell, the Carolinas, Virginia, and Maryland would follow. The reason was simple. They ''are Cultivated by Negroes, and there is near Ten Slaves to one free Person.'' The Spanish gained access to the houses of the planters by utilizing ''Irish Priests, who pass for Physicians, Dancing Masters, Clock Makers, and other such kinds of Rambling Professions.''[44] Only two weeks after this April 1741 letter Oglethorpe pressed Walpole again, this time predicting a general Negro revolt as far north as Pennsylvania if Georgia fell. The Carolinians would be no help whatever, having been seduced by ''Pamplets, Sartys [*sic*], and Spanish Agents.''[45]

Oglethorpe's feeling that the Salzburgers at Ebenezer and the Scots at Darien were the backbone of the colony was enhanced when these settlements compiled petitions supporting his fight against the discontented.[46] As the dark days on St. Simons, following the 1740 disappointment in Florida, went slowly by, and as Oglethorpe nervously awaited Spain's counteroffensive, he fell back on the Scots, his Indian allies, and the Trustees' regulations for security. The absence of rum at Frederica made the place healthy, the inalienability of lands gave an air of stability and suppressed ''the stock jobbing temper,'' and the fact that in Georgia the inhabitants were ''white and Protestants and no Negroes'' meant there were few internal enemies whom the Spanish could subvert.[47] Still his hyperactive imagination conjured up conspiracies. ''The mutinous temper at Savannah'' had demonstrated its Spanish origin, he asserted, but that was only one aspect of the whole story.[48] The Spaniards' contacts with the Negroes up and down the seaboard had resulted in disastrous fires at New York and Charles Town as well as in the Stono insurrection. The dupes of the enemy had blindly agitated for blacks so ''that Slaves would be either Recruits to an Enemy or Plunder for them.'' But, he optimistically predicted, the Spanish clique in Savannah was on the wane.[49]

Spanish clique or no, the various pieces of legislation expressed for Georgia by Trustee action and introduced into the colony by Oglethorpe himself could not long survive his departure from America in 1743. The rum and land provisions had been either altered or abandoned well before Oglethorpe took ship. The Indian Act stayed on the books, but more as a token than as an example of enforced policy. The Negro Act remained operative longer than the others, and it was from this goal—to keep Georgia a refuge for free, white, Protestant yeoman farmers—that the Georgia Board retreated most reluctantly. Finally, in 1750, the original act was overthrown and to the joy of many of the inhabitants the black ban was removed.[50]

The administrative story of Trusteeship Georgia is like looking at a scene through the wrong end of a telescope: instead of an official on the scene being magnified with more power to cope with the intricacies of the local situation, be that official called governor or by another title, the reverse is true. Oglethorpe was slowly shorn of his civil duties, and the colony was even divided into northern and southern segments after 1740. His old favorite, Savannah, was taken from his control, and when Oglethorpe left for England in 1743 it was as a military figure, one whose reputation was under a cloud at that. Oglethorpe's soldierly training helped him not at all as an administrator. Taught by his mother and sisters and by his military experiences to expect or even demand victory, he found it next to impossible to settle for compromise.

Over and beyond aspects of Oglethorpe's personality and training, it must be said in his defense that he had a clear notion of what he thought Georgia should be. With his parliamentary experience he also could see how each regulation related to the whole of Trusteeship Georgia and how that whole fitted into the empire. He posed the issue of the creation of a new kind of colony that would change the orientation of the southern provinces by directing them away from the plantation system. His and the Trust's experiment with free white labor was a variation from the eighteenth-century norm and showed not only considerable courage but more common sense than is usually credited to it. As Richard Dunn has noted, although the Trustees have been derided as "impractical idealists," they "were at least practical enough to induce the British government to pay for their new colony when private funds proved insufficient."[51] No colonial leaders before had ever pulled such weight.

Georgia as a purveyor of silks, oils, and wines was not to be. It is an irony, however, that many writers who consider themselves in the forefront of contemporary American historical interpretation have scorned Oglethorpe and the Trustees for being so foolish as to fail to see that the injection of Negroes into Georgia was inevitable. These authorities view the introduction of slavery into Georgia after 1750 as liberating the province from the most objectionable of the Trust's restrictions. In this light slavery was a kind of reform and Georgia was at last redeemed from the clutches of the Trustees and Oglethorpe, who only too long had ruled over "the victims of philanthropy."[52]

Such contentions of inevitability are based upon the assumption that Georgia could succeed only as a colony growing staple crops with slave labor, but no law, natural or man-made, dictated this. It was just as economically feasible for Georgia to have developed as a colony oriented toward the Indian trade with one urban focus at Savannah, another at Augusta, and perhaps a third at Darien-Frederica. It was also feasible for Georgia to have taken on strong secondary characteristics as a self-sufficient province with a backbone of white farmers and a mercantile element in the towns trading timber products on world as well as imperial markets.

These possibilities were dependent on Oglethorpe and the Trust knowing how to bring such ends about and being elastic enough to make provisions for human (that is, even Trustee) error. In the final analysis they could not do it. To develop the Indian trade Oglethorpe and the Trust would have had to meet such influential men as Samuel Eveleigh halfway. A more fluid and reasonable position concerning land grants, too, would have helped. Even so, the Carolina merchants and traders were so alarmed by Savannah's potential that the older colony's traders took out licenses in Georgia as well as Charles Town. But the old Puritan, Oglethorpe, sensed a principle at stake and vetoed any trend toward compromise.

Similarly, it would seem madness to expect a colony to develop a powerful and effective yeoman-farmer base while insisting that the original grants, often made in ignorance of the lay of the land, be rigidly adhered to. Apparently the proper military configuration of the province was so dominant in

Oglethorpe's mind that the quality of the grant was secondary to strategic location. And even Oglethorpe had no right to expect miracles from those who had the misfortune to find their fifty acres comprised of marsh or pine barren. Reason and common sense would seem to dictate a pragmatic stance here, but reason and common sense were not always uppermost in Oglethorpe's thinking. Obsessed with the notion that his settlers plotted property accumulation, he vehemently opposed alteration of grants and inheritance provisions. Their petitions rejected, the discouraged landowners could only flee or give in.

The trouble with Georgia and its administration lay, then, not so much with the nature of the scheme as with its execution. There is more than enough ammunition to turn the charges of "impracticality" back on the critics of Oglethorpe and his fellow Trustees. Perhaps the militants and the malcontents were the unrealistic ones in the final accounting. Had slavery been permitted in Georgia, the question that immediately presents itself is one Oglethorpe time and again articulated: What would the Negroes in a new colony do in time of war, particularly if the province were invaded? The question is moot but needs no less to be asked: Could Georgia have survived a Stono?

The most disappointing aspect of Oglethorpe's administrative career in Georgia is that had it been more carefully thought out and had Oglethorpe been able to put the regulations fully into effect, the results might have been remarkable. Instead of a study in eighteenth-century reformist dilettantism, as some have considered her, Georgia might have proved a stunning pacesetter. Had the colony actually developed as the Trustees envisioned it, the pattern of southern colonial slaveholding might have been dramatically broken. With neither economy nor geography necessarily dictating a planter-staple crop province, Georgia could have acted as the buffer that not only could have protected South Carolina from the Spanish but, far more important, might have given the institution of slavery its limits in the British continental provinces by drawing an invisible line up the Savannah River to the foothills of the Appalachians. Slavery might have been confined, for a start, to the old British colonies from South Carolina northward. Cut off from access to new fields west of the Savannah and unable to expand feasibly into the remote fastness of the mountainous Indian lands, slavery could conceivably have been turned back upon itself. Although Oglethorpe may be faulted for failing to secure permanent acceptance of the Trustees' plan in Georgia, the enormity of the task and the almost revolutionary conception of the colony, in the light of eighteenth-century thought and action, must be considered when all accounts are finally closed.

6   Oglethorpe and the Indians

In no area of colonial endeavor was James Oglethorpe more successful than he was with the Indians. Prior to
1733 he had had no dealings with red men, but he appeared
somehow inherently to understand them. He enjoyed his
contacts with them. This feeling was transmitted to the natives
and they returned the affection warmly.

Before Oglethorpe's arrival in Georgia, Indian-white relations
in the Guale-Carolina area had fluctuated widely from decade
to decade and even from year to year. When the Spaniards
controlled the Georgia coastal region, their contacts with the
tribes were usually friendly. The Franciscan priests at the Guale
missions led basically lonely and dedicated lives, and because
they concentrated more on Christianizing the Indians and
teaching simple farming habits than on the development of
trade, their associations with the natives were generally satisfactory. There were periodic uprisings against the leadership of
the friars, but the overall relationship was one of mutual trust.[1]

The coming of the English to the southern frontier changed
all that. With one hand on the pocketbook and the other on a
loaded rifle, the aggressive Carolina traders and merchants
exploited the natives in every way they knew how. The Carolinians also experimented with the use and exportation of
Indian slaves. In the backcountry the English traders fanned
out, exchanging their wares for deerskins, hides, and other
items. Although they found that they could compete for the
loyalty of the Indians on more than equal terms with the
Spanish or the French, largely as a result of their superior
commodities and lower prices, grievances mounted. Coupled
with the allied problems of speculation and unplanned expansion these grievances resulted in the bitter, costly, bloody

Yamasee War, 1715–16, a war almost fatal for South Carolina. The colony suffered a terrible setback.

Following the Yamasee War Carolina felt more vulnerable to her Indian and European enemies than ever before. The trade in deerskins and pelts was slow to revive, and as a result of the contraction of the frontier Carolina's traders lost their favored position in the backcountry. A new brand of leadership was needed; the time appeared ominous for the English in their struggle with Spain and France for the friendship of the tribes on the southern frontier.[2] Into this situation came the colony of Georgia and the figure of James Oglethorpe.

Hardly had Oglethorpe and his colonists climbed the bluff on which Savannah was to be located than the first contingent of Indians arrived to parlay. Tomochichi, the Yamacraw chief, his queen, and the trader John Musgrove approached Oglethorpe and welcomed him officially. After much saluting and volleying of small arms the Indian procession, led by "one of their generalls," came toward Oglethorpe. Following a friendly conference between the Indians and the whites, the former returned well satisfied to their town upriver.[3] And Oglethorpe seemed satisfied with Tomochichi as well. He and his tribe "desire to be subject to the Trustees to have land given them and to breed their Children at our Schools." Tomochichi also professed interest in being taught the fundamentals of Christianity.[4]

Showing a keen appreciation of what the Indians' role in his colony might be and being careful to consult with them on important issues, Oglethorpe was at his diplomatic best in the earliest days of his American experience. He had made it a point to befriend Mary Musgrove and Tomochichi, the two figures who, along with himself, dominate the history of early Georgia-Indian relations. In his incisive manner and conciliatory attitude Oglethorpe displayed the sort of leadership the Indians could accept and respect.

Oglethorpe had high hopes that Georgia would be able to develop a profitable trade with the Indians, and he understood that the first step along this road must be securing a treaty with them. Accordingly he sent invitations to the Lower Creek chiefs to come to Savannah to parlay. By 18 May 1733 kings, chief men, and their advisers from all over the Creek country had assembled in Savannah, "to treat of an Alliance with the new Colony."[5] Nearly one hundred Indians were present, representing the eight tribes that comprised the Creek nation. Gifts were exchanged, "the great guns were fired" upon the Indians' arrival (surprising many who had "never heard a cannon before"), and the Georgia settlers were lined up "under arms" from the riverside to the little wooden house where Oglethorpe was to meet with them.[6] The Indians were dressed in their finest costumes, and the townspeople of Savannah tried to look as impressive as possible. The various chiefs sat with Oglethorpe during the talks, with interpreters standing before them. In this fashion they worked out a treaty. Afterwards they all smoked tobacco, and two Carolinians saw to it that the wine glasses were kept filled.[7]

Chief Oueekachumpa of the Oconees, "a very tall old man, stood out, and with a graceful action, and a good voice, made a long speech" welcoming the English to Creek country. He offered any lands "which they did not use" and thanked Oglethorpe for the kindnesses shown to his relative, Tomochichi. The chief men of each Indian town then presented Oglethorpe with eight separate bundles of skins, symbolic of their welcome.[8]

Tomochichi, who was being curried for leadership by Oglethorpe, made the most dramatic representation. Although his little group of Yamacraws had been living away from the main body of the Creeks since about 1730, Oglethorpe hoped to build up the chief's stature among his red kinsmen to the point that his word would be listened to all along the southern frontier. At a pertinent moment during the discussion Tomochichi rose and addressed the gathering in the following fashion:

> I came here [Yamacraw Bluff] poor, and helpless, to look
> for good Land near the Tombs of my Ancestors, and the
> Trustees sent People here; I fear'd you would drive us away,
> for we were weak & wanted Corn, but you confirmed our
> Land to us, gave us Food, and instructed our Children:

... The chief Men of all our Nation are here, to thank you for us; and before them, I declare your Goodness; and that here I design to die; for we all love your People so well, that with them we will live and die.[9]

The mico of the Cowetas, Yahou-Lakee, delivered an eloquent address appealing to Oglethorpe to use his influence to reunite the Creek Nation. The Yamacraws and the Yamasees, the latter the foe of the British since 1715, should be reconciled to the other Creek towns so that the nation could once again play the full role to which it had been accustomed in the past.[10]

After many speeches and the distribution of presents the treaty was signed on 21 May 1733. The Indians made a general grant of land to Oglethorpe, the treaty specifying only that the Creeks ''freely gave up their Right to all the Land they did not use themselves,'' provided only that whenever new towns were established a conference be held to set aside certain lands for the use of the Indians.[11]

In their turn the Trustees promised ''to see Restitution done'' should Georgia traders in any way destroy or molest Indian property in the backcountry. Such offenders, when reported ''to the Beloved Man'' Oglethorpe, would ''be tried and punished according to the English Law.''[12] Oglethorpe and the Trust, furthermore, agreed to set up a schedule of rates and prices to be adhered to when the colony sent items into the Indian country. This effort reflected the Trustees' determination to establish fair prices and to eliminate wherever possible cheating and poaching by the traders in the backcountry. The Creeks promised that English traders would ''not be robbed or molested'' by the Indians, but if such offenses occurred the perpetrator would be handed over to the Georgia leaders to be tried either under English law ''or by the laws of our Nation as the Beloved Man of the Trustees shall think fit.''[13] A schedule of rewards was created for the return of runaway slaves.[14]

The Treaty of 1733 can be viewed as the Georgia Indian Act of 1735 in microcosm. Once again, as with slavery and landholding, the Georgia leaders were trying to profit from Carolina's mistakes.

Once the treaty was signed Oglethorpe presented each leader with a coat trimmed in lace, a hat, and a shirt. To every warrior present went a gun and other minor items. Even the attendants received "coarse Cloth for cloathing." Linen, gunpowder and bullets, pipes, "8 Belts and Cutlasses with gilt Handles," colored ink, and ironically, in light of subsequent events, "8 Cags of Rum" were also parceled out to the pleased natives.[15]

Oglethorpe had clearly thought it of the first importance to secure a treaty with the Creeks—the most powerful, diplomatically astute, and unpredictable of all the Indians on the southern frontier. He had succeeded. In a stroke he had reached a level of accord with the Indians that the Carolinians had never approached. His graciousness to the halfbreed Mary Musgrove, wife of John, and to the venerable Tomochichi may have prejudiced the Indians in his behalf, but whatever the cause, the fact stands out that the alliance proved an enduring one.

For the remainder of Oglethorpe's first stay in America, Georgia and Carolina concerted Indian measures nicely, Oglethorpe going to Charles Town to discuss with the Assembly the multifarious problems of trade regulation.[16] His salutary effect on the hitherto cool attitude of the Lower Creeks was recognized in a Carolina memorial to the king, taken to the mother country by Oglethorpe himself.[17]

One of the direct effects of Oglethorpe's dealings with the Creeks bore fruit in early July 1734, not long after Tomochichi and Oglethorpe sailed for England. The numerous Choctaw Indians, far removed from Georgia geographically and generally thought to be pro-French in orientation, consented to meet with the Georgia authorities in Savannah. Undoubtedly they had heard of the new colony and of its treaty with the Lower Creeks, their rivals. Quite unexpectedly the Choctaws expressed interest in having a trading path opened between them and the seaboard colonies, with Savannah, presumably, being the entrepôt. They pointed out the town's superior location, and Chief Redshoes poured salt in the Carolina wound by saying that the older colony had long attempted to lure the Choctaws to Charles Town but that they preferred to do business with Georgia.[18] Mary Musgrove, the interpreter at the meeting, gleefully reported these happenings to Oglethorpe and reveled in Carolina's discomfort when, after a three-week stay in Savannah, the Choctaws turned down an invitation to go on to Charles Town and returned to their own territory.[19]

While pressure between Georgia and South Carolina was building because of competition for trade with the Indians and while his early coup with the Creeks seemed to be paying off with the other tribes, Oglethorpe was having the time of his life playing the social and political lion in England. Upon his return home he had brought with him the ancient chief Tomochichi, as well as his great-nephew and successor, Toonahowi, his queen Senauki, and five of his Yamacraw warriors. If Oglethorpe had wanted to create a stir and if he wanted to draw attention to Georgia by putting the natives in the limelight, he succeeded as well as P. T. Barnum did at a later day. There had not, apparently, been such a brilliant American Indian visitation to England since Anne's reign, when a party of Iroquois had been the hit of the London season. (A Carolina contingent that had recently visited had been accorded but slight notice.)

It is difficult to say why Oglethorpe decided to bring the Indians with him, but it is certain that he had more in mind than simply teaching them the English language. Being a member of Parliament, he probably sensed that that body could be swayed into an economic commitment to Georgia by a political stroke such as his tour with the Indians. Bringing over Tomochichi and his followers was like showing off a piece of the debatable land itself, and if the visit caught the public imagination Tomochichi and Oglethorpe might come to symbolize the British effort to wrest this territory from Spain. Here would be something tangible—the noble savage and the philanthropist arm-in-arm resisting the infringement of the black-hearted Spaniard. Some said he brought the Indians to draw attention from his own weaknesses as a colonizer; there is no doubt Oglethorpe also wanted to impress the Indians with the strength of English society.[20] But there was still another facet to his Indian policy that would be furthered by the visit to England. Oglethorpe's tactic of building up the prestige and influence of Tomochichi in the eyes of the Indians back home would be forwarded nicely. Presumably the other natives would be envious of Tomochichi for having been singled out and he and his tribe would rise in their estimation.

The tour itself was a complete success. The Trustees seemed fascinated by their Georgia wards and arranged for apartments over the Georgia Office near Parliament for the duration of their stay. The visitors were fitted out with new, brilliantly colored clothes for their public appearances, Tomochichi in a "fine scarlet bainan" trimmed with gold lace and rabbit fur, the queen in a matching costume, and the rest of the Indian party in blue.[21] Although one of the warriors died during the visit, the survivors, after a period of mourning, went on with their arranged schedules. When several of them became indisposed, Oglethorpe called on none but the best for treatment and consultation, Sir Hans Sloane, old friend, noted physician, and founder of the British Museum, who proved, fortunately, equal to the task.[22]

Oglethorpe and his Indian friends had a crowded, ambitious schedule, with the Indians being exposed to the most influential people in the realm. Tomochichi had audiences with George II, Queen Caroline, the Duke of Cumberland, and the Archbishop of Canterbury. Canterbury was woefully sick at the time, but rather than risk missing the Indians, the prelate appeared at his audience propped up on either side by an attendant.[23] The sensitive Tomochichi, taking in the situation immediately, canceled his set speech and cut the meeting short.

Walpole himself was pressed into service to see to it that King George's own horses and coaches were used to carry Tomochichi and his party to the royal audience. He was also asked to assign a guard—and did—to stand watch at the Georgia Office "to protect them [the Indians] from the curiosity of the Mob who begin now to grow troublesome."[24] Finally, their visit to the Trustees was memorialized on canvas by William Verelst.

Over ten years later the cynical Horace Walpole used a reference to Tomochichi's 1734 visit to illustrate a point concerning the then current invasion by Bonnie Prince Charlie. In London, Walpole reported in September 1745, all was calm in spite of the fact the Stuarts and their allies might be at the city gates in two weeks. Everyone pretended that Prince Charles was "only some Indian king brought over by Oglethorpe: Tooanohowy, the young prince [Bonnie Prince Charlie] has vowed he will not change his linen till he lies at St. James's."[25] It is noteworthy that Walpole could recall, so many years later, the name of Tomochichi's heir.

During Oglethorpe's eighteen-month visit to England he was constantly occupied and at the top of his physical and mental powers. Besides attending to his red guests he had to play his usual parliamentary role, present his financial statement to the Trustees, try to counter critical rumors flowing into London from Carolina, blunt opposition to himself on the Georgia Board, and push for the passage of the three acts to be made operable in Georgia. In all these activities he proved to be exceedingly effective. And although he laid himself open to charges of using the Indians to distract attention from his own flaws, his subsequent behavior toward the natives should absolve him of any such accusations. That he answered all his critics successfully is borne out by eulogistic poems in London papers:

> Let nervous Pope, in his immortal lays,
> Recite thy actions, and record thy praise;
> No brighter scenes his *Homer* could display,
> Than in thy great adventures we survey.
> . . . .
> Thy great example shall thro' ages shine,
> A fav'rite theme! with poet and divine:
> People unborn thy merits shall proclaim,
> And add new honours to thy deathless name.[26]

By now, after fifteen months' experience in America, Oglethorpe considered himself something of an expert on the Indians. And he was, particularly when measured against his associates in Great Britain. To an old family friend, Dr. Samuel Wesley, father of sons soon to be entering the Georgia scene themselves, Oglethorpe wrote two long and revealing letters during the last weeks of 1734. In the first, he outlined the rugged day-to-day life of the average Georgia colonist and warned that one who went as missionary to the Indians, as old Samuel once planned and as his sons now proposed, must be prepared for a challenging experience in every respect. In the same letter he showed real sympathy for the Indians and respect for their customs. It was in the Indians' songs, Oglethorpe explained, that their history and heroic tales were to be found. Their heritage incorporated a story of the deluge and a tale that their "Ancestors formerly inhabited great Cities ... and ... came from the Setting Sun, over a great Sea of Salt Water." The legends of the Indian religion were "too long" to go into in a letter, but the natives had a firm belief in "the Immortality of the Soul and expect an Instructor & Mediator."[27]

Wesley's response to this letter was gratifying,[28] but it was Oglethorpe's second letter, dated Christmas day 1734, that shows him at his best. On the subject of the Georgia climate, he mentions the notable "Thunders and Lightnings in Summer" and the heavy rains "which greatly refresh the Earth, and cause a fragrancy superior to the most blooming Spring in Europe." And again his admiration for the Indians was high. They are "of an excellent Temper," and would hear "with Pleasure" what was preached to them. But they were shrewd and "will Sift everything that is alledged with great penetration." Unlike Englishmen, Oglethorpe seemed to say, the Indians "always give up their Opinion to Reason." They desired knowledge, but were satisfied with learning for its own sake, "not being pressed by Poverty nor Clogged by Luxury." Their "Expressions" were "high and lofty" and "their Sentiments noble. In their manner of Living they resemble much the patriarchial age." They live "under the Shade of Oak, Laurel or Pine," sleep on "Skins of Beasts," and hunt for their meat while the women cook, bake, and tend the fowl and children. The Indian dwellings are in their corn fields and have dirt floors. "In these Mansions," Oglethorpe reflected, "they live much more contented than our great men in palaces."[29] The Indian king, he said, told his followers "when to hunt, when to Sow, when to fish." Also, "They think the English very unwise who waste Life in Care and Anxiety merely to heap up Wealth, for to raise Discord amongst their Heirs and to build lasting Houses for to make their

Children incapable of bearing the Inclemency of their native Air.''[30] His letter concluded with a section outlining the sense of mission a minister must have "to take up the Cross and follow his Crucified Master" to Georgia.[31]

Revenge and rum, he commented elsewhere, were the Indians' two greatest weaknesses, but he felt he had made an impression, at least concerning the latter. "I have weaned those near me a good deal from it." Furthermore, theft was unknown among the Creeks and they would not tolerate adultery, murder, or polygamy. Their kings, being the elders of the tribes, were experienced and, therefore, cautious and sane, helping the entire tribe to "reason together with great temper and modesty." Oglethorpe, impressed by the native ways, concluded that the Indians were "thorough masters of true eloquence.''[32]

Oglethorpe must have been aware of the parallels between his own leadership and that he described as characterizing Indian society. The similarities were particularly apparent when he was preparing to lead the second transport to America in 1735. Then he even went so far as to parcel out specified amounts of garden seeds—turnips, cabbages, beets, sandwich beans, and the like—to each of the settlers for their Georgia planting.[33] That he told his new colonists how to build their houses, when to plant, demonstrated his fishing prowess, and gave advice on how to act in America is clear from his letters and from accounts left by others. The strong resemblance between Oglethorpe's paternal approach and Indian leadership customs was probably emphasized by his close contact with Tomochichi. Consciously or unconsciously Oglethorpe in Georgia may have tried to emulate Indian societal organization.

After his return to Georgia in 1736 Oglethorpe was pleased to discover that the faith he had put in the Yamacraw chief had not been ill-founded. He wrote the Trustees that in spite of the efforts of the French, Spanish, and alienated Carolinians, Tomochichi, who had returned to Georgia before Oglethorpe, "has maintained the Trustees Interest among the Creeks till my arrival."[34] In fact, the mettle of the agreement with the Creeks and the personal relationship between Oglethorpe and Tomochichi was tried time and again. It proved true. Toonahowi and Tomochichi joined Oglethorpe at the new settlement of Frederica and promised continued loyalty. They pledged to "live & die by us," Oglethorpe proudly remarked to the Trustees, and Tomochichi had sent friends into the backcountry to bring allies down to St. Simons to help out in case of hostilities with the Spanish.[35] The chief even accompanied Oglethorpe to the outskirts of Spanish Florida to demonstrate his devotion to the British cause. His men were so anxious to strike a blow against the Spanish, with whom the British were still at peace, that Oglethorpe quieted them only "with much Difficulty."[36] He used the Indians' supposed rage at the Spanish as a diplomatic ploy to intimidate the officials at St. Augustine, and even posed as the protector of Florida because of his calming influence on the Indians. Governor Moral de Sanchez was assured that an important meeting of the Indians would soon be held at which Oglethorpe promised to do all he could to prevent the natives from attacking the Spanish.[37]

The summer of 1736 was critical in the field of Anglo-Indian relations in Georgia. In addition to reaffirming friendships with Tomochichi and the Creeks, Oglethorpe spent a good part of June and July conferring with other natives in Savannah. He was interested in lining up backing for Georgia's Indian Act, but his primary consideration was to make certain of the red man's support should war break out. It says something for the strong position in which Oglethorpe had placed the English through his handling of Indian relations that he was able to parlay with contingents from the Chickasaws as well as from the Upper and Lower Creeks during a period of less than three weeks.[38] As during his London tour, Oglethorpe was in top form. He promised to regulate the Indian trade fairly and see to old grievances, and at the same time he pointed out that the Spanish and French were untrustworthy. He was openhanded with tobacco and wine and himself drank a toast to the Indians. As a further token of esteem he asked Tomochichi and Chigilly, principal mico of the Lower Creeks, to confer alone with him in order to show special favor to the two chiefs.[39] In a characteristic gesture Oglethorpe presented the influential Chigilly with "the Coat off my own Back" so that he would be remembered and so that Malachi, son of Brims and intended successor to Chigilly, would remember him as well.[40] Chigilly was flattered, accepted the gift, put it on then and there, and professed to have been delighted with the outcome of the Savannah talks. Upon leaving, Chigilly was given many other gifts to distribute among his tribe's women and children as a sign of his standing with the English.[41] Mary Musgrove again presided as interpreter during most of these gatherings. (Oglethorpe never became completely fluent in the Indian dialects.)

The Chickasaws were especially curious about Oglethorpe, whose name had spread far and wide in the backcountry. It was rumored, they informed him, that his mother was a "red-woman." After seeing him with his own eyes the chief who reported this said he was now satisfied that Oglethorpe had "as white a Body as any in Charles Town."[42] Oglethorpe disarmed the Indians by his reply. He *was* a red man—"an Indian, in my heart, that is I love them; do they love me the worse for that?"[43] What could the Indians respond except to try to match Oglethorpe's compliment? He had won the day, and with it the affection of the Chickasaws.[44] This tribe, only recently attacked by the French, emphasized the French threats on the frontier. Oglethorpe, the French said, was short of bullets and powder, and what powder he had was faulty and "makes no Noise."[45] Furthermore, British "Balls drop down as soon as they come out of the Guns."[46] Hearing this, Oglethorpe told the Indians to inspect his stores for themselves and to take what they needed.

The Chickasaws dramatized to Oglethorpe the threat of French encirclement. By drawing ever larger circles in the sand to represent the three forces the Indians pointed out not only their own weakness and vulnerability but the English weakness as well. The large French circle encompassed the Anglo-Indian marks with ease. Unless something was done, they said, the French would "kill us like Hogs or Fowls."[47] Oglethorpe advised the Chickasaws to steer clear of political squabbles and to keep mobile; French grenades and weapons of war could not penetrate forests. He reminisced about his earlier military experience as a young soldier in Europe fighting the French with Eugene of Savoy:

> I was bred to war, and know these things.... In our Wars with them we have come so near the French as this Room is wide, and yet could not come quite close. Then we threw these things [grenades]. I have taken them up and thrown them back again.[48]

The Chickasaws, who had wanted powder and shot to resist the French, got what they asked for.[49]

Oglethorpe was brilliant in his handling of Georgia's Indian relations, as William Bull of South Carolina and others knew he would be, but the real test still lay ahead. Although some of the Carolinians were nettled by Oglethorpe's successes, particularly with the Chickasaws, and although trade regulation caused misunderstandings between the provinces, when it became obvious that war with Spain loomed, the older colony began to reassess the situation. Oglethorpe's stature among the Indians was unquestioned, and so it would be up to him to assure them that the English would triumph; he must reaffirm the Anglo-Indian accords. With Broughton dead, Oglethorpe and Bull coordinated backcountry relations in a spirit of unity and cooperation.

Upon his third and last return to Georgia, in 1738, Oglethorpe found the colony fallen on dark days. There were almost daily alarms that the Spanish intended to invade, Frederica was rent by internal tensions, and Savannah was in its usual muddle confounded by the inadequate bookkeeping of Thomas Causton. On top of all this, Oglethorpe found that the Spanish had eroded some of the good will built up with the Creeks during his previous visits to Georgia. He felt that his arrival would buoy the colony's morale, just as the regiment he brought with him would buoy its defense capability, but the Indian situation bothered him. The Creeks must be given assurances, and their ties to England strengthened.[50] By late November 1738, Oglethorpe had met with about eighty representatives of the Creek nation, including "Four Kings," and had secured promises "of their Fidelity to His Majesty and that they had rejected the Spanish offers."[51] Indian affairs were still unsettled, however. Anxious to choose a winning side the backcountry tribes were probing and testing to determine which of the contending European powers had the strongest hand.

To the astonishment of Savannah and William Stephens a delegation of between thirty and forty Choctaws appeared in February 1739.[52] Though provisions were short, Stephens and Thomas Jones, Causton's successor, did what they could to entertain the Indians with wine, biscuit, beer, and "a small Hog, which they would barbacue themselves."[53] Oglethorpe was summoned from St. Simons, but he was unable to come to Savannah until after the Indians had departed.[54] Stephens did what he could to put a brave face on things for the sake of making an impression on the Choctaws. Tomochichi and some other chiefs came to call on the Indian visitors, probably to encourage them in their leanings toward the English, but Stephens and Jones were both nervous to have so many uninvited guests on the bluff. The Indians were not only "troublesom and expensive,"[55] but they took surprising liberties with the English settlers by entering their houses and "laying their Hands on any Thing they liked." In despair Stephens wondered in his Journal if Oglethorpe's failure to come when he was so desperately needed was not a final proof that he "had given over all farther Regard to Savannah."[56]

It seems reasonable to assume that the Choctaws came to Savannah simply to take stock of the English position. They left a message for Oglethorpe, however, asking him to prepare himself for a journey into the Indian country for a kind of "summit meeting" with the native leaders on the southern frontier. His absence from Savannah had made a later trip to Creek country a necessity.

During March 1739, Oglethorpe made some effort, with the invaluable help of Stephens, to make sense of the administrative chaos surrounding the Trustees' accounts in Savannah,[57] but he felt that more important affairs needed his attention. England, in spite of Robert Walpole's opposition, was drifting into a warlike frame of mind owing to the reported Spanish outrages against British shipping.

On the southern frontier, Oglethorpe, who welcomed a fight, was yet realist enough to know that the key to defending Georgia rested with the Indians. In the early months of 1739 he began to hear more and more about growing discontent and disaffection among the natives. Spain was trying to bribe the Creeks, he explained to the Trustees, and Chigilly and Malachi, with whom he had talked so successfully in 1736, "insist upon my coming up to put all things in order." The trip would be "fatiguing and dangerous," but the chiefs were called together at Coweta and Cusseta to meet him and so he must go. It would be expensive, but such expenditures were essential for the welfare of Georgia. Tomochichi agreed he had no choice, especially as the Chickasaws and Choctaws would be represented.[58] Probably this was Tomochichi's last bit of advice to Oglethorpe, for shortly after the latter's return from Indian country the old Yamacraw mico died.

In July, with about twenty-five attendants in addition to a number of Indians, Oglethorpe set off cross country to the Lower Creek strongholds on the banks of the Chattahoochee River. Provided by hunters with venison, turkey, and honey in abundance, they forded the great Ogeechee on the twenty-seventh, observed large herds of "Buffaloes," and passed gradually into hillier country. On the last day of July, from high on a promontory the group looked out over tree-filled valleys and saw a column of smoke rising far off which, it turned out, came from a party of Spanish horsemen.[59] Here was evidence of the enemy's presence and interest in the region.

On 6 August, a Georgia Indian agent came into camp with two friendly chiefs, who greeted Oglethorpe warmly, and on the following day as they trudged along, they found "Cakes and Bags of Flower" put in the trees along the trail by the Indians to satisfy the hunger of the English. They camped near the Indian town the next night and were feted with various delicacies including watermelons, potatoes, squashes, and more venison. On the next day Oglethorpe was escorted, with ceremony, to the main square of Coweta and welcomed by the king, who held a small English flag as a sign of friendship. A ceremonial drink, made from casena berries and held in a conch shell, was drunk, after which Oglethorpe was given an Indian banquet and taken to observe the natives as they danced in the square.[60]

Oglethorpe and the natives conferred for several days at Coweta, from which talks only a few details emerge. On 11 August, acting "in behalf of his Majesty" he "Opened the Assembly by a Speech."[61] On the following day the Assembly adjourned to Cusseta,[62] where the whole procedure was repeated and the talks continued until 21 August.[63] The friendship between the English and the Creeks was reaffirmed, apparently with fanfare and ritual. Oglethorpe, sick with a fever, distributed gifts and began the long homeward march on 25 August.[64] He arrived in Augusta, on the Savannah River, 5 September 1739.[65]

From his illness he was, he reported to the Trust, "perfectly well recovered," and that he was jubilant there can be no doubt at all. The Creeks had "very fully Declared their rights to ... all the Land as far as the River Saint Johns, and their Concessions of the Sea Coast, Islands and other Lands to the Trustees, of which they have made a regular Act."[66] Had Oglethorpe himself not gone to meet with the Indians, he wrote, war might have broken out because of Spanish and French agitation against the Carolina traders. But his appearances in Coweta and Cusseta blunted the efforts of the agitators. Now "every thing is entirely settled in peace." As he remarked, it was "impossible to Discribe the Joy they expressed at my Arrival."[67]

Although Oglethorpe can hardly be accused of false modesty, there is no doubt that his actions were bold and effective. With Anglo-Creek relations strained, with France as well as Spain agitating in the backcountry, with the Choctaws and the Creeks on the verge of a war that could only damage England's position, with France plotting an attack on the Chickasaws and also on the brink of war with the Creeks, Oglethorpe had calmed the almost Byzantine situation to the advantage of the British. Furthermore, he patched up the relations between the Indians themselves. He wanted the Choctaws to be able to oppose the French, but he also wanted to avoid a Franco-Creek confrontation as he needed Creek support against the Spanish in Florida. Overall it was an astonishing achievement and one that left the Spanish with only the Yamasees as reliable allies.[68]

Insofar as a grant of land and recognition of the legitimacy of Georgia were concerned, the Indians confirmed what they had before given, and with the exception of the larger sea islands along the coast and a small area above Savannah, they granted to the English all land between the Savannah and the St. Johns rivers as far up as the tide flowed. A stunning victory for Oglethorpe and the British, these negotiations and this agreement have been cited "as the basis for Creek-English friendship" for the entire period leading up to the Great War for Empire.[69]

While Oglethorpe was recuperating in Augusta the Cherokees, often at odds (or even at war) with the Creeks, sent down a party to treat with him. They could not afford to ignore the man who seemed to dominate affairs in the Indian country. Oglethorpe "Received them with all Tenderness" on 6 September, and on the eighth they followed him downriver to a fort on the Carolina side. Three days later "a Peace" was settled between Oglethorpe and the Cherokees, and on the thirteenth he distributed gifts among them.[70] In exchange for provisions and promises of support Oglethorpe apparently wrung verbal assurances from the Cherokees that they would send him six hundred warriors to render assistance against England's enemies.[71] He in turn sent them fifteen hundred bushels of corn to tide them through hard times brought on by a smallpox epidemic, and by Carolina rum too, the implacable Oglethorpe claimed. The Cherokees had been so hard hit that they had been unable to till their fields.[72]

On 13 September Oglethorpe received news that England was on the brink of war with Spain.[73] He hurriedly terminated what business he had in the Augusta area and on his way downriver to Savannah was informed of a Carolina slave uprising in the Stono River area near Charles Town. He paused to await developments in Carolina should he be needed there, and when he heard that the main body of insurrectionists had been put down, he hurried on to Savannah on the twenty-third, arriving "well, and healthy," late in the afternoon.[74] During a long talk with Stephens, Oglethorpe claimed that Georgia now "unquestionably" had the alliance of the Upper and Lower Creeks. Since hostilities with Spain had broken out, this consideration was of prime importance, for with their location the Indians could appropriately be thought of "as a Wall of Defence" protecting Georgia's western and southwestern flanks from Spain or France.[75] Oglethorpe now found it necessary to spend time in Savannah coordinating plans to confound the Spanish.

The entire settlement had to pause, however, for the funeral of Tomochichi, who died on 5 October and was buried with signal honors the next day in one of the town's squares.[76] Oglethorpe, Stephens aptly wrote, "always esteemed him a Friend of the Colony, and therefore showed him particular Marks of his Esteem, when living; so he distinguished him at his Death, ordering his Corpse to be brought down [to Savannah]; and it was buried in the Centre of one of the principal Squares, the General being pleased to make himself one of his Pall-Bearers."[77] The Tomochichi-Oglethorpe friendship had not been one-sided. As the object of the Georgia policy to build up the prestige of a nearby native leader and rely upon him to defend the colony's viewpoint with other Indians, Tomochichi had been shown all the favors Oglethorpe and the Trust could give him. For his part, Tomochichi respected Oglethorpe, whose attitudes seemed so much like his own. When the old mico was leaving England in November 1734 after his memorable tour, Oglethorpe asked him if he was not pleased to be returning to Georgia. Yes, Tomochichi replied, but parting with Oglethorpe *"was like the day of death"*; this was considered a "very elegant" response by Egmont and his friends, especially as it was extemporaneous.[78] Oglethorpe, when Tomochichi's real "day of death" arrived, could only have felt a strong sense of loss for an ally, and even more for a friend.

With Tomochichi dead, Oglethorpe relied more heavily on Mary Musgrove, not only for her interpretive skills, but for advice as well. Generally speaking, although she was opinionated, egocentric, and probably not very smart, Mary performed with competence as long as Oglethorpe was around. Her taste in husbands, after the death of the reliable John Musgrove, may have left one wondering about her judgment in personal affairs, but her devotion to Georgia was never in doubt when Oglethorpe was there to help her maintain her equilibrium. Stephens felt Oglethorpe made too much over Mary and that he spoiled her by deferring to her opinion. He treated "her very kindly on all Occasions," and "would advise with her in many Things, for his better dealing with the Indians."[79]

While Mary Musgrove is usually given credit for marshaling the Indian forces to Oglethorpe's side,[80] in actuality Oglethorpe had already done that himself. Through his patient and considerate leadership, his concern for the welfare of the native population, and his unobtrusive empathy with Indian ways and wants, he made a lasting impression upon the tribes and gained many loyal red friends. Although the visitor to Ebenezer who, in 1736, said "Oglethorpe was both God and King for the Indians" dealt in hyperbole,[81] he did not overstate the case by a very wide mark. And as Thomas Jenys of South Carolina said later, in 1744, "noe Man in Life is soe well Acquainted wth. the Nature and turn of the Indians."[82]

The effectiveness of Oglethorpe's dealings with the Indians was emphasized during the campaigns and guerrilla warfare between the Spanish and English on the disputed frontier. The natives rallied to Oglethorpe's standard during the skirmishing in the early months of the war and were a useful, though not large, part of the expedition against St. Augustine. They also served with distinction during the bleak days that led to the defeat of the Spanish on St. Simons in 1742.[83] Their services as scouts, hit-and-run raiders, observers, and messengers really went beyond mere usefulness and can be considered instrumental in the ultimate outcome of the war in the Georgia-Florida sector.

Once the strong hand of Oglethorpe was withdrawn, however, the story was different. The officials who followed Oglethorpe in Georgia had to concede reluctantly that the Indians were gradually departing from their old pro-Georgia habits. In 1751 Henry Parker, vice president of Georgia, admitted to

Governor James Glen of South Carolina that the Choctaws and Cherokees had not been to Savannah ''in a Body since General Oglethorpe left.'' He did, however, defend Georgia's record insofar as the Creeks and Chickasaws were concerned, claiming they had been to Savannah as often as they had been to Charles Town.[84]

As in almost everything else Oglethorpe did, there was an ironic touch that can be detected in his handling of Indian affairs. Although not fluent in the Indian tongue, he seems to have had better luck communicating with the natives than with his English colonists. With the latter, he was apt to be peremptory, intransigent, impatient, or arrogant. Because the Indians often seemed content to accept Oglethorpe's counsel he, who had been accustomed in England to considerable authority, may have trusted the word of the red men over that of many of his own settlers, particularly when Georgians showed signs of questioning his decisions. For one thing, he wanted to secure an act from the Georgia Board of Trustees that would make Indian evidence acceptable in colonial courts.[85] His efforts were never to succeed, but as a result of his obviously good intentions the sophisticated Creeks, the most powerful Indians with whom he had to deal, sensed a man greatly concerned for them. Accordingly they put their trust in him to an extent that they rarely accorded a European.

Like Governor George Clarke in New York, Oglethorpe had an overall view of the Indian problem as it pertained to the colonies and how the colonies related to the challenges from Spain and France. It was Clarke's notion, he wrote Oglethorpe, that delegations of southern Indians should be sent to a general conference of all tribes allied to the British to work out a peace of their own. Governors William Gooch and Bull, of Virginia and South Carolina respectively, had been told that such a conference would gather in May 1743.[86] Oglethorpe sensed immediately the scope of Clarke's plan. It was, he said to the Trustees, ''one of the noblest designs'' that could be conceived for the British colonies. If all England's Indian allies could be convinced to make peace with each other, then not only would both colonist and Indian profit, but the English Indians would be able "to act with more vigour & greater numbers against the Spaniards" or whoever else might mount an attack. The Chickasaws, he pointed out, would never be able to help meaningfully against the Spanish or French until they could be reassured by some sort of general treaty that their old "back Enemy," the Six Nations, would not attack when they were busy fighting for England.[87] Oglethorpe was so impressed by Clarke's ideas that he sent a copy of the New Yorker's letter with his own to the Trustees, commenting that he could "add nothing" more.[88] For Oglethorpe, quite an admission.

That Oglethorpe did not always act idealistically where the Indians were concerned was obvious. As the head of a colony surrounded by potential enemies he could not afford to ignore the reality that France and Spain were always aiming to undermine his work with the natives. Hence he had no choice but to view the Indians in one light as military allies against Georgia's enemies. He therefore supplied them with guns, ammunition, and other articles of war, but this should not obscure the fact that Oglethorpe had a sincere respect for the Indians' life, culture, beliefs, and social organization. Had the situation on the southern frontier been less perilous he might well have emerged as one of the eighteenth century's best scholars of Indian lore. As it was, however, he had most importantly to look at the natives in a political light. The continued existence and prosperity of Georgia always came first in his mind.

Edmund Gray, who petitioned the Board of Trade in 1752 to ensure that Georgia was maintained as a colony separate from Carolina, accurately summed up Oglethorpe's Indian policy. Georgia, he said, was established with the approval of the natives, a formal treaty recognizing this was drawn in 1733 between the Indians and the Trustees, and another agreement negotiated in 1739. Each side adhered to the provisions in good faith and had "Since lived in perfect Peace, Confidence, and Friendship."[89] Unlike the French officials, who went into Indian country only when escorted by guards and attended by pomp and circumstance, Oglethorpe, in his own words, "relied entirely on the good Faith of the *Indians*." He reaffirmed the honest intent of the English in Georgia, settled the fears of the natives, and "unravelled" the cloth of deceit that the Spanish and French had been so laboriously weaving.[90] Largely as a result of Oglethorpe's policies Georgia was spared, almost alone among southern colonies, a major internal Indian war during the formative years.

It is also true that the decision to keep Georgia as a distinct and separate province may have resulted from the accord and friendship with the Indians for which Oglethorpe was responsible. Certainly had Georgia's relations with the natives been unsatisfactory, the government would have been more likely to dissolve the colony and merge it with Carolina. If indeed Georgia owed her separateness to the fact that Oglethorpe handled the Indians ably, then the British Empire as well as Georgia is doubly beholden to him. Oglethorpe not only founded the colony, but by his dealings with the Indians he made certain her existence as a distinct and contributing province inside the Empire.

7 Alarums and Excursions: War Comes to the Southern Frontier

From the time of Georgia's permanent settlement the Spaniards looked with increasing uneasiness upon British encroachments in Florida. It had been bad enough when earlier the missions were forced to retreat gradually southward down the coastal islands, leaving an unsettled area between the limits of Spanish and English spheres, but when Oglethorpe arrived on Yamacraw Bluff fear and consternation in St. Augustine reached a peak.

Spanish imperial strategy had in fact been jolted by Oglethorpe's activities. Spain's planners had originally hoped that Florida and the region to the north could be transformed into a basically pastoral province of empire. Although it seemed at first that their goal might be reached, French and British raids in Guale, a lack of direction from Old Spain, periodic Indian uprisings, and the settlement of Carolina all spelled doom for it. The expeditions sent by the Carolinians into Florida during Queen Anne's War resulted in the nearly total destruction of the mission as a factor on the southern frontier, and the erection of Fort King George on the Altamaha was another step toward British victory in the land that was later to become Georgia. The abandonment of Fort King George in 1727 seemed to promise new hope for the Spaniards, but then, only a few years later, Oglethorpe arrived and his intentions were clear: his colony would be permanent, and if Spain challenged his right to be there he would fight.

Although by 1733 Spain had ceased to think of Florida as a center from which new settlements could radiate into the surrounding areas, she still looked upon this beleaguered outpost as essential: Florida must be held to protect Spanish shipping in the Bahama Channel. The colony's role by the time of Georgia's founding was primarily to act as a buffer between the British and the Spanish stronghold of Cuba. The Gulf of Mexico, regarded as a Spanish lake, must also be kept clear of English outposts. So the Castillo de San Marcos at St. Augustine was virtually rebuilt and was made more formidable. It was no longer expected that Florida would be self-sustaining within the empire; she would be a drain on the economy of Cuba and Spain, but still she must be held. If Georgia was considered, in one of her many functions, as a buffer colony for Carolina, Florida was even more a buffer for Cuba and the Gulf.[1]

As long as Spain and England remained at peace no important military actions along the southern frontier were to be expected. Oglethorpe knew as well as any that his colony was weak; he had been instructed by Walpole not to nettle the Spanish unnecessarily and he heeded the instruction. Spain, more concerned with affairs elsewhere, was also willing to let the situation alone and contented herself with diplomatic protests against the British presence in Georgia.

South Carolina and Georgia were expected from the start to coordinate measures involving military affairs and imperial defense. As a result of mounting tensions on the frontier, Newcastle told Lieutenant Governor Broughton in 1735 that the independent company of troops, previously stationed at Port Royal, would be moved southward to protect Georgia. Broughton was also informed that he "should recommend" to the Carolina legislators that every possible encouragement be given to Oglethorpe in his effort to fortify a strong position on St. Simons Island, where a new fort and town would be situated in 1736. Oglethorpe, who had shown "so much Zeal and Concern" for South Carolina, was a "very usefull" person with whom to consult.[2] It is doubtful the testy Broughton, who was already involved in stirring up a fight with Georgia over the Indian trade, accepted Newcastle's advice with equanimity.

By the summer of 1736, after Oglethorpe's intentions of putting a fortress on St. Simons Island were unmistakable, the

Spanish authorities in Florida and Europe were thoroughly aroused. The fort was menacing enough, but when Oglethorpe put a frontier outpost—imposingly named Fort St. George—at the mouth of the St. Johns River, the Spaniards acted. Antonio de Arredondo, soldier, frontier diplomat, and capable engineer, was sent from Cuba to treat with Oglethorpe and secure withdrawal of the British beyond the Beaufort–Port Royal area. Oglethorpe, who entertained Arredondo as though he were an eastern potentate, countered by telling the Spaniards to evacuate all of Florida north of the twenty-ninth meridian. Both demands were equally preposterous and the men knew it. A crisis impended, but after a number of consultations (where Oglethorpe showed off his Indian support to advantage) they reached an agreement that cooled the immediate situation. In exchange for Oglethorpe's promise to withdraw from his extreme southern positions, Spain agreed that she would not settle the area either. She recognized the validity of Britain's title to the region, and the determination of an exact boundary was left up to the European diplomats.[3]

Knowing Oglethorpe, Samuel Eveleigh remarked that the Georgia leader acted cleverly here. By the time word was sent from Madrid and London, Oglethorpe "will be capable of finishing his Forts, mounting his Guns and furnishing them with Men" so that the Spaniards would be unable to turn the Georgia colony out by force.[4] And in part, this is what Oglethorpe did: he negotiated with the enemy and put on a peaceful face until he felt strong enough to bare his true intentions.

But before Georgia could be relatively secure, the province must have some sort of semipermanent and dependable military element to protect it. It was to obtain permission from the crown to raise a regiment, of which he would be commanding officer, that Oglethorpe returned to England early in 1737. Through astute maneuvers Oglethorpe was able, by midsummer, to answer his critics on the Georgia Board, respond to Carolina's challenges, play the most prominent role in getting a generous defense appropriation from Parliament, secure the appointment of Samuel Horsey as governor of South Carolina, and get permission to raise his regiment.[5]

In September 1738 Oglethorpe, just arrived with his soldiers off the island that bore Sir Joseph Jekyll's name, wrote that Georgia "bridles the Spaniards in America & covers the English Frontiers."[6] He was spoiling for a fight. He got, ultimately, almost more than he wanted, but that he was for the present confident was demonstrated by the way he handled a mutiny among the soldiers that came, according to most reliable reports, near to ending his life.

On the frontiers in November, at Fort St. Andrews on Cumberland Island, Oglethorpe suddenly found himself face to face with a situation that was full of danger for himself and the colony. Some of the seasoned troops he had brought with him to Georgia had grievances concerning sea pay and provisions. The complaints took an ominous turn when dissatisfied elements tried to take over the fort. Acting quickly, Oglethorpe personally disarmed one of the leaders who had shot at him. The bullet "grazed his Shoulder, & the powder Singed his cloaths."[7] As a Charles Town source noted, "he so narrowly excap'd that the Bullet went thro' his Periwigg."[8] This near miss was followed by another unsuccessful effort to gun him down, after which the mutineers were seized, one of them by Oglethorpe himself. He offered pardons on the spot to the other disaffected troops if they would disperse, "which they immediately did."[9] Later, Oglethorpe spoke individually to each man in the two companies involved and mollified all of them. Typical of Oglethorpe's positive attitude during his career in Georgia was his candid remark to a friend on the Georgia Board that though he labored under extraordinary conditions the challenges "rather animate than daunt me."[10] His reaction in the face of mutiny was immediate and typical.

Oglethorpe was informed of the outbreak of war with Spain after his successful trip to Creek country in 1739. Actually it had been only a question of when, not whether, hostilities would occur. One thing that had seemed particularly frightening to the British was the proclamation issued by the Spanish in the spring of 1738 that all slaves fleeing South Carolina or any other English colonies would be granted freedom and would be given land and protection in Florida.[11] This open invitation to a slave uprising was precisely what the Carolina whites feared most. Spain's invitation to the slaves at first seemed to have little effect, but as the word spread among the Negroes, desertions to Florida mounted. Oglethorpe was able, he wrote, to capture most of those who tried to use the land route, but those who, one way or another, managed to make their flight by sea were another matter. Although he had been careful, in the interests of peace, not to offend the Florida officials, the Carolinians "complained" to him about the slave losses. Understandably edgy, the planters claimed to have suffered severe financial setbacks and were in constant fear. If Spain continued to lure slaves in such number, the older colony "will be entirely ruined."[12] Even William Bull admitted as much to British authorities[13]—and this, it must be recalled, was prior to the Stono troubles.

Manuel de Montiano, governor of Florida, almost had cause to rejoice at the turn of events. He was able, at the end of 1738, to report to his superiors that twenty-three Negroes "from Puerto Real" had arrived in St. Augustine and that he was placing them at "Moze" (Mosa, Moosa), close to the Castillo de San Marcos, where thirty-eight free Negroes were already settled.[14] Because the village began to assume considerable proportions, a fort, frequently referred to simply as "the Negro Fort" or "Fort Mosa" was built. It was here that the decisive battle of the St. Augustine expedition of 1740 was to be fought.

Montiano was also encouraged by other turns of events. He had sent Pedro Lamberto as his emissary to Charles Town to sniff out whatever plans the enemy might have, and though he had hardly been permitted the run of the city, Lamberto had uncovered chinks in the British armor. Montiano hoped "the discord prevailing between the latest squatters [the Georgians] and the people of San Jorge [Charles Town], and between the latter and Don Diego Ogletorp, whose supreme command they refuse to recognize" would be helpful in fending off the advances of the British. His province was ill-prepared for war, but perhaps there might be reason to hope after all.[15]

In England, Walpole, although anxious above all to keep England out of war, was "trapped between the Scylla of empire and the Charybdis of peace with Spain."[16] Eager to negotiate with Spain, he reached a tentative agreement, called the Convention of El Pardo, on 14 January 1739. Oglethorpe was strictly enjoined by Walpole to obey the decision of commissioners who were to determine the Georgia-Florida boundary.[17] But the Pardo agreement was unacceptable, for many reasons, to Walpole's enemies, who demanded his political scalp. The opposition combined to force the ministry down a path which could lead only to war. The government capitulated. If the nation wanted war, then war it must be.[18]

England did not actually make an official declaration of war until 23 October 1739,[19] after which Spain followed suit.[20] Oglethorpe had jumped the gun somewhat in Savannah on 3 October. With the armed freeholders drawn up, drums beating, and the magistrates dressed in their official robes, he spoke to the gathering and congratulated them on the "Chearfulness which he observed to be in all Ranks." He assured the townspeople that his trip into the backcountry had protected them from possible Indian raids but warned that everyone must be on the alert for runaway blacks who might be trying to take advantage both of the confusion in Carolina society following the Stono Rebellion and of the Spanish proclamation of 1738. Official papers were read aloud by William Stephens, including Newcastle's instructions to Oglethorpe. Georgia's leader then returned to "his Lodgings" to the boom of cannon and the rattle of "three handsome Vollies" from the militia.[21] Although he wrote to the Trustees that he was overwhelmed with work, he was again "in good health" after his illness in the Indian country and was on his way "to anoy the Spaniards."[22] Cautious Charles Town did not publish England's formal decree until 28 April 1740. The solemn procession there included even "French Horns on Horse-back."[23]

To Walpole, whose pacific preferences Oglethorpe knew well, he confided that he had unleashed the Indians against the Spanish, but that he had done nothing more. He had interpreted his orders from Newcastle to mean that the point was to bring Spain "into Terms, so as to continue the Peace." If it was to be a full-scale war, Oglethorpe continued, he had evolved a plan to cause a "revolt" in one of the enemy's "richest Provinces" and "hinder their Treasure from coming to Europe."[24]

He revived his scheme to overthrow the Cuban government after the failure of the St. Augustine expedition and perhaps to distract attention from it, but his other letters at this time were not so mild as the Walpole note. In spite of the peaceful intent he expressed to the prime minister, Oglethorpe had already informed William Bull, almost two weeks before, that he had sent into Indian country for as many allies as could be spared. Oglethorpe expressed the desire that "the People of Carolina will give the necessary Assistance that we may begin with the Siege of Augustine before more Troops arrive there from Cuba."[25]

Only one day before writing Walpole he had communicated again with Bull: "All is in Action." He hoped the Assembly would take advantage of "this favourable Opportunity of getting rid of their Neighbours at Augustine."[26] Two weeks later Oglethorpe's peaceful intent advanced just about as far it could go. He would do his "utmost," he said, to take St. Augustine before it was reinforced. "If we do not attack, we shall be attacked."[27] This was not the way to reestablish cordial relations with Spain, but Oglethorpe was never really serious on that point. He had longed for a fight for years and now that it was upon him he had every intention of taking advantage of the situation; the planning and the waiting were almost unbearable to him.

But Mars could not be served every minute. Thanks to the indefatigable William Stephens, history has been left an appealing picture of the warlike Oglethorpe working on a cleanup detail in Savannah. Taking time off from his preparations for war, he ordered all male inhabitants "whether Freeholders, or Inmates, and Boys of a competent Age" to gather on the morning of 17 October for a town-wide brushup. He had noticed that the common land and the squares, having been cleared of trees since Savannah's earliest days, had become clogged with an "Abundance of Shrub-Wood" and "an offensive Weed" that grew shoulder high. Not only did the bushes and weeds keep grass from growing; they also "harboured and increased many troublesome Insects and Vermin" and constituted a fire hazard as well. The townsmen cooperated wholeheartedly with Oglethorpe on this project, and he himself worked with them "and every Body, without Distinction, took Pains to do what he could." Oglethorpe was pleased, not just to get the undergrowth cleared away, but because the willingness of the inhabitants showed their "Disposition to obey." (It also gave him a rough head count of the number of men who could bear arms in an emergency. This total, Stephens reckoned, came to "very near two hundred.") In high good humor, Oglethorpe presented the workers with bread and beer in the morning and at the close of day as well.[28]

The figure of two hundred able-bodied men is by no means unimpressive, particularly in light of criticisms leveled by the malcontents who claimed Savannah was a dying settlement unable to care for itself. The town's spirit buoyed hopes that Georgia would be able to repel the best the hated Spaniards had to offer.

Although Oglethorpe had first told Bull of the impending crisis with Spain as early as September 1739 and had written at least twice in October, the Carolina leader did not think the situation serious enough to warrant calling the Assembly into special session, and so the legislators simply convened at the regularly scheduled date of 7 November. Bull's opening address focused on the crisis, but he added that he had no recent intelligence of specific Spanish designs against Georgia. Pledging Carolina's full support to Georgia, he asked that committees be set up to study how his province would best be able to render aid to the colony to the south.[29] The legislative committee did not report out until 12 December. If Oglethorpe ordered a siege at St. Augustine and could give strong assurances that it would be successful, then "the best Assistance" the colony could afford would be put at his disposal. The Commons House and Upper House endorsed the report promptly.[30]

Oglethorpe arrived at Frederica from Savannah on 8 November and six days later learned that the Spanish had delivered the first blow along the frontier by raiding Amelia Island and

killing two of the inhabitants.[31] The experience only strengthened Oglethorpe's determination. He wrote the Trustees that he
and the people in the colony were "resolved to dye hard and
will not lose one inch of ground without fighting." He
understood that England's advantage in the situation lay in the
fact that their fighting men were also inhabitants of the area.
With this in mind, he thought it expedient "to strike first."[32]
On 23 November, Toonahowi, Hillipsilli, and other Indians set
out on a punitive expedition "vowing" to avenge the Amelia
dead, and they were followed by Oglethorpe himself at the
head of a mixed party that pressed beyond the St. Johns River
but failed to make significant contact with the enemy.[33]

In Frederica about a month later, Oglethorpe wrote Bull of the
kind of aid he needed to take the Spanish stronghold "whilst it
is weak." He envisioned a total force of almost thirty-five
hundred men, not including his own regiment and troops raised
from the residents of Georgia. He was confident Carolina could
raise ten companies of sixty men each, provide eight hundred
pioneers, thirty-five rangers, and one hundred and sixty other
men for miscellaneous duties. He estimated the cost at £139,
637,[34] a figure the Assembly thought too low for a force of such
size. It was recommended, however, that the colony appropriate
£120,000 local currency if Oglethorpe would give reasonable
assurances that the projected expedition would succeed.[35]

Time was passing, but still the Carolinians hesitated. Discussion in the Commons House was put off, on 7 February, because
attendance was so poor—a comment in itself; the following
morning "wet Weather" forced an additional postponement.[36]
On the ninth, progress was made. A tax on slaves and land was
approved to raise the largest share of the money to support the
expedition, but the number of troops voted was cut sharply.
There was a good deal of other hedging as well. For instance,
the Carolina men could be used for no longer than six months;
the troops were subject to South Carolina's orders; they were to
have equal votes in the councils of war as well as equal shares of
the anticipated booty; and the Carolina contingents were to
punish their own offenders. Fears that another slave insurrection
might develop hung heavily over the Assembly. Both houses

agreed to the aid measures and to the restrictions too. Bull was instructed to inform Oglethorpe, after which the Assembly adjourned for fifteen days.[37]

In the meantime Oglethorpe had been demonstrating the utmost energy and activity along the Georgia-Florida frontier. On 1 January 1740, with almost two hundred men, he set out from Frederica by boat and by the sixth the force had landed on the south bank of the St. Johns River. On the following day he moved against and captured two small forts on either side of the river, one of which, called Picolata, was found abandoned. Fort St. Francis de Pupo, however, offered stiff resistance until Oglethorpe could bring a battery to bear on it. When it was apparent the British had an overwhelming superiority, the tiny garrison surrendered.[38] He reveled in his triumph. St. Francis was ordered repaired, and a garrison of fifty men stationed there. Oglethorpe considered the victory at the fort "of great consequence" because it cut communications between St. Augustine in the east of Florida and St. Marks and Apalache to the west. In addition, it blocked a possible invasion route the Spanish might use if they wanted to invest the Creek Indian country.[39]

He sent out reconnaissance parties on 9 January to probe Spanish strength near St. Augustine, but two days later he himself returned to St. Simons, arriving there on 17 January.[40] He busied himself with more letters, urging on Walpole the importance of his most recent incursions[41] and telling Bull of improvements that had been made in the defenses at St. Augustine. "The longer we delay attacking them," he counseled, "the stronger they will be."[42]

Montiano, meanwhile, was frantic over the state of the Florida defenses. In the strongest language he could muster he said the situation there amounted to "a rebuff of His Majesty's sacred honor, a foul stain on his catholic arms, and an insult exciting the rage of our nation." He begged for reinforcements from Cuba. If they were not forthcoming, Spain must be prepared for the worst.[43]

And, indeed, in his position it is no surprise that Montiano was in a frenzy. The British had already made two virtually unopposed sorties into the heartland of his province and there was no predicting when Oglethorpe might make up his mind to give Florida another of his sudden and inexplicable visits. Under the circumstances Montiano, who was forced to fight a defensive rearguard action, did what any sensible commander would: he avoided a confrontation with the enemy, kept his scouts and Indians active in their observations of Oglethorpe, and withdrew the main bodies of the garrisons from outlying forts and concentrated all his strength at St. Augustine. Finally, he wrote desperate letters to his immediate superior in Cuba outlining his plight.

For Oglethorpe, affairs in Charles Town seemed not to advance speedily enough. On 20 March he paused briefly at Thunderbolt, while on his way from Frederica to Carolina, in order to issue "his Commands in divers Matters" to Stephens and Thomas Jones.[44] By the twenty-sixth he was in the Carolina port city "to consult Measures" with the Assembly how best (and most economically) to bring St. Augustine to its knees.[45] Three days later Oglethorpe expressed his anxiety to be off to the frontiers. If the troops were not raised and ready to leave in fourteen days, he was not optimistic as to the ultimate outcome of the invasion. The Commons House expressed its "unanimous Opinion" that such speedy mobilization was impossible, and then returned to its squabble concerning the makeup of a committee that was to confer with Oglethorpe.[46]

Although things appeared to be moving very slowly, Oglethorpe was still able to write one of his optimistic letters to Newcastle predicting that St. Augustine would "very probably" surrender after a short bombardment. But he had found Carolina's finances so shaky that he himself had been "obliged to advance them £4,000 Sterling upon the Credit of their future Taxes, without which the Siege could not be carried on."[47] The prominent Carolina merchant Robert Pringle, who was not so intimately associated with the St. Augustine effort, wrote "that the Expedition is goeing on with all speed."[48]

By 3 April 1740, the Assembly had appropriated the necessary money, had named Alexander Vander Dussen as commanding officer of the Carolina regiment, and had cut the six months' period of service to four. Oglethorpe had been forced to accept a series of concessions in relation to his command to which, under ordinary conditions, he would never have consented.[49] But at last the way seemed clear to make the push against Florida. Ironically, on the same day the aid was voted, six half-galleys armed with nine-pound brass cannon, arrived in St. Augustine harbor from Cuba. It was the presence of these ships that thwarted Oglethorpe's plans to take St. Augustine.

8   The St. Augustine Expedition of 1740

The St. Augustine expedition of 1740 was a study in frustration for Oglethorpe and the English. It was not until well into May that he and some of his allies landed again on the south bank of the St. Johns. Then Oglethorpe proceeded to march toward St. Augustine where Fort Diego, on the lands of Diego Espinoza, stood in the army's way. An engagement on 11 May was followed by the surrender of the fort the next day. At this battle were captured a number of cannon and prisoners, arms and ammunition, and a good many horses.[1] Neither Oglethorpe nor his Indian and Carolina allies knew it at the time, but this was to prove the only real ''victory'' of this expedition.

Oglethorpe then returned to the mouth of the St. Johns, joined forces with Carolina troops under Vander Dussen, and went back to Diego on the sixteenth. After several false starts he moved with his main strength toward St. Augustine, overrunning the Negro fort, Mosa, early in June[2] but returning to Diego after setting fire to parts of the former Negro stronghold. Apparently intimidated by the presence of the half-galleys in St. Augustine Bay, situated so that they controlled entry to the harbor and afforded extra protection to fort and town, Oglethorpe considered how best to proceed. With his original plan of a concerted land-and-sea attack endangered, he moved his greatest strength to Anastasia Island opposite town and castle. The island was of little tactical value as long as the Royal Navy was in control outside the harbor, and the distance between Anastasia and St. Augustine rendered the artillery that was taken there virtually useless. What he did was divide his forces between Anastasia, Point Quartell across the harbor entrance from the island, and the mainland where he put a third force. The latter group he instructed to keep St. Augustine's garrison and townspeople from foraging in the neighboring countryside. The Spanish must be prevented from bringing in provisions to stockpile against the possibility of a siege. (A siege was in fact being recommended to Oglethorpe by the sea captains who at the same time blandly informed him that they would no longer be available for blockade purposes after the fifth of July.)[3] Although the move to Anastasia makes sense in light of an effort to destroy or render useless the half-galleys, it also served to advertise to Montiano that Oglethorpe had divided his army and that his command must, perforce, be weak somewhere.

It is difficult to say what happened to Oglethorpe's usually decisive manner during the first month of operations in Florida. Apparently he suddenly became irresolute in his approach to the problems which faced his expedition, for he demonstrated a lack of imaginative leadership that made some wonder if he had not lost his nerve. He fell back on sterile tradition and on a series of marches and counter marches designed, he claimed, to draw the Spanish out of their fortification. The Spanish had no intention of being lured out by his drum beating and banner waving. The more Oglethorpe's tactics are analyzed the more they seem almost designed to camouflage the fact that he did not know what to do once his first plan for a joint land-sea assault went awry. When goaded about his refusal to rush the town of St. Augustine in a sudden move, forcing the inhabitants into the castle for protection, he denounced the plan as "too hazardous." Instead of being typically forward and aggressive he said "he knew what he had to do; that it was the Custom of Armies always to shew themselves to the Enemy first and to make a Feint." So he and Vander Dussen, after taking Mosa, marched toward the Spanish to observe the castillo while drums beat "the Grenadier's March"; at dusk he sent his drums out again and succeeded in getting the enemy to fire randomly.[4] All of this seemed to demonstrate Oglethorpe's failure to comprehend that it would take a serious effort, as well as bloodshed, to capture Montiano's command.

Early in the morning of 15 June the Spanish made a surprise sortie from the gates of St. Augustine. Their target was the isolated group on the mainland, a mixture of Highland, English, and Carolina Rangers, Highlanders from Darien under John Mackintosh, about forty-five Indians, and a detachment from Oglethorpe's regiment. The total number of troops ran to about a hundred and thirty-five, but there was bitter dissension in the group and they were outnumbered two to one by the Spaniards.[5] Much as he had advised the Chickasaws earlier, Oglethorpe had instructed these men, who were under the operational command of Colonel John Palmer of Carolina, to keep mobile and, above all, to be wary of spending more than one night in the same place. Oglethorpe's warning was ignored, the consequence being a general relaxation of discipline by Palmer's men, who were also separated by a marsh and tidal creek from Vander Dussen's headquarters at Point Quartell. To make a dangerous situation worse, the Highlanders had taken to pitching their tents within the breached walls of Fort Mosa. The troops seemed to feel so secure that apparently not even an adequate line of pickets was posted on the road that led to the gates of St. Augustine. These blunders and feelings of false security proved fatal. After putting up a relatively stout fight, all things considered, the English were overcome by the superior Spanish force. Those who were not killed in the melee either ran for their lives or surrendered. Although records are wildly contradictory on the subject of the affair at Mosa, it appears that the British suffered about sixty-eight killed and thirty-four taken prisoner.[6] The rest, presumably, made their way to Vander Dussen's command.

From Mosa on, all was anticlimax. On the day following, Vander Dussen and Lieutenant Colonel William Cook visited Oglethorpe on Anastasia and "found Things in a good deal of Distraction; Resolutions taken and not put in Execution."[7] On 17 June, Oglethorpe ordered Vander Dussen to come to Anastasia with his regiment, leaving a guard behind on Quartell to protect the cannon and stores. Vander Dussen was incredulous. What he feared, of course, was not only the lack of an effective overall plan, but also that by dividing his forces again, another

Mosa might be in the offing. Vander Dussen and his officers issued a demurral which the Carolina colonel personally delivered to Oglethorpe. When the general bridled and asked if this was disobedience, Vander Dussen mildly replied that it was opinion only and if ordered to Anastasia, there the regiment would go.[8] Still there seemed to be no realistic planning in the commanding officer's camp, or so apparently thought Vander Dussen.

There was almost no firing either at or from the enemy from 17 June through 19 June. On the afternoon of 20 June Oglethorpe, satisfied now that he had his artillery and mortars in position, wrote to Montiano demanding that he surrender St. Augustine and admonishing him to take proper care of the prisoners he held. There was no fighting at all on that day, but the bombardment of fort and town, with the Spanish giving as well as they got, was renewed on 21 June after Montiano's indignant rejection of Oglethorpe's ultimatum. He would fight, he said with resolution, to the last extremity.[9]

On 23 June the transference of the Carolina regiment to Anastasia was completed, with some of Oglethorpe's troops taking their place on Quartell. He and the entire regiment, with only a few exceptions, had returned to the mainland by the evening of 24 June.[10] It sounds almost like motion for motion's sake, and although Oglethorpe probably wanted to bring the expedition to a head his imagination seemed gone; with Vander Dussen, the Indians, and the Carolina volunteers all anticipating action, Oglethorpe was paralyzed by indecision. Reluctant to call on others for advice and too proud to admit that he was at a loss over what to do, Oglethorpe wrote Bull for reinforcements in the form of additional soldiers and a schooner to frustrate the annoying half-galleys.[11]

Affairs continued in such a desultory fashion to the point that Vander Dussen, who now seemed to be the only leader with any nerve, began to explore the possibilities open for the English. He hatched a scheme to destroy the half-galleys, a scheme rejected out of hand by Commodore Vincent Pearse and the naval contingents as too risky. Vander Dussen followed up this idea with another one: set up a battery to control access to the mouth of the St. Sebastian River, which emptied into St. Augustine harbor just south of the town. If this spot could be covered and if Matanzas Inlet could be kept under surveillance, the Spanish would be circumscribed in their actions. Most important, supplies could not be run into Matanzas and St. Sebastian, and thence to St. Augustine. In order to create this new battery, however, a contingent of about two hundred men from the seven ships blockading the harbor would be necessary. Vander Dussen asked Oglethorpe to write Pearse to detach temporarily the necessary men to be used at the new battery. Once the hurricane season had passed, Pearse and his ships could resume their patrolling and could pick up their men at that time. Oglethorpe did as he was bid, but neither he nor anyone else could convince the naval arm that this plan or any other had merit. It was, probably, too close to the navy's departure date of 5 July. It is hard not to reach the conclusion that the ship captains were anxious to be through with this particular operation.[12]

By the end of June Oglethorpe seemed almost resigned to the failure of the expedition. He wrote Bull complaining again of the shortage of men but also announcing that he had "recovered" Mosa—as though it were some feat of military significance. But in his aforementioned letter to Pearse, where he requested the sailors, he let slip his opinion that with the departure of the ships went the last hope of taking St. Augustine. He expressed concern how the men and artillery already on Anastasia could be removed without the navy's help. With the king's ships gone, the half-galleys would be free to range far and wide, laying waste the Georgia coast, including Frederica, "and all the Sea Settlements of Carolina."[13] Such a vision of destruction perpetrated by six little half-galleys, powered by oars and manned by fewer than two hundred men, smacks of panic and must make serious students of the expedition wonder if Oglethorpe's judgment had not been seriously impaired.

On 3 July the operation, already staggering, was given its coup de grace. Vander Dussen spotted Spanish launches and a sloop that had come up the Matanzas Inlet with the aim of running supplies to the beleaguered town and fort. He tried to prevent their getting through, but the galleys rushed "to their Protection" and he was forced to fall back,[14] leaving the way open for the relief boats to be escorted to the Spanish town.

On the same day, Oglethorpe was brutally rebuffed by Pearse and the council of war. Not only was he denied sailors for the projected battery to control the St. Sebastian, but the council let it be known that no help would be given in patrolling the St. Johns River area, thereby leaving Georgia and Carolina open to an attack if Spain could mount one. The next day the blockading ships prepared to leave Florida waters and Oglethorpe, apparently almost with a sense of relief, ordered a withdrawal.[15] The whole ambitious project had failed.

The expedition itself was over, the controversy as to who should be blamed for its unhappy end had hardly begun. At the very heart of this new battle was the spare yet imposing figure of James Oglethorpe, standing tall and erect as always, but surrounded by a cloud of suspicion and doubt.

As an example of the rancor between Georgia and Carolina, a letter from a prominent Charles Town merchant, written even before the expedition broke up, is revealing. Oglethorpe, wrote Joseph Wragg, "follows no advice" and was primarily to blame for the failure in Florida. He seemed determined to march his soldiers in circles "only to harrass the men, without any Design of coming to Action." Although Carolina forces began to leave the expedition in its last hours, Mosa was the cause, and the disaster there was wholly owing to Oglethorpe. Wragg noted quite frankly that "our Voluntiers are daily coming away, as they see there is no prospect of Succeeding under such Mad conduct." Had an officer other than the general been in command, said the merchant, St. Augustine would have been taken early in the war.[16]

As criticism of Oglethorpe's leadership became more pronounced, so did his defense. Before the end of June he wrote Charles Pinckney that the Mosa affair was not his fault but Palmer's, for Palmer had permitted his men to camp at the Negro fort in direct disobedience to Oglethorpe's strictest orders.[17] Pinckney, then in Boston, found time to write Carolina agent Peregrine Fury in London the full "Mellancholly Account" of the expedition. Pinckney feared that Spain would speedily invade and conquer Georgia. Then the Carolina situation would be desperate "with regard to our s----s." It was a thought so fearful that Pinckney dared not spell it out. Fury must pull any string he could to get aid in Britain.[18]

The mood of the London journals gradually changed from one of incredible overconfidence to keen disappointment when it became clear that Oglethorpe had failed. Indian desertions were cited by *The Champion* as the cause of the frustation of Oglethorpe's designs, but the Mosa affair was called inexcusable. The troops placed there were "so remote from the main Body, that they could not in time be supported."[19] Captain Hugh Mackay, who was in actual command of the troops at Mosa, was in England not long after the retreat and was disgusted to hear the criticism of Oglethorpe voiced even in the "Coffee houses" to "defame" Georgia's leader. Palmer at Mosa had got nothing more nor less than what he deserved; Oglethorpe's leadership had been above reproach.[20] And on and on.

Oglethorpe was keenly aware of the criticism he would receive; it was a chance one took when one was in command. So even before leaving Florida for the friendlier confines of Frederica, the weary leader wrote Bull what might be called his apologia for the expedition. He defended his division of troops by saying that owing to the lay of the land at St. Augustine the town "cannot be closely shut up" except by such a move. It must be recalled, Oglethorpe said, that he had informed Bull that St. Augustine was short of food, the defenses weak, and the garrison only partial. But this had been early in the game, when Oglethorpe had urged the necessity of haste on Carolina. He had feared that St. Augustine would be provisioned and reinforced, and that the time of year when hurricanes and heat might be serious factors would come before an attempt on it could be made. He had been right. Every one of his fears had been realized, and it is clear he thought each of them important in bringing about his frustration. The sea captains, however, came in for a special denunciation. Unless the Spanish half-galleys were taken, Vander Dussen could not successfully attack the town from Anastasia, and the sea lords refused to move against the Spanish boats. The time of year had caused fevers and dysentery to strike the men, but in spite of all discouragements Oglethorpe bravely concluded that he could easily march back to St. Augustine and make a fight of it.[21] But there was really no question of rushing down there again. The men were tired, disgruntled, and sick, and they needed rest and their families.

Once back in Frederica Oglethorpe suffered something that sounds like a physical and mental collapse. He "was much weakend by a lurking Fever," Egmont wrote in his journal,[22] but the information came from William Stephens, who, in turn, originally heard the news of Oglethorpe's illness from Vander Dussen himself. On his way to Charles Town from the southern frontiers, the Carolinian stopped by Savannah and spent about twenty-four hours. It was during this visit, when Vander Dussen and Stephens were much together, that the former told Georgia's secretary "that the General was in so ill a State of Health at Frederica, as he was at the Time when he now left him, being (as he said) reduced to an extraordinary Weakness, by a continual Fever upon him, with some Intermission, for two Months past." In that period "his Spirits supported him under all Fatigue; but the Disappointment of Success (it is believed) now galled him, and too great Anxiety of Mind preyed upon him."[23]

Here was an interesting development. If Vander Dussen is to be credited, and there is no reason to doubt his word, then Oglethorpe was plagued with his sickness and fever during the days of lethargy and indecision that led up to the affair at Mosa. How typical of the proud Oglethorpe to hide his illness from the army, but Vander Dussen, who saw him regularly, could not be misled. Oglethorpe, a bit disdainful of physical frailty, had succeeded in keeping his incapacity out of the official dispatches of the expedition and out of his semiofficial correspondence as well.

Not long after receiving this report Stephens had occasion to go to Frederica, where, to his alarm, he found that the lingering fever had eroded Oglethorpe's strength. Oglethorpe stayed mainly upstairs "on his Bed," and although obviously feeling ill he still possessed the old "Vivacity of Spirit in Appearance to all whom he talked with, though he chose to converse with very few." Stephens waited for Oglethorpe to say when he was ready to do official business. After about ten days he felt somewhat stronger and so the two men transacted the long-neglected affairs of the province.[24]

By January 1741, Oglethorpe had shaken his fever, ennui, and depression, and was found once again defending his old postures and showing a willingness to assume new ones. To the Trustees he vindicated his conduct in surprisingly mild tones, but the letter was written considerably before the invective against him had begun to flow in earnest. He complained against the Carolina Assembly's conditions and said he could easily have taken St. Augustine had aid come early.[25] To Walpole he once again raised the possibility of the capture of Havana. Obviously he was thinking of himself and his experience in Florida when he said the "Moor" castle in Cuba could "be easily surprized." It would take a bare minimum of British soldiers, Admiral Edward Vernon's squadron, some artillery, and Indians he would muster for the occasion.[26] His spirits had revived even if his military judgment had not improved.

But the principle he enunciated was correct. As he told the Trustees in 1743, Florida's main fort and town would both have fallen to his "litle Strength" if he had been joined in March by the Carolinians. May was too late. Defensive measures had been taken, and the half-galleys had arrived. Vernon, with a small force, could have taken Cartagena easily in 1741, but once the Spanish were reinforced and warned, his numerical superiority had no effect. The analogy to St. Augustine was obvious.[27]

Vander Dussen was safely back in Charles Town on 13 August, but before his arrival the Assembly, upon receiving final word of the failure of the expedition, formed the inevitable committee to look into the reasons for the disappointment.[28] The complex history of the committee report itself, and of its separate publications, is told elsewhere.[29] Suffice it to say that this report, with its one hundred and thirty-nine appendices, ultimately appeared in print and blamed the miscarriage of the expedition on Oglethorpe. A regular pamphlet war broke out in London between the advocates of Oglethorpe and the supporters of Carolina.[30] The air was filled with venom over this expedition—an expedition called by *The Champion* the most "romantic" and irregular in its leadership since a more famous one some years before against Troy.[31]

From the vantage point of twentieth-century America, what can be said about the St. Augustine affair of 1740 and Oglethorpe's role therein?

For one thing, although the Carolina volunteers left the scene of action early, the desertion charges so often heard against the South Carolina contingents appear to be almost totally groundless. The Carolinians made good and loyal troops, contrary to the charges made by some officers of Oglethorpe's regiment. And Vander Dussen himself, although apparently a bit forward in suggesting alternate plans to his commanding officer, comes out well in any objective survey of the 1740 British effort in Florida. Positive documentary evidence is lacking, but it seems reasonable in light of Oglethorpe's health that the general was at this crucial point lacking his usual decisiveness and may actually have relied on Vander Dussen to do some of his strategic thinking for him. If this is true, it is unfortunate Oglethorpe could not have gone one step farther and adopted Vander Dussen's schemes as his own. He recognized that the Carolinian's advice had merit and referred to his "several handsome Proposals," but beyond that point he could not go.[32] He was too accustomed to making his own decisions to change overnight or under the abnormal stresses of war and unaccustomed illness.

That the expedition was not very professionally organized and carried out is apparent to one who explores its intricacies. The communications were poorly arranged; the logistics of the blockading forces were faulty; and the food supply for the army was handled inefficiently. Perhaps most astonishing of all, Oglethorpe's reactions to the lay of the land around the Spanish town and fort would almost lead one to believe he had never seen a map of the area and had never heard a report from a spy or an informer as to the strength and position of the Spanish

garrison. Actually, his innumerable reconnaissance parties, sent
almost within sight of St. Augustine for months before the
expedition was in fact underway, perhaps told him too much
about the territory he was to invest but never to win. He could
not see the forest for the trees. Each palmetto hut and each dune
or fort seemed important, but one hardly more so than another.

In effect what happened to Oglethorpe was that he lost his
sense of proportion. Everything took on the appearance of being
of equal weight; hence, for example, his ''recapture'' of Mosa
was made to seem of almost the same significance as the Spanish
victory there. This is a dangerous delusion for a military man,
particularly one in command of a large number of troops.

It should be pointed out in defense of Oglethorpe that he was
not very familiar with day-to-day warfare. Of command he
knew little more than what he may have learned in his reading
or picked up in his youth while fighting briefly in Europe. He
was apparently an afficionado of military tactics, military
science, and military decorum, but as a commanding officer on
the field of battle he was hardly more than a novice. It is a
tribute to his ability to project the image of himself as a
qualified military figure that no one—not even Walpole or
Vander Dussen—questioned his competence to lead such an
expedition against a capable and well-entrenched foe. But there
was a world of difference between marking the disposition of
troops on a tablecloth with a finger dipped in wine—which
Oglethorpe did, to the delight of Boswell, Johnson, and
Goldsmith, in 1772 to illustrate the battle of Belgrade—and
actually distributing his forces properly before St. Augustine in
1740.[33]

Robert Pringle in Charles Town was one of the few to isolate
Oglethorpe's inexperience as a factor in assessing the cause of
the Florida disappointment. In addition to the usual references
to the ''Inglorious Expedition,'' and Oglethorpe's ''un-
accountable Bad Conduct & Ill Management,'' Pringle wrote
that the general had exposed for all to see ''his want of
Knowledge & Capacity in Military affairs.''[34]

Although Oglethorpe's original ideas were predicated upon
the notion of a sudden assault, he assumed that the time of year

in which this assault would be made would be early spring. By the time he actually put his invasion into full operation it was May and already getting hot. The marches and countermarches must have exhausted as well as annoyed the private soldier. There are records surviving which indicate that he drove his men to the limit—but for what? On 21 May, on one of the frequent scouting parties, Oglethorpe, Vander Dussen, and another rode out from the camp on the St. Johns to look over the St. Augustine harbor entrance. The pace was so quick that the Indians left the group and even the Highlanders "dropt down by the Way." When the three men returned that night at 2 A.M., all the way to Fort Diego, their horses were so exhausted that they were scarcely "able to walk" and had to be led into camp.[35]

Oglethorpe's idea of a quick attack against St. Augustine may, technically, have been the correct procedure to follow, but his own modest thrusts and probes left a good deal to be desired by such standards. His defense was that he did not have enough troops to make the decisive move he originally had in mind, but surprise in some cases makes up for numbers. He also failed to consider that the enemy was far less prepared for war than he. A determined move by Oglethorpe's regiment alone, with a few Indian allies, might have overwhelmed the undermanned and disoriented Spanish positions and resulted in a victory as startling and electric as Vernon's at Porto Bello. Oglethorpe, however, was cautious and chose to wait until he had been reinforced before moving in strength to the south bank of the St. Johns River. By that time succor had been sent to the Spanish at St. Augustine, and with the Cuban aid the morale of the Spaniards improved.

The behavior of the Royal Navy must also be put high on the list when considering reasons for Oglethorpe's frustration. Pearse was constantly finding fault, and the warships, in effect, acted as a separate command. Through their own councils they controlled not only their own fate, but the fate of the land forces as well. As long as the harbor was effectively blockaded there still was a chance the Spaniards could be starved into submission, but the defection of the *Hector* on 1 July, four days before the date set by Pearse for the departure of the squadron, was a sure sign the expedition was doomed. Two days later supplies were ferried up the Matanzas Inlet and in two more days' time the entire squadron was under way. There was no reasoning with Pearse; no appeals, either from Vander Dussen or Oglethorpe, could touch him.

Probably the worst single blow, insofar as the naval aspect of the contest was concerned, was the failure of Captain Simonds, on the fifty-gun *Colchester*, to show up off the Florida coast. It was Simonds who carried with him the orders to Pearse and the others to give total cooperation to the besieging forces. As it was, all Oglethorpe could do was to plead.

Benjamin Martyn, Trustee secretary, wrote with considerable justification that the divided command was most unfortunate and that the Royal Navy acted too independently in the whole affair.[36] The most thorough work on the role of the navy during this entire war, however, concluded that both Oglethorpe and Pearse "proved themselves indifferent leaders; the former, though he developed the idea, was incapable of putting it into execution; the latter saw difficulties everywhere but made little effort to overcome them."[37]

One factor that has never been given adequate consideration was the stubborn and intelligent opposition by the forces under Montiano. Perhaps because they were Spaniards and therefore to be given no credit, it never seemed to occur to the British that Florida's governor conducted a careful, effective defense. Instead of a healthy respect for the enemy, the newspapers and journals of the day, both in England and America, were exuding confidence in the capacity of a single Englishman to handle easily six or seven Spaniards. But when the siege was lifted in July, even Governor Montiano was mystified why the English plan misfired. "My wonder," he wrote, "is inexpressible." What he alluded to as the British army's "shameful flight" was beyond his ken. He wistfully reported to his superior, Cuban Governor Juan Francisco de Güemes, that he wished he had the sort of force that could pursue the British as they retreated northward; Spanish arms would prevail because relations between Georgia and South Carolina had reached a new low. The latter colony would never cooperate with the former again, he wrote.[38]

Edward Lyng, of Oglethorpe's regiment, captured during the action at Mosa and later released, testified upon his return that in spite of appearances Montiano would have surrendered in four more days had the British stayed before the town.[39] In light of the fact that provisions were reaching St. Augustine by 3 July, Lyng's story suggests Charles Town polemics calculated to embarrass Oglethorpe. The mulatto Felix Argular had in fact earlier appeared before the Carolina Council and reported that the stresses in the English camp were common knowledge in St. Augustine, and that the dissension gave the enemy courage to continue the struggle.[40] Certainly Montiano knew the disposition of the British and the morale and health problems faced by Oglethorpe. He had twelve English deserters with him in St. Augustine who, he reported, supplied him with valuable information and encouraged the garrison to stand up to the unpredictable tactics of "Don Diego Ogletorp."[41]

The fact remains that Montiano was clever to concentrate his strength rather than permit himself to be gradually whittled down to the point of impotence. He drew the English into the wilds of Florida and thus extended their supply lines and threatened their communications. He surrendered to Oglethorpe only fields of palmetto and, with the exception of San Diego, forts with breached walls and poisoned wells. Montiano had been briefed concerning the best possible Spanish defense measures and the castillo had only recently been strengthened. Arredondo, the engineer-diplomat over whose interpretation of the debatable land Spaniard and Britisher fought, had introduced new touches at St. Augustine that negated the superior fire power enjoyed by the English. In the words of the specialist on the subject, Florida's "defenses were equal to the emergency, justifying the long years of preparation and suffering that had attended their construction."[42]

It is also not quite fair simply to blame Oglethorpe, Palmer, Mackay, or even others for the affair at Mosa. To do so is to look at the incident in a negative light. Although it is difficult for those whose sources are English-oriented to take an objective stance, anyone who is anxious to give credit where it is due must concede that Montiano chose precisely the right time and place for his lightning-like stroke. The early morning raid against the isolated English camp resulted not only in an immediate victory for Spanish arms, but it boosted the morale of the defending forces and caused a corresponding loss of élan by Oglethorpe's army. In the final analysis the fate of the expedition was sealed at the breached walls of the Negro fort, Mosa. If Oglethorpe is to be blamed for failure of leadership, then it is only just to give credit to his opposite number for possessing what Oglethorpe lacked. Only David Ramsay has seen fit to give the Spaniards credit for conducting an effective opposition to the British push. But St. Augustine, he wrote, "was so strongly fortfied, both by nature and art, that probably the attempt must have failed though it had been conducted by the ablest officer, and executed by the best disciplined troops."[43] Unfortunately for the English side, the expedition had neither.

With Oglethorpe eager to get started and with South Carolina having been asked as far back as September 1739, for material aid, it seemed only reasonable to expect Carolina elements of some sort to join Oglethorpe for his planned "sudden assault" by the time six months had passed. Had the province done so it is likely the outskirts of the Spanish stronghold could have been reached before the half-galleys (as well as the heat) had arrived. Had these boats not been present Oglethorpe could have proceeded as he had originally planned, but it was well into May when the final rendezvous was made. Although Oglethorpe's leadership is open to dispute from that point on, it is hard to defend Carolina's response when it took the older colony over seven months to raise and equip troops for service. The truth of the matter is that Carolina had been lulled into a sense of false security caused, in part, by the settlement of Georgia in 1733, and more particularly by the presence of Oglethorpe's regiment there since 1738.

Jack Greene has uncovered yet another reason for Carolina's foot-dragging. The Commons House was engaged in an effort at that time to get into the gray area between executive and legislative authority. The Lower House would earmark no money for Oglethorpe's expedition until it was shown specifically how the funds would be spent. Bull and his Council claimed that such appropriations were executive functions, but the Commons was adamant. Finally, even Oglethorpe was "required" to come before a committee and give "an itemized estimate" of what he planned to spend. The elected body had its triumph, but it all took time, and the enemy was not idle.[44]

One other—and final—factor should be mentioned. The failure of the expedition was in part owing to the imperfect functioning of a virtually untried idea, at least in the southern colonies. The expedition against Spanish Florida seemed to be an effort by England to have her provinces rely more on one another and less on the mother country. Results were not encouraging. Initial planning had been faulty, and the colonials were poorly informed as to Spanish strength and determination. Even the urbane William Byrd offered his opinion on the question of seizing St. Augustine by stating that "it would be very easy to take the Nest of Pyrates."[45] There is no question that the experienced and able Governor Belcher of Massachusetts put his finger on one of the worst blunders made by the English when he indicated that underestimating the strength of the Spanish may have been fatal.[46]

Former North Carolina Governor George Burrington, an able and informed man, concluded, however, that poor colonial planning lay at the heart of the problem. Oglethorpe's army, numbering only slightly over one thousand effectives, was not large enough to do all that was expected of it. As Burrington pointed out, the other colonies nearby should have been instructed to send men to swell the size of the force. So the miscarriage of the campaign should be ascribed partly to debilitating provincialism and intercolonial rivalries, but also to the absence of effective leadership by the ministry in London.[47] Belcher's estimate of the affair concurred with Burrington's: Oglethorpe lacked sufficient force to accomplish what was expected of him.[48]

As Oglethorpe had his difficulties in 1740, so Vernon and Wentworth had even more severe problems before Cartagena one year later, and Shirley and Pepperrell faced the same kinds of odds in 1745 at Louisbourg. Gradually the kinks that went along with this kind of Anglo-American expedition were worked out, as seen in the stirring triumph at the proud French fortress on Cape Breton Island. By the time the Great War for Empire opened, colonial and British interests seemed to be working more effectively together toward a common goal. Such was not, unfortunately, the case for Oglethorpe in 1740, but it may well be that some of the lessons learned at Point Quartell and on Anastasia helped make later joint expeditions more successful. If so then the Mosa affair was not fought and lost in vain.

9 The Spanish Invasion of Georgia

As the ill and dispirited Oglethorpe led his troops and Indian allies back into Georgia in the summer of 1740, Florida's Montiano expressed not only relief but also the hope that the Spanish might counterattack. In any future undertaking Oglethorpe, in spite of his "authority and restless spirit," could expect little aid from the Carolinians, who were jealous of the general and afraid of their slaves. For the same reasons any renewal of British invasion efforts, especially under the unpopular Oglethorpe, was therefore, for the present, highly unlikely.[1] Montiano was right. With the dispersal of the expedition in 1740, Oglethorpe and the remnants of his forces were thrown into a defensive posture. The initiative passed to the Spanish.

For a number of years Spanish informers had gone into Georgia and Carolina and brought back information on the defenses of the two colonies.[2] The Spanish king had not forgotten his claim to Georgia and even to South Carolina as far as Port Royal, and what Philip V and his queen, Elizabeth Farnese, wanted they often got by one means or another. Still, offensive action by Spain in the Georgia-Carolina sector was unthinkable in 1741 because of the English thrusts in the Caribbean, first against Cartagena and then at Santiago de Cuba. After Spain repelled these attacks and upon arrival of reinforcements for Florida from the mother country, Spain was ready to assert herself on the southern frontier.

The St. Augustine garrison was stiffened in June 1741 by additional soldiers and provisions.[3] English prisoners who had escaped from their Spanish captors in Cuba reported that Havana was a beehive of activity. Ships were being built and fitted out to invade the Bahamas, and almost forty recent prizes had been sent in by Spanish privateers. It was reported in Havana that Carolina must be "a sleep, otherwise they'd not let us take their Vessels *even* on the Bar of *Charlestown.*"⁴

Georgia was never held in lower esteem in England than after the failure of the St. Augustine expedition. The Trustees were discouraged while Oglethorpe was in a state of despondence and ill-health. Toward the end of August 1740, Oglethorpe was able to rouse himself enough to send a letter to Walpole emphasizing his delicate situation. He was expected to fend off the Spanish, but he had neither material aid nor encouragement from England. Therefore he was forced to make the decision whether to draw upon his own personal wealth or to abandon his colony.⁵

From his post in Frederica Oglethorpe initiated a one-man campaign to keep Georgia before the eyes of the ministry. While so doing he resorted, as is frequently the case in such circumstances, to exaggeration. To the harried prime minister, who was doing a desperate domestic balancing act to stay in power, Oglethorpe ventured the horrid possibility that if Georgia fell the Carolinas and Virginia would follow. One of the chief reasons the other provinces were so vulnerable, claimed Oglethorpe, was the number of blacks in those colonies. The Spaniards insinuated themselves by every means, promising the slaves whatever they wanted if they could escape to Florida. Slave insurrection, like the Stono River uprising, was encouraged.⁶

In a letter two weeks later Oglethorpe added Maryland to the list of colonies that would go under if Georgia fell. A Spanish conquest of his province might well result in a general revolt of the "Black Slaves" as far as Pennsylvania. Carolina was undependable—its militia "inconsiderable for Courage as well as Numbers" and its people oblivious. Lulled into a sense of false security, the colony was unaware of the danger just over the horizon.⁷ He even had no help from the king's ships in Charles Town, so he was forced to fit out his own vessels from Frederica to defend the southern frontier.⁸

By the fall of 1741 it was fairly obvious that, in spite of Oglethorpe's efforts to secure support for Georgia, the colony would be left on its own. His efforts to commit the government to Georgia's defense and to the capture of Florida were dismissed and he was instructed to introduce economies. It was recommended he "make monthly returns upon honour" as to the strength of his command and the expenses he was undergoing on the frontier.[9]

As a crowning irony *The Champion* suggested, as Santiago de Cuba was under siege, that when it was taken it should be held permanently by the British. The climate was "temperate," the soil "fertile," and "Should the Government think proper, it would be much to the Advantage of those poor Wretches at *Georgia* to remove to this Place."[10] The notion of transplanting Georgia's inhabitants to Cuba must have been bitterly resented by the Trustees, and had Oglethorpe heard the suggestion it would have made his blood boil and his temper flare.

Governor General Güemes of Cuba designated Montiano "Commanding General" of the Spanish expedition that would win back Georgia, and together they laid plans for an invasion. The year 1742 seemed a propitious time to begin the process of destroying the plantations and settlements of the English interlopers.[11] Oglethorpe was aware of the Spanish activities and began to search in America for the reinforcements he felt would be denied him from England. A North Carolina correspondent, writing from the Wilmington area, reported that on one of these efforts "Capt. *Higginbotham* from *Georgia* is raising Recruits here, but meets with great Obstruction."[12] What this "great Obstruction" was is not clear, but it would be futile, apparently, to expect help from that quarter.

As Spain's activities picked up, so did Oglethorpe's. By late summer 1741 he was on the frontiers again harrying the enemy, and by winter he seemed to be physically and mentally as good as ever—and as indefatigable.[13] Still he found himself unable to accomplish anything lasting because he had so few troops. He had his regiment, and his Indian allies remained faithful, but beyond these he had little more than what he could pay for out of his own pocket. Also, since Georgia had to be protected from a possible flanking attack by the French from the backcountry, Oglethorpe had to make sure that troops were manning the strongholds he had set up for Georgia's protection. With these garrisons tied down, his offensive parries into Florida could be primarily only reconnaissance and observation forays.

Early in 1742 the danger signals of renewed Spanish activities became more and more apparent. Reports in London spoke of the aggressive tack now taken by the once somnolent Spaniard and of the countermeasures resorted to by Oglethorpe.[14] Along these lines Montiano, who was impatient to invade Georgia and Carolina, spoke of the necessity of having three thousand men. He was rebuked by Güemes, who knew that raising such a force was out of the question. At most, the Cuban official confided, he could spare thirty ships and thirteen hundred men from Havana. To this nucleus Montiano, who was given direct charge of the upcoming expedition, was to add five hundred men from St. Augustine's garrison. Such a force, the Cuban governor predicted, should succeed "with happiness and without risk," but Montiano was warned that delay might prove fatal. Surprise was to be a necessary part of the main plan for the invasion: a mortal blow against Carolina. First Oglethorpe must be rendered harmless—a job thought not too difficult—after which everything up to Port Royal was to be laid waste. From Port Royal Montiano was to send into the surrounding country "negroes of all languages . . . to convoke the slaves" and offer them, in Philip V's name, their freedom and to promise them lands in Florida where they could settle.[15] Speed was essential, however, as Havana would be left with only a skeleton force to protect it.[16]

As the crisis of invasion approached, Oglethorpe assumed a kind of serene self-confidence. After his bitter complaints of the year before, his idyllic description of St. Simons at the end of May 1742 sounds a little unreal. A fine wheat crop had just been harvested, the vineyards grew "prodigiously," the corn looked promising. "The Soldiers hold the spade in one hand and the sword in the other and both successfully for since we destroyed seven Spanish Forts in Florida in the Campaign against Augustine, we have held them into this very hour so that they have not been able to rebuild any one of them."[17] This kind of optimism was for the benefit of the Trustees and the English public, but as usual Oglethorpe was stimulated by the odds being against him. Now that he was well again the Spaniards had a tenacious foe awaiting them.

By early June Oglethorpe knew that large Spanish reinforcements had arrived in St. Augustine. A letter to Lieutenant Governor Bull, written shortly thereafter, reflected the old Oglethorpe of the pre-St. Augustine expedition. He expected an attack, he said, and was determined "to give them a warm reception and make them sick of it." Should he fare badly, it would be wisest for Bull to reinforce his defense position at Port Royal, for there the Spanish would go after Georgia. From Port Royal the enemy would incite a slave insurrection. Bull was clearly warned that as commander Oglethorpe would hold the governor liable should the Carolina position crumble as a result of negligence. "If there's any trifling in this and an accident thereupon should happen," said Oglethorpe bluntly, "You may depend on it you are answerable for it."[18]

As a result of weather and provision problems the Spaniards found themselves running two weeks behind schedule. Although their spirits were dampened by the rains and delays, chief engineer Antonio de Arredondo took solace in the report that Oglethorpe was weak and might be easily overcome. "Carolina," it was rumored, "was not of a mind to give the help which Oglettorp was seeking" without specific orders from the king.[19] His information was accurate. The older province dawdled as the invasion threat mounted, and it was not until after Bull had received notice of Spanish landings on Cumberland Island that he finally called a special session of the Assembly to deal with the crisis.[20]

As early as 4 June Oglethorpe had warned Bull of the "powerfull Succour" sent to Florida. In spite of "the idle conversations" of Charles Town traders in the Indian country, he planned to make "a considerable stand" at Frederica. By defending South Carolina on St. Simons "Carolina will reap the benefit they already have by not so much as feeling there is a War." There followed the phrase clung to by the Carolinians after Oglethorpe had defeated the Spanish in Georgia without substantial assistance from the older colony. Considering the situation in Carolina, Oglethorpe said he expected at the time "no Assistance Since you can spare non'."[21] However, he did ask immediate aid of the navy in a letter of 18 June to Captain Charles Hardy[22] and early sent two of his most trusted officers to plead with the Carolinians. The warning of Lieutenants Hugh Mackay and Primrose Maxwell were ignored and no relief forces, Patrick Sutherland later reported indignantly, arrived in Georgia waters until after "all the Danger was over."[23]

South Carolina might have been under financial stress had she offered the aid Oglethorpe wanted, but her casual attitude seems in retrospect almost suicidal. Maxwell, for example, reported that he came to Charles Town "about" 10 June and personally informed Bull of the Spanish reinforcements. Bull disputed Maxwell's word, saying that the ships and soldiers at St. Augustine amounted to only eleven craft and three hundred men—merely "the usual Relief sent from the Havannah ... and That the same Vessells carryed back the like Number of Men." Later advices concerning the arrival of fifteen more ships elicited "the same Answer" from Bull who "seemed to take no Notice" of Maxwell's pleas for help in raising supplies in Charles Town for Oglethorpe's forces. Seeing that his mission had failed, Maxwell returned to Frederica.[24]

When the Spaniards actually invaded Cumberland Island, Oglethorpe, in one last effort to stir the Carolinians, sent his articulate and able secretary, Francis Moore, to Charles Town with "the utmost expedition."[25] It is from Moore's pen that the best account came of the happenings in South Carolina during the last days of June and the first few days of July.

Moore arrived in the Beaufort–Port Royal area on 29 June and proceeded immediately to Bull's plantation at Waspee Neck where the governor was relaxing. He "seemed sorry at the News" of the Spanish invasion of Georgia and suggested Moore go on to Charles Town to tell the ship captains. Bull promised he would arrive in town on 1 July. Late on 30 June Moore discovered from Charles Hardy that Oglethorpe's "frequent Advices" to the navy had been completely ignored. Even more appalling, Bull had told the captain of the *Rose* that the ships off St. Augustine were only the yearly "common Relief" for the

Spanish garrison, and so the *Rose* had already left Charles Town for another station.[26]

The first of July came and went. No Bull. His absence "gave the People room to imagine that Georgia was not any way invaded," for if the Spaniards were at Carolina's back door then surely the colony's chief official would be properly informed and would be working to thwart the enemy.

The Carolina Council finally met on 3 July without Bull. Moore repeated the particulars of invasion and asked Joseph Wragg what could be done. Wragg said that the sloops *Hawk* and *Swift* would be sent out to join whatever other English ships might be at sea, but that without Bull the councillors lacked power to do more. Everyone admitted that they "were very much surprized" by Bull's tardiness and that he had not kept the Council informed of Oglethorpe's letters to him.[27]

Just as Moore, in despair, was preparing to leave Charles Town, Bull arrived on 4 July.[28] Two days later the Commons House convened, passed a resolution, and voted money for Georgia's relief. On the next day news of the Spanish landing on St. Simons reached Charles Town, additional aid was voted, and Vander Dussen was appointed commander of the troops to be raised for Georgia's relief.[29]

Carolina's delay in supporting Oglethorpe must be attributed partly to factional disputes in Carolina but also to efforts to escape the authority of Oglethorpe, whose official position was commander-in-chief of the king's forces in both provinces. There was at this time a move afoot to have three companies of troops stationed in South Carolina independent of Oglethorpe's command, and discussion of this took up precious moments when the more immediate defense questions should have been under consideration.[30] It also must be borne in mind that the controversy over publication of the report concerning the St. Augustine expedition was still very much alive. But regardless of how the issue is approached it must be concluded that Bull acted indecisively, perhaps even irresponsibly. As Eugene Sirmans, a Bull apologist, noted, the colony was visited by a "curious lethargy" after the St. Augustine failure. Although the Carolinians were rudely awakened by the Spanish activities in

Georgia, Sirmans concluded that Oglethorpe's charges against Bull for lack of support had "some justification."[31]

The Vander Dussen appointment, too, threw the town into a partisan frenzy. The controversy became so heated that Vander Dussen said he "was willing to resign." Bull stuck by his appointee, even though petitions were circulated to the effect that Vander Dussen was "unfit for such Command."[32] The end result, Moore observed with disgust, was "that for three or four days, a full stop was put to every thing, except Mobbing, Quarrels &ca."[33] Even the local newspaper denounced the dissension and turmoil that had caused such a delay in sending help to Georgia.[34] It was an episode that showed Carolina in a poor light, and Oglethorpe was never to forgive or to forget that his former friends failed him when the crisis came.

The long-awaited invasion of Georgia followed Spanish attacks on British positions at Cumberland Island. Oglethorpe felt constrained to abandon Fort St. Andrews, on the northwestern tip of Cumberland, but he reinforced Fort William, on the southern point nearest Florida. He himself, having forced his way through a dozen or so small Spanish ships to relieve St. Andrews, personally supervised the evacuation of the northern part of the island and fell back on his base on St. Simons.

On 28 June 1742, the main elements of the Spanish fleet anchored off the St. Simons bar. Oglethorpe, just before their arrival, had engaged in feverish activity to strengthen his defenses. He had called down the Highland elements from Darien; he brought in the Rangers from their stations on the rivers and sounds nearby; he freed the indentured servants in the neighborhood on the provision they fight to defend Georgia; he brought in Mark Carr's marine company from its station on Turtle River; and he asked Mary Musgrove to send as many Indians as possible to him. By the time of actual hostilities on the island, therefore, Oglethorpe's forces may have totaled as many as nine hundred men (though the precise number will never be known).[35]

On 5 July, the wind and the tide being finally right, the Spanish ships formed a line of battle and prepared to brave the narrow entrance to St. Simons Sound and the British batteries on the tip of the island. Oglethorpe went aboard one of the British ships still in the Sound and gave the men a rousing talk, which was well received.[36] There were probably about thirty-six vessels in this Spanish flotilla, some of them modest in size, and the exchange of fire with Fort St. Simons, on the southern tip of the island guarding the entrance to the harbor, was hot. It was a tribute to Alexander Parris, ex-Carolinian who acted as the pilot and led the Spanish through the tricky channel, that they passed by the guns of the fort without serious mishap. In Montiano's victorious words, the entrance to the harbor was "gloriously forced" by Spain's invasion fleet.[37]

Oglethorpe, realizing that Fort St. Simons was now outflanked, ordered his troops to render the artillery and supplies there useless. At midnight the flag was struck from the ramparts and the British began their retreat to Frederica. They arrived at this still unfinished fortified town about daylight on 6 July.

Meanwhile, Montiano and his men cautiously disembarked from their ships, now riding at anchor in the safe harbor of St. Simons Sound. The strategic withdrawal by Oglethorpe along the military road linking Forts Frederica and St. Simons seemed to catch Montiano somewhat by surprise. He later admitted that he could probably have "overtaken" the British during this retreat, but added that it "did not appear to be prudent, so long as I was ignorant of the road and of the ground."[38] Prudent Montiano remained during his stay on St. Simons Island.

The contending forces consolidated their positions on the next day—Oglethorpe making last-minute adjustments in his defenses and Montiano trying to secure himself against surprise attack. The most conservative British estimates were that Montiano had at least three thousand men under him, and Sutherland, whose account of the battle is otherwise a valuable one, estimated "about 5000," a preposterous claim.[39]

Considering that Güemes could spare from Cuba only about thirteen hundred soldiers, Montiano probably commanded in the vicinity of two thousand men. When it is borne in mind that not all these were operational fighting men and that a number of troops did not arrive until after the decisive battles with Oglethorpe, the differential between the size of the British and that of the Spanish forces was not so great as is usually claimed. Finally, Oglethorpe fought on familiar soil and with an undivided command; so the imbalance on paper that seemed to exist between the two forces all but vanishes.[40]

On 7 July came the most important contacts between the armies during the campaign. Montiano sent two columns of troops on separate paths in the general direction of Frederica. Becoming confused, these two groups joined forces and came within a mile and one half of the walls of Frederica before being detected by a small party of Oglethorpe's Rangers. The Rangers exchanged fire with the larger Spanish force and hurried back to inform their commander of the frightening development.

Oglethorpe immediately mounted a horse and ordered a group of Indians (Toonahowi being one of them), other reinforcements from the regiment, and Highlanders to follow him in a sally against Montiano's troops. It was, Oglethorpe said, essential to stop the advance of the Spaniards before they reached the open ground or savanna near the fort where they could form properly for an attack on Frederica itself. The fort would be defenseless, Thomas Spalding wrote, if the Spanish could concentrate their strength on "the prairie in its rear."[41]

Oglethorpe's sortie proved enormously successful. The Spaniards were demoralized by his pell-mell attack on their center, and their defenses collapsed. The Spanish were, in fact, "entirely routed," to use Oglethorpe's words. The English, who now had the initiative, followed closely on the heels of the enemy back down the military road for perhaps as far as two miles.[42]

What happened next is confusing, and the effort to construct an accurate picture of the fighting that took place is made no easier by the fact that surviving accounts are either too brief and conflicting or hopelessly romantic in the light of modern scholarship. Apparently after moving up the road some two miles, Oglethorpe stopped his forward advance at what looked to be an advantageous spot where there was a clearing surrounded on three sides by dense woods. When troops from his regiment came up to the location from Frederica, "He posted them with the Highlanders in a Wood with a large Savannah or Meadow in their Front"[43] so that the placement blocked any attempted new advance by the Spanish on the Frederica position via the military road. Oglethorpe then hurried back to Frederica, apparently fearing that Montiano's probings on the road were feints intended to disguise the fact that the main push might be an assault by water against the town. When he discovered that all was quiet at the fort he took along additional troops and headed back in the direction of the position where his troops were already deployed.

Meanwhile the Spanish camp became fretful. Montiano, who never budged from his base near the abandoned St. Simons fort, was unsure what was happening in the interior of the island. When he heard the news of the initial repulse of the Spanish column near Frederica, he sent three additional companies into the wilds of the island to reinforce the first group and cover its retreat if need be.[44] The crack Grenadier company under Antonio Barba led the advance into the wilderness. According to Barba, his command had proceeded about two leagues down the road which, he said, was in actuality no more than a footpath, when they had to cross "a causeway made of brush wood no wider than the trail." The only way to get through or across this point was by "single file" for if the men "went beyond the fascines [they] became mired." At this point the scouts and Indians who had been with the early morning group when it came this same way noticed something different.

> There was something new on the road, a felled tree and part of the branches like a breastwork on some sides where it was not before. He [Barba] halted to reconnoiter it, and at the same time they began to fire on him from right and left without [his] seeing more than the flare of the powder flashes.[45]

Barba and his company were in a most uncomfortable spot. He and his veteran troops did what they could in the circumstances, and although pinned down and fighting an enemy they could not see on terrain they did not know, the Spanish fired back gamely at their assailants.

Judging from the accounts that have survived, the English

were almost as much befuddled by the fog of war as the
Spanish. It is particularly difficult to get Barba's account of the
battle (as narrated by Casinas) to gibe with the English ren-
ditions of the skirmish. There is, for instance, no reference to a
felled tree, or a kind of breastwork, or even to a causeway close to
the scene of battle in the British versions of what happened on
this muggy, showery 7 July, from three to four in the afternoon.
It may well be that Barba's view of the battlefield was such a
brief and unsatisfactory one that he mistook the lay of the land,
for the English all mention that their troops were deployed
facing a savanna or meadow through which the Spanish must
pass on their way to Frederica.[46]

The British, though prone to denigrate the Spanish at every
turn, were impressed by the determination of the enemy not to
give in, even when caught in an extraordinarily awkward
position. Oglethorpe admitted that the Spaniards "fired with
great spirit," but their efforts caused no casualties. Because of
the dense undergrowth, Barba and his troops could not see where
they were firing.[47]

Two wounded grenadiers and two cadets found their way
back to Montiano's camp by four-thirty in the afternoon and
noted candidly that the Spanish had "suffered a frightful fire,"
but that they were giving as good as they got.[48] Possibly because
some of the Spaniards actually penetrated the extended line of
the British (and if this is true it must have been Barba and the
vanguard of his company who did so), the contact was too close
for several of the English platoons. They wilted under fire "and
a shower of rain," and hurried back toward Frederica.[49] But
Oglethorpe, rushing up the military road to the scene of action,
"prevented their Retiring far" and "immediately ordered
them to Rally."[50] It may well be that it was this defection, at a
crucial moment, that permitted the Spanish to regroup their
forces and withdraw "in good order" from the scene of their
confusion and surprise.[51]

Oglethorpe continued along the military road to the scene of
the battle. Some of the defectors had told him that Patrick
Sutherland, the commander of one of Oglethorpe's regimental
platoons, had been killed and the English "quite beaten." He

felt that if the story was true his appearance at the struggle "might preserve them," and so he "spurred on." When Oglethorpe arrived on the scene he must have had mixed emotions: elation to see "the Spaniards intirely routed,"[52] but chagrin at not having been there to take part. Little did he suspect, too, that this battle would be the last exchange of any importance between the British and the invaders on St. Simons Island.

By five in the afternoon Barba and his troops were back at the Spanish camp recounting their tales to Montiano. The news that the British were nearby caused everyone to be "stood to arms" for the entire night and, as it turned out, for the duration of the Spaniards' stay on St. Simons.[53]

After surveying the situation Oglethorpe marched his men in the direction of the Spanish camp and posted himself on the road to prevent enemy stragglers, who might have become separated from their commands, from reaching their camp. He passed the night there, checked the Spanish defenses the next day and deemed them too formidable to attack "with so small a number," and then marched his entire command back to Frederica "to refresh the Soldiers."[54]

On the day following, English-allied Indians set upon a boat sent by Montiano to seek out good drinking water for his troops. The boat's crew was killed "by hostile Indians," adding to Montiano's anxiety and sense of impending doom. An indecisive junta on the ninth did little to reassure him that the Spanish position was a happy one. It was decided, however, that an effort should be made to invest Frederica from the water side. Three ships were sent up the Frederica River to take soundings and to see if there might be a convenient place to land troops from which operations against the fort might be recommenced. But Oglethorpe "fired at them with the few Guns we had so warmly that they retired."[55] This, in effect, was the last half-hearted effort by the Spanish to penetrate the St. Simons defenses.

Oglethorpe and a sizable force crept quietly to within less than two miles of the Spanish camp on 12 July only to have their presence betrayed by a soldier who discharged his gun and fled to the enemy's lines. Oglethorpe realized that the deserter would inform Montiano of Frederica's weakness and that, so encouraged, the Spanish commander might make a more determined effort up the military road. Something must be done to counteract the new advices Montiano would receive from this informer, but first Oglethorpe felt that he must withdraw at once, having been discovered by the Spanish. Accordingly he divided the drums he had with him, presumably to make the army seem larger than it was, and ordered them to "beat the Grenadiers march for about half an hour." After this characteristic display of military histrionics he and his men quietly returned to Frederica.[56]

The Spaniards were finally convinced on the day following that their plans to reconquer "Gualquini" had gone thoroughly awry. For one thing, Oglethorpe's stratagem of sending a man to the Spanish camp with a letter for the deserter to the effect that he should continue to deceive the Spanish as to the English weaknesses, must have left a suspicion in the minds of Montiano and his officers. They were not really taken in by Oglethorpe's rather juvenile trick, but early that same afternoon an outpost reported seeing five British ships near the horizon "to the north." Oglethorpe's ploy might be bluster, but the British sails were real. As one of the Spaniards accurately noted in his journal of the Georgia proceedings, it was not so much the five ships on the horizon that the Spanish feared as the unknown number that might lie just beyond.[57]

On 14 July some of the Spanish force hastily left St. Simons, the Cuban forces going the following day in twenty ships by the open sea and the St. Augustine contingent following Montiano in the smaller boats and schooners down the inland waterway. They laid waste William Horton's plantation on Jekyll, spent a night at abandoned Fort St. Andrews on Cumberland, made a semi-feint at Fort William (still doggedly held by the English), and were back in the relative safety of Florida by 20 July. Oglethorpe pursued the St. Augustine troops at a distance but felt that his numbers were not adequate to attack.[58]

Thus the invasion of Georgia was repulsed. The ramifications for both England and Spain were enormous, even though the number of troops engaged and the casualty lists were not. Wholly reliable figures are unavailable, but as was the case in the assault against Florida, the Spanish reports have more the ring of truth than do the English, where the numbers of bleeding and dead Spaniards stretch even the most credulous imagination. Oglethorpe himself reported that the enemy lost at least two hundred killed in the two encounters,[59] and Patrick Sutherland's estimate of a total of two hundred and fifty-nine Spaniards missing, though relatively restrained when compared to later assessments, is still far too high.[60]

Montiano's own narrative, being the Spanish official account and the one intended for the eyes of investigative officers, should probably be taken as definitive where Spanish losses are concerned. At the first encounter near Frederica, Montiano suffered twelve killed, ten wounded, and thirteen captured—one of whom, a captain, subsequently escaped and made his way back to friendly lines.[61] At the second encounter, where Barba and his command were pinned so uncomfortably by British fire from the undergrowth beside the road, the Spanish apparently had seven men killed and eleven wounded.[62] When allied actions and their losses are taken into account it seems safe to assume that no more than two score Spanish lost their lives during the invasion of Georgia. British losses were negligible—a tribute to Oglethorpe's tactics, Montiano's hesitancy, and inaccurate Spanish marksmanship.

As in most battles, the Almighty was invoked by both sides to help explain the outcome. J. Smith, an observer of the early maneuverings by the Spanish, remarked that the British were outnumbered, but that Oglethorpe was ready "for all dangers." He "relied upon the valor of his men, and he did not doubt, with the aid of God, they would be victorious."[63] After the enemy withdrawal, Oglethorpe wrote the Trustees telling them in what a "wonderfull manner God has been pleased to defeat the Spaniards in their invasion of this Colony."[64] It was one of the few times in his career that Oglethorpe was willing to share the credit.

To Montiano the feeling that his defeat was preordained made it easier to take and, he hoped, the same idea might deflect some of the criticism heading his way. His elaborate and well-considered plans would have worked, he pointed out, "had not the All Powerful, who disposes of all things, brought to naught the plan I had in mind."[65]

Oglethorpe, however, was in a rage against his old friends in Charles Town. He indignantly noted that it was only after news of the Spanish defeat that "a number of Carolina People raised in a hurry set out and came off this Barr [at St. Simons] after the Spaniards had been chased quite out of this Colony."[66] Hardy and his squadron of the Royal Navy behaved even worse. After their momentary appearance on the seas near St. Simons, they decided the Spanish had too many ships to risk attack. Feeling that discretion, in this instance, was desirable, the squadron turned tail and was safely back in Charles Town on 15 July.[67] The enemy was left in unquestioned control of the seas and used this control to effect an orderly and unopposed withdrawal.

If Oglethorpe was enraged, Güemes in Cuba was incredulous. He had been certain Montiano's forces would ravage all the British plantations up and down the Georgia-Carolina coast. Though "profoundly astonished" and "mortified" by the failure of Spanish arms, he felt some good had been done by the invasion of "Gualquini,"[68] but he was worried that the onus of failure would fall on him. Güemes did not have to worry long, however, for before fall was out assurances came from Old Spain that he was not at fault. The frustration of the invasion was ascribed instead to the "poor direction, lack of diligence and inefficiency" of Montiano.[69]

The Florida governor's defense was eloquent and reasoned. The "impenetrable" forest, the island being "full of swamps and lagoons," the "tempestuous weather" to be expected in August and September, and the shortage of supplies must all be weighed when considering the reasons for the withdrawal from Guale, he said. Montiano also indicated more cogent reasons for abandoning the project that Güemes and others assumed would succeed. For one thing, English naval strength off Carolina was "superior to ours," the initial delay in getting the invasion operation underway gave Oglethorpe time to prepare his defenses, and a storm which struck the armada as it lay off Florida prevented a number of vessels and troops from joining the invasion. Most important of all in determining him to evacuate St. Simons was that he had been told specifically not to jeopardize the army; he had to bear in mind not only that his troops were trying to lay waste Guale but that they were defending Havana as well. Güemes had been specific in cautioning Montiano not to take risks that could result in leaving Cuba and Florida open to easy conquests by her enemies. What Montiano was trying to do, in effect, was to throw the blame for the failure on St. Simons back to the governor.[70]

There are numerous similarities between Oglethorpe's 1740 invasion of Florida and the Spanish attempt against Georgia and South Carolina. The invasion of Georgia in 1742 resulted in as much frustration for Montiano as the expedition against Florida did for Oglethorpe. The invading forces of the Spanish, like those of Oglethorpe two years before, were numerically superior, and though the tactics of the two commanders differed widely each enjoyed defensive positions that were difficult to penetrate. Oglethorpe was familiar with the lay of the land in the vicinity of St. Augustine, but Montiano apparently knew almost nothing of St. Simons. In retrospect, it seems almost mad for the Spanish to have landed upon an island about which they were so little informed. It is not a tribute to their scouts and spies that Montiano lacked basic knowledge of the defensive arrangements at Fort St. Simons and at Frederica. That the Spaniards had to rely upon a renegade Carolinian even to get them across the bar into St. Simons Sound is a comment needing no elaboration.[71]

Though outnumbered, the defenders in 1740 and 1742 found themselves with certain advantages. Their positions were more maneuverable, they had intimate knowledge of the terrain, and they were both blessed with the presence of a strong and well-located fort as a focal point from which to execute defensive raids and sorties. Furthermore, each defensive commander enjoyed the luxury of facing an indecisive opponent. It was even written of Montiano at the time that he acted as inoffensively on St. Simons as Oglethorpe had before St. Augustine.[72]

As the real battle between Oglethorpe and Montiano was being fought, another engagement was taking place between noncombatant advocates of South Carolina and Georgia. Oglethorpe's victory was reported in Charles Town on 19 July, but his triumph was later ascribed to the fact that the enemy had caught a glimpse of the ships sent from Charles Town to aid the general. Merely the sight of the British navy caused Montiano to evacuate *"with the utmost Confusion."* Oglethorpe, thanks to the naval aid, was left "Master of the *Island*."[73]

Oglethorpe's allies felt differently. Stephens reported significant unrest in Charles Town against Bull for his dilatory behavior in the days before the invasion.[74] Francis Moore indignantly wrote that the Carolinians refused to believe Oglethorpe's messages, but when the invasion actually materialized they were the ones who were "the most terrified."[75] Georgia schoolmaster John Dobell waxed eloquent over Oglethorpe's triumph: "Poor and dispicable as it is yet hath it Phinehas like stood in the gap, deserted of all assistance but Divine, and hindred the destruction of its Sister Province."[76]

The more Oglethorpe thought about the lack of support from South Carolina the madder he got. He began, in fact, to address his dispatches meant for Carolina not to Bull but to John Fenwicke, president of the Council. Oglethorpe minced no words. He explained to Fenwicke that Bull was found to take "no kind of notice of the Early Accounts I gave him of this design [the invasion plans] and even spoke very Slightly of those Intelligences." Anyway, Oglethorpe concluded, as Bull was "oftner at his Plantation than in Town Letters which go to you [Fenwicke] will be more immediately Communicated to his Majestys Council and Assembly."[77]

Although Carolina opinion appeared on the surface to be overwhelmingly anti-Oglethorpe, in reality there was apparently a sizable body of the population that thought he had performed an invaluable service by repelling the Spaniards. The Port Royal–Beaufort area residents went so far as to memorialize the Georgia leader to the effect that his "late wonderfull Success under God" prevented the invasion of Carolina. Had Spain won, her troops "would have intirely destroyed us and laid our Lands waste." Home and countryside would have been the scene of awful "blood and slaughter." Only the Lord could have saved Carolina had Oglethorpe not won at St. Simons. The memorialists said their area would have granted all Oglethorpe wanted in the way of military aid "were we assisted and put in a Condition to have been of Service to you." Criticism of the ruling Charles Town clique was implicit.[78]

To Oglethorpe it was all but inconceivable that after his triumph over the Spaniards he and Georgia should be left to fend for themselves just as they had been before 7 July. But the government, more particularly Newcastle and Pelham, who had taken power upon the fall of Walpole in 1742, remained silent. Even more galling, the Trustees were unresponsive too. In fact Egmont, who had been the guiding light of the group, particularly when Oglethorpe was in Georgia, resigned from the Common Council in the summer of 1742. And by coincidence, Egmont stepped down on 7 July, the same day that his friend, half a world away, was vanquishing the Spanish along the narrow military road between Forts St. Simons and Frederica.[79]

Oglethorpe's dispatches to Newcastle seemed to have no more effect than his 1740 barrage on the Castillo de San Marcos.[80] Characteristically therefore, Oglethorpe decided on another strike against Florida, and a modest invasion was mounted early in 1743. Most of his time was spent trying to lure the defenders from behind the walls of their fortress. The idea was for the Spaniards to make sallies, with Oglethorpe "destroying them by Piece Meals."[81] He claimed that his Indian allies killed "upwards of forty" Spanish in the initial encounter.[82] Later, he tried to ambush the enemy, "but they were so meek that there was no provoking them."[83] Lacking materials and troops, Oglethorpe found that he had to withdraw once more to Frederica.

These activities proved diverting to the Carolinians. All he had done, it was said in Charles Town, was to have "knock'd a few People on the Head about the Country." In an obvious reference to Oglethorpe's strategy in 1740, the *Gazette* said he tried to induce "*the Enemy by all possible Means to Sallies, in order to bring the Place to a Condition of being surpriz'd.*"[84] Andrew Rutledge wrote at this same time that the "Majority" of the people in Charles Town "are delighted with nothing more than to lay hold on all Occasions to villify the Man, to whom they owe their Preservation." He hoped that "even the Nonsence or Malevolence" of the Carolina metropolis would not undo Oglethorpe's work among the Indians. The 1743 expedition against Florida had positive results, even though there was criticism "because he was the Actor."[85]

Oglethorpe's strategy was defended in London,[86] and a Carolina letter was extracted and printed in the *London Magazine* to show that opposition to the Georgia Trustee was not so widespread in Charles Town as Rutledge implied. Oglethorpe's second invasion, it was said, "kept the *Augustiners* at Home," and the sloops and schooners fitted out by him helped clear the Carolina coast of the Spanish privateers that had "infested" the area—in spite of the Royal Navy. "*Georgia* is a *Gibraltar* to this Province and *North America,* however insignificant some People may make it."[87]

After returning to Frederica from his second effort at the Spanish stronghold in Florida, Oglethorpe began to plan for his return to England. It is impossible to say whether he thought this would be his farewell to America, but he had received no cooperation from the mother country in a year or more and it must have been hard for him to feel he still had a useful role to play in the New World. In addition, one of the officers from his regiment was bringing official charges against him and his own financial affairs were in a sorry state, and so it is not surprising that Oglethorpe sailed for the last time and without fanfare from Georgia to London on 22 July 1743.[88]

No defense of the later stage of Oglethorpe's colonial career is so eloquent as his own letter of 22 January 1743 to Newcastle. It was only "by the great Blessing of God that we defeated the Enemy," for they had the time and the wherewithal to crush the English on the southern frontier. Had Georgia gone, then like dominoes the Carolinas would have fallen "for the Negroes would have certainly revolted." The troops in Georgia were all that stood between the Spaniards and the Carolinians, and "they had nothing but what would have run from them."[89] He did not write from a desire to promote his own fame but "to prevent future ill Consequences by dear bought experience." His remarks about the unsatisfactory arrangement of having the navy in Charles Town, as well as his contentions concerning the power and ability of the Spanish to mount an offensive blow, had all been justified by events of 1742. It was important to profit from the mistakes made during this episode.

Oglethorpe concluded his defense with a moving section that is an accurate reflection of his sense of mission as well as of his remarkable personal generosity.

> It is the duty of that Office and my standing orders to defend
> the Provinces I saw the danger every day more certain and
> too near to receive support or orders from England on such
> an Emergency therefore as in duty bound made all the
> Preparations I could, these occasioned expence and that ex-
> pence was crowned with success and I drew for sums towards
> defraying it, had I done otherwise and for want of these
> necessary assistances of Indians, Vessels, Rangers, Provisions,
> &ca. and had lost these Provinces I should have deserved to
> have answered it with my life.[90]

As he had written earlier to Newcastle, his realization of what the loss of Georgia would mean had "made me expend my fortune and expose my person much more than by the strictest rules of duty I should have been obliged to do."[91]

Personal courage, generosity, energy, dependability, a ca- pacity to be a leader of men—all these things Oglethorpe had in abundance. But what, particularly, of his military prowess?

Oglethorpe loved command in the field; he reveled in the intricacies of war. He enjoyed each march as well, if not better, than its equal and corresponding countermarch. But what he enjoyed and what he excelled in were not necessarily the same. Faced with a problem like the 1742 invasion, he was able to rise to the occasion. His victory, however, is not so remarkable as it may seem. He enjoyed many tactical advantages and the allegiance of his troops was unquestioned. Unlike the Spanish force of regulars, militia, Indians, convicts, and Negroes the troops under Oglethorpe, including the Indians, understood and had confidence in one another. They also had confidence in Oglethorpe, who was willing to endure any hardship the common soldier underwent as long as the cause was Georgia. This force on St. Simons was his hard-core following, purged of the faint-hearted. There was no questioning Oglethorpe's honesty when he said he would die, if need be, for his colony. This was the sort of spirit that imbued his men too. They were willing to go down by their commander's side.

On the other hand Montiano, uncomfortable in offensive command, apparently inspired little more in his men than the desire to be back at home. Once the Spaniards landed, Montiano suffered a dimming of his imaginative powers. Considering the makeup of his "expeditionary force," however, his caution is understandable, and when it is borne in mind that his camp was riddled with dissension, Margaret Davis Cate's claim that he could easily have captured the incomplete fortress at Frederica had he acted decisively is unreasonable.[92] Finally, the available evidence seems to indicate that Montiano did not enjoy the overwhelming numerical superiority he was long thought to have.

All of this is not to downgrade Oglethorpe's achievement, but to attempt to put it in proper historical perspective. His victory, though not Caesarean, was still important, particularly in the light of England's tricornered colonial conflict with Spain and France. Ettinger's claim that Oglethorpe's triumph was as decisive as Wolfe's at Quebec or Washington's at Yorktown seems exaggerated,[93] whereas Trevor Reese's efforts to downplay the battle to the point of insignificance seem only an exercise in antithesis.[94]

Oglethorpe's victory on St. Simons did not save the southern continental colonies from imminent destruction and ruination. Even had Montiano vanquished Oglethorpe it is difficult to conceive of his makeshift flotilla and his makeshift army leap-frogging up the eastern seaboard bringing destruction wherever they went. Particularly in the light of the cautious orders given him it is doubtful he would have attempted an invasion much beyond Port Royal. The time of year was not "right" to continue such operations and, even more important, the British navy yet had to be met and defeated. Still, a Spanish victory on St. Simons, culminating in the capture of Frederica and the capture or death of Oglethorpe would have completely upset the balance of power on the frontier. Savannah might have been the next target, and it would have fallen easy prey to any relatively determined foe. The invasion route to Carolina would have been opened, but whether the Spanish could have followed up their victories is questionable.

Enmeshed in local feuds and partisan politics, South Carolina stood by and allowed Oglethorpe to meet the Spanish threat virtually unaided. The Charles Town power group was jealous of Oglethorpe and yet, at the same time, was wary of his influence at court.[95] When asked for help Carolina tried to steer a middle course which might be construed in England as adequate to Oglethorpe's needs. Remembering the 1740 expedition, Carolina had no desire to grant Georgia massive aid, but considering what the older colony stood to lose, it is hard to say why the Carolinians were willing to take such a risk. Narrow parochialism, complicated by a dislike of Oglethorpe, seems to have won the day in Charles Town while the broader objectives of British imperial policy and intercolonial cooperation went begging.

The Carolinians blamed Hardy and the navy for the failure of intercolonial cooperation.[96] Oglethorpe too denounced the naval arm, and in a letter to Andrew Stone, the influential secretary to Newcastle and a good friend of Oglethorpe, the usually austere Georgia leader permitted himself a rare bit of levity at the navy's expense.

> We did beat them at land but did not persue them so that they are now capable of undertaking a second Expedition, I have given notice of it to the Men of War but can get none to stay here and unless I should punn I can't say we have any Balls to entertain them with.[97]

Where Bull and the Carolinians were concerned, there was no

joking. Oglethorpe blamed Bull for the failure of the Charles Town squadron to act more decisively. As he said in the same letter to Stone: "At Charles Town they were so stupid (not to say worse) that they prevented the Men of War from coming hither tho' I gave them very near a month's notice."[98] Once back in England, he kept up his attack on them.

In spite of the spilling of much ink, there was never an effective reply to Oglethorpe's oft-repeated charge: Carolina sat on her hands at the climactic moment of eighteenth-century Anglo-Spanish relations along the southern frontier. Oglethorpe it was who rose to the occasion.

Epilogue

In spite of not being successful in every phase, James Edward Oglethorpe's American career should be deemed positive and fruitful. His attempts to keep Georgia free from slavery and liquor, his efforts to be scrupulously fair to the Indians and to articulate a policy that was in many ways geared toward them, have an especial appeal to the twentieth century, but caution must be exercised lest modern ideas be read into an eighteenth-century situation.

Among those who have distorted the image of James Oglethorpe none have been more seriously at fault than his biographers. He has been pictured variously as an early advocate of prohibition, a forerunner of Abraham Lincoln, and a colonial leader who was motivated by philanthropy alone.[1] It is ironic that he is best remembered in those three areas where he was unable to make his will felt permanently. Of his lasting achievements, on the other hand, little that is meaningful has been said.

Like most men with a mission, much of what Oglethorpe tried to do was bound up with his own ego. Unfortunately, almost all of Oglethorpe's correspondence from the Georgia period is official or semiofficial in nature. His private correspondence, if he had any of note during this stage of his life, either does not survive or has not yet come to light. Indications are that if it existed, it was skimpy. He wrote in 1776 to James Boswell: "I have a strong Aversion to Writing as a bad Scribe, but glad to recieve Letters from my Friends particularly you, whose Attick Wit gives a Zest to Life."[2] Boswell, fortunately, hounded Oglethorpe in his later years and carefully saved the letters he wrung from the old general, but by no means everyone possessed the charm—much less the "Attick Wit"—

of Oglethorpe's Scottish friend. There was no Boswell during the Georgia years to draw Oglethorpe out of his shell. Nevertheless by careful examination of his letters from, to, and about Georgia, and by judicious use of the observations of those around him it is possible to reconstruct, with some accuracy it is hoped, the figure of James Oglethorpe.

Oglethorpe was no bloodless saint; he was a passionate, garrulous, headstrong, confident man. As such a man he should be judged with the other founding fathers who, just as Oglethorpe, must be pulled off their pedestals before a close look at them can be taken.

Once the restructuring begins Oglethorpe is found to be complex and many-faceted. His complexity should be emphasized, particularly for American historians who tend to assess his exploits in Georgia but gloss over his youth and his accomplishments once the Georgia phase of his life was finished. All indications point to the fact that Oglethorpe was a voracious reader, particularly in his later years. He passed the tedious time during ocean crossings in this fashion. As he said to Boswell, when you are on the open sea and are not in the habit of drinking, there was little else to do *but* read.[3] His later correspondence is spiced with literary allusions and at the sale of Samuel Johnson's library in the winter of 1785, less than six months before his own death, Oglethorpe attended every session and made numerous purchases. His own reading preference seemed to be ancient history, but it is a tribute to his optimism as well as to his probing mind that at the Johnson sale he bought a Gaelic grammar, presumably to study Irish in his spare time.[4] Even as a young man he was highly respected at Corpus Christi, Oxford, and when after the death of Queen Anne a book of poems was put together to celebrate the accession of George I, Oglethorpe was asked to contribute. His effort, in Latin, is wooden, and, true to his Jacobite upbringing, shows more sorrow for Anne's death than joy for the accession of George I. Nonetheless the fact that he, a young man under twenty years of age, was asked to take part was a tribute to his standing among both faculty and students at Oxford.[5] He retained an interest in poetry and poets the rest of his life.[6]

Oglethorpe had no time for poetry or Latin in Georgia. In a new country, faced with the basic problems of life and death, Oglethorpe, just as other colonial leaders before him, found there was scarcely time for sleep, much less for reading or contemplation. Fortunately for the early settlement Oglethorpe had a rugged constitution that could endure almost any hardship. He kept himself physically fit, ate lightly, and was extremely careful about his intake of beer and wine. Rum or harsher liquors he never drank. He was tall, slim, hawk-nosed, and erect. According to Thomas Coram, Oglethorpe and Baron Philipp Von Reck, the distinguished Salzburg leader, looked alike, though Von Reck was not "so thin in his face." Both men were deemed handsome, with aristocratic features; the prominent nose was an Oglethorpe family trademark. Writing in 1717 to the Duke of Mar, Fanny Oglethorpe said her sister Molly "hopes you don't think like all the world that he [James] had her nose; she will never forgive you if you have observed it."[7] Probably because Oglethorpe was so moderate in his habits he developed an endurance that struck many as extraordinary. Many settlers sickened or died, but Oglethorpe thrived on the stresses of a new environment—at least until 1739. Like many bachelors his work was his life, and Georgia, from 1732 to 1743, was his work.

Oglethorpe's willingness to face physical and mental strain was marked. There are several instances in his Georgia career when he seemed almost to defy death and, to the uneasiness of some, to expose himself to unnecessary danger. He may have been following the dictum of a distant and crusty relative, the Marechal Brown, who advised Oglethorpe when the latter was a young officer to demonstrate fearlessness to his men by facing danger openly in order to engender confidence and respect in his troops. Brown approved, too, of his "Cousin Nell," Oglethorpe's mother, who reared her son to be tough and ready for any exigency. As Oglethorpe reported to Brown, Lady Eleanor "cut holes in his shoes, when he was a boy, that he might have his feet wet" in order to inure him to discomfort.[8]

Oglethorpe made many financial sacrifices for Georgia. Naturally he expected to be reimbursed by Parliament for expenses he undertook while shoring up the English position on the southern frontier, but he had no assurance that this would actually be done. In 1740 one of Oglethorpe's cousins pointed out to Egmont that he must return from Georgia or otherwise "he will ruin himself." Oglethorpe felt that the whole situation —left alone as he was on the southern boundary of British America—might be a plot "to sacrifice him."[9] Whether he really saw developments this way is conjectural, but it is known that he sent a power of attorney to England to raise funds against his estate "without limitation of the sum, as also to employ all his salary from the Government for answering the bills he should draw."[10] It does little credit to the government to note that his total expenses, which reached a figure in excess of £90,000, were not fully repaid until 1792, seven years after his death.[11] What his elder brother Theophilus referred to as the Oglethorpe family's "natural zeal" was as strongly apparent in the ninth child as in his older brothers, older sisters, or, most zealous of them all, his mother.[12] No sacrifice, be it physical, emotional, or financial was too great for Oglethorpe to make if he found the cause just.

Oglethorpe was ill-prepared by spirit and emotion to perform the methodical acts required of the best administrator. He was too impatient to be good at paperwork; he tended to be unsympathetic toward those who lacked ambition, but he was also suspicious of those who had it. His judgment of character was sometimes clouded, witness his choice of the imperious Thomas Causton to be storekeeper and chief magistrate in his absence. Causton, though too much maligned at the time, was incompetent with figures and often dealt too abruptly with his fellow colonists.

That Oglethorpe was vain and enjoyed flattery was obvious. This weakness was played upon brilliantly in *A True and Historical Narrative*, and his tendency to display something of a Caesar complex was derided in the special dedication to this work that appeared in London in *The Champion*.[13] Much later, and over a bottle of Tokay, Oglethorpe recounted tales of his youth to Boswell, General Pasquale Paoli, and Bennet Langton. He told how, when in France, where he had spent so much time as a youngster, he had *"walked* over Caesar's progress in Gaul, and traced it with the *Commentaries* in his hand."[14] He was also an admirer of Raleigh, whom he may have aspired to emulate.

In letters directed to Oglethorpe, no flattery seemed to be too gross. Henry Newman of the SPCK, to give only one example, praised Oglethorpe for his many "wise Maxims," and continued by saying how "America is much beholden" to his sort, for had he not come to the fore the Indians "might have slept on to the End of the world." Newman concluded with the "hope" that Oglethorpe was "the *White Man* that will . . . deliver them from the darkness" in which they have stumbled for so long.[15]

Oglethorpe could never be accused of false modesty, but it was not a modest age, and those who insisted upon hiding their light under a bushel usually found that it stayed there. He took some of his cues from William Penn, whose promotional feats on behalf of his colony were well known to the Georgia leader. The Penns and the Oglethorpes had in fact been family friends for years. In the colony, Oglethorpe assumed that he was the indispensable man; he wanted in the worst—or best—way to make his mark in America. In 1736 from the southern frontiers he wrote that he wished he could be in Ebenezer to help settle the situation there, but that the orders of George II "& my own Reputation require me to be where most danger is."[16] He was acutely aware of his own importance.

The platitudes in verse about Oglethorpe were incredible. Almost every American as well as English paper and journal overflowed with the work of bad poets singing Oglethorpe's praises.[17] Having been coached by his mother and sisters to feel that he had a special role to play and having this apparently confirmed by adulation from all around him, Oglethorpe was remarkable for being no more of an egoist than he was. Curiously enough his vanity was physical as well as social and intellectual. This seemed a family trait too; both his sister, the Marquise de Mézières, and her daughter were keenly sensitive about the appearances of aging.[18] The old general's reluctance to disclose his own birthdate, even when he was well into his eighties, caused a misunderstanding about his age that still crops up occasionally. In Boswell's notes on Oglethorpe's life, taken during personal conversations between the two men, there is a blank where the year of Oglethorpe's birth should be.[19] The old general had apparently even refused to tell his Scottish friend and would-be biographer.

Although Oglethorpe lived in a time of generally relaxed morals he was not, in this sense, of his time. He often strikes the observer as spiritually fastidious, even demanding that a stern moral code be observed by those under his tutelage. If the meaning of the word "puritanical" can be extended beyond its religious connotations and if it may be used without the distortions often associated with it, the term might suit James Oglethorpe well. Without stressing salvation or advocating covenants of grace or the like, he by his actions implied that good Christian living went hand in hand with good government. He and the Trustees hoped Georgia would be as much a beacon to the rest of the world as the New England Puritans had intended Massachusetts Bay to be a century before. To help assure the purity of the Georgia experiment lawyers, who were thought to play on the ignorance and superstitions of their clients in order to secure control of the legal process and, ultimately, the government, were banned from the province. Each person in court would argue his own case the way it had been done in England long before. Roman Catholics, too, were banned from the Protestant colony.

But the three laws discussed earlier were to be the cornerstones of the Trustees' southern Zion. The Indian trade act would establish standards of fairness and morality with the natives who, upon benefiting from just policies, would show their thankfulness not only by rendering aid if war broke out but also by converting to the Christian religion. The prohibition of the rum trade, it was thought, would be beneficial for everyone. The health of the province would be assured, no group would evolve by owing its livelihood to taking advantage of the people's weaknessses for alcohol, and in the backcountry much of the cause for friction between settler and native would vanish.

It was the prohibition on blacks, however, that was to be the crucial point in the view of Georgia as a colony guided by the best eighteenth-century principles of reason, morality, and the dignity of white labor. To forbid slavery and black labor would be to strike a blow at an institution many in England were coming to consider reprehensible. The Trustees, and particularly the ministers who exhorted them yearly at their annual meeting, felt that black labor also caused the white populace to become more prone to drinking, gaming, and litigating. With the amount of land one could hold being limited, lacking access to Negro labor, and with each Protestant landowner (under tail-male restrictions) living on and protecting his own property, Georgia might actually become the most enlightened British province. Not worried by slave revolts, land speculators, or lawyers, the Trustees felt they had a good chance to create the sort of Eden they wished.

Oglethorpe not only agreed with these sentiments, he was the prime mover of them. He was given the responsibility for bringing the theory of Georgia into reality. It was, of course, part of his and the Trustees' failure that a unique English province was not successfully created.

The main problem with Oglethorpe's principles as they related to his colonists was that they were too demanding for the average man. In his constitution and his predilections he may have differed from many of those around him. But his own abstemiousness concerning strong drink, his idealistic attitude toward the opposite sex, and the fact that although he was apparently virile and physically attractive there was rarely a bit of gossip associated with his name, all illustrate the point that he did not set up rules and regulations for others to observe while ignoring them himself.

Several years after Oglethorpe's final departure from Georgia, William Horton, left in charge of the southern reaches of the colony, wrote to the Trust that the province would remain "in a melancholly State" until those who caused trouble "are made Examples of or at least discountenanced." He continued: "I wish to God the General or either of the Trustees were to come over here" to resolve the problems. "The Volumes of private and publick Scandal" from Savannah had reduced it to a "tottering Condition."[20] A strong moral hand pointing the path of rectitude was needed, but Oglethorpe by that time had found himself a wife and his once burning interest in Georgia had cooled as its early guidelines were either repealed or ignored. The chances that he would return were remote indeed.

It is easy to blame Oglethorpe for a doctrinaire approach and scold him for failing to secure the permanency of the Trustee legislation, but it is difficult not to admire him for articulating simple, straightforward principles at a time when to do so was something of a rarity. More than any other member of the Trust he was conscious of the dependence of each Georgia law on the other; permit one to be changed and they would all be changed. He was repulsed by the prospect of meeting the Georgia malcontents, whom he considered to be motivated by selfish considerations, on some sort of middle ground. Principles, where Oglethorpe was concerned, were not negotiable.

Although he had long been accustomed to positions of leadership in England, had been effective in helping secure the Georgia charter, and had been most influential in organizing the original expedition, the situation changed abruptly when the scene shifted to American shores. Oglethorpe had read and studied about the New World, but he had never actually experienced its reality. The environment, climate, attitudes, land, trees, pests—everything—proved different or at least modified from what he had known in England. Fairly abruptly Oglethorpe and his colonists found themselves in a venture the ultimate outcome of which was suddenly in doubt. Where there had been a wide gulf separating Oglethorpe from the generality of his settlers as long as they remained in England or even on board ship, this gulf was narrowed perceptibly by the realities of the New World. Not only were his colonists being tested in the crucible of American experience, Oglethorpe too was being tested. His "right" to be a leader in Parliament and in British life had been based, to a large measure, on the happenstance of family and wealth. But suddenly in America these factors seemed not so important, as everyone faced questions that could not have been foreseen by the Georgia Office where the Trustees met to settle the fate of their province.

After arriving in America, Oglethorpe chose superior locations for his main settlements. Savannah, his first colony,
proved to be his most effective, but the surrounding town sites,
picked without adequate knowledge of the quality of the soil,
were not well selected and most of them soon perished.
Although Frederica did not survive the withdrawal of Oglethorpe's regiment, it had been chosen because of its strategic
military location on the inland passage at the Altamaha's
mouth. It served its purpose and died, although Oglethorpe
obviously had high hopes for this town which, he asserted, was
virtue and rectitude personified as compared to Savannah. The
sites of Augusta and Darien were fairly routine. Oglethorpe had
less to do with their selection than with the others, but they
were established at sensible locations and proved to be contributing factors in the success of Georgia. The first site of
Ebenezer, suggested by Oglethorpe to the Salzburgers, was a
mistake, and he was ultimately convinced to permit the settlement to move to a more fertile spot.

After the initial phases of settlement Oglethorpe's leadership
struck many as being too authoritarian. No one dreamed of a
democratic arrangement for Georgia, but Oglethorpe, main-
taining that the colony must have strong guidance to survive,
took everything upon himself. He then became so jealous of his
power that he was reluctant to part with the slightest shred. This
was, at least in some measure, the fault of the Trustees, who laid
out and specified only a few areas where Oglethorpe was
positively licensed to act. Perhaps this failure to give Oglethorpe
significant authority was the fatal flaw of Trusteeship Georgia.
Had Oglethorpe received the perquisites and powers of a
colonial governor (even without the official title), he might have
acted in a less arbitrary manner. But as it was, to his enemies he
was guilty of a kind of coup and some of his associates on the
Board thought him guilty, at the least, of usurpation.

The result of Oglethorpe's assumption of power was an
incredible workload for himself, high-handed tactics that alienated colonists and Trustees alike, and the evolution of a group
in Georgia that gradually became more and more outspoken in
its criticism. Every person who posed a threat to him received

Oglethorpe's immediate and often vitriolic opposition, be he a man of the cloth like Whitefield, a medical man like Tailfer, or an appointee of his own Trustee colleagues like Stephens. It was unthinkable to Oglethorpe to take a back seat or even to share the position of eminence in Georgia.

In their fervor the Trustees wanted to be privy to every decision taken in Georgia. Oglethorpe found this was quite impossible because of the multitude of day-to-day determinations that had to be made on the spot. It was unrealistic, he said, to defer to England for each important decision. By the time the Trustees had been consulted the circumstances might have changed drastically; instantaneous judgments had to be reached daily on an astonishing variety of issues.[21] He found out what leaders before him had already discovered: the distance from London alone made the proper running of a colony tremendously different from home government. He was thrown more on his own initiative than he had envisioned and was faced with making significant as well as trivial judgments. He did not draw back from the challenge, however, and met the problems as they came. In the long run he acted maturely and by so doing placed himself in the ranks of responsible British colonial leaders.

Oglethorpe's most striking failure was his inability to make the black prohibition stick. Considering that the land and Negro regulations, along with the rum and Indian legislation, were all related to one another it is hard to censure him for failure in this instance. Once the provisions for small landholdings and the procedural questions touching upon alienation and inheritance were undermined, it was likely that the anti-Negro restriction would fall too. It should be pointed out, however, that there were no environmental or geographical laws that said Negroes or slavery were essential for the prosperous life of the province of Georgia, but she shared the Savannah River boundary with an aggressive, expanding province that daily emphasized the institution of slavery. It would have taken a superhuman effort for Oglethorpe and his allies to reject the concerted agitations of the proslavery elements in both colonies.

The prime reason Oglethorpe and the Negro Act failed is not

a rigidly deterministic one. There is little question that the slave restriction would have stood a better chance had Georgia been blessed with more fertile soil for agricultural purposes, similar, for example, to Pennsylvania's rich fields, but geography does not fully explain the failure. And the notion that Georgia was preordained to be a slave colony falls under the weight of its own rhetoric. Where Oglethorpe and the Trust missed their best chance was in not creating an economic climate where Georgia might develop an effective alternative to the slave and the plantation. Indentured servitude was never a success in Georgia, for many servants fled to Carolina and elsewhere. They would have been more likely to stay if they had had bright prospects for the future, after their indentures had expired. But land grants were severely limited, property was entailed, and transferrals of grants were difficult at best. These factors and more worked against the development of a yeoman-farmer class and against Oglethorpe's dream of a colony broadly based on his concept of agrarian equality. Furthermore with rum taboo, trade based on rum and molasses in exchange for grain and forest products was out of the question. For this and other reasons the early attempts by Samuel Eveleigh to develop a strong Indian trade in Georgia were futile.

The only alternative to slavery for the development of an import-export trade that the Trust held out seemed to be an almost mystic faith in silk culture. Although it became apparent that silkworms did not prosper in Georgia and that the patience, experience, and initial investments involved were all beyond the means of the average Georgia landholder, Oglethorpe clung tenaciously to his belief that silk would offer salvation to his colony. Together with wine and olive oil, silk would make Georgia into a sort of American Paradise. In the grand manner he sometimes affected Oglethorpe wrote in 1734 that those products were to be Georgia's exports—as though preordained because he wanted it so. He ignored the fact that profitable culture of all three took years of painstaking work. How he thought the colonists would survive and "live comfortably" in the meantime Oglethorpe did not say.[22] Had more emphasis been put on the Indian trade and forest industries, and had extensive efforts been made to produce on Georgia's little farms goods that might have found a ready market elsewhere in the British Empire, there is no valid reason to maintain that slavery's expansion into the colony would have been economically or intellectually inevitable. In fact there is at least as good a reason to hold the opposite view.

What Oglethorpe and the Trustees did not perceive as clearly as the twentieth century were the psychological, economic, and political repercussions if the institution of slavery actually had been prevented from crossing the Savannah. With the westward experience in American life having the stirring effect it did, the potential implications of such a barrier to slavery and to blacks are staggering. If the Trust and Oglethorpe had acted in a slightly different fashion, Georgia might have become far more a southern Zion than anyone in his wildest dreams could have envisioned. There might then be some real substance to the parallel drawn by Ettinger between Oglethorpe and Lincoln.[23] Georgians, far from being, in Daniel Boorstin's unhappy phrase, "the victims of philanthropy," would have proved themselves the dispensers thereof.[24]

Some of Oglethorpe's feats of military daring on the southern frontier are reminiscent of scenes in Italian opera buffa, but the effects of his stance in the Georgia-Florida area were of far-reaching importance. Oglethorpe's immediate aim was the capture of St. Augustine, and to this end he spent untold hours of planning and execution only to be frustrated. In spite of the bravado, his failure before the Spanish stronghold haunted him. In retrospect, however, it was his repulse of the Spanish invasion of Georgia that was by far the more important military action. Oglethorpe's dramatic defeat of the Spanish in 1742 provided a needed morale boost for a nation that had expected one easy and brilliant victory after another once war with Spain was declared. The bright promise of Porto Bello had been succeeded by shocking setbacks in the Caribbean. The battle of St. Simons helped restore the confidence of the English in the war effort and placed the name of Oglethorpe alongside that of Vernon as a hero of the moment.

Oglethorpe returned to England in 1743, and after easily

refuting some groundless charges placed against him by a dissatisfied officer of his regiment, he resumed his seat in Parliament and picked up his English career where he had left it over a decade earlier. After he married in 1744 he came to the Georgia Office less and less frequently. Still, he retained a strong interest in the course of American affairs generally and was vitally concerned in the events associated with the American Revolution. When he was well over eighty years of age he tried to secure a compromise arrangement that would allow the colonies to remain in the British Empire. He and John Adams, first American ambassador to be received in London, exchanged lengthy visits just a few months before Oglethorpe died, on 30 June 1785.[25]

July 1743, the month of Oglethorpe's departure from the New World, was marked by severe weather in Savannah. On 3 July a bolt of lightning "Shatterd our Flag Staff into Small pieces," Stephens reported. Almost a week later, as the founder prepared to leave for good, another stroke blasted two of the five trees left standing on the bluff where Oglethorpe had originally landed and where he had first "pitched his Tent." The trees had remained, Stephens noted, "as a Standing Monument" to Oglethorpe and the act of settlement; but now they were gone.[26] He failed to add, however, that the surviving pines still stood, symbolic of the boldness and strength of James Oglethorpe and symbolic, too, of the permanency of the colony he founded, settled, protected, and led.

Notes

Chapter 1. VOYAGE AND SETTLEMENT

1. James Oglethorpe to the Trustees, 13 January 1733, The Phillipps Collection of Egmont Manuscripts, University of Georgia Library, 14200:13. (Hereinafter cited as Egmont Papers.)

2. Ibid.; Charles Town *South-Carolina Gazette*, 20 January 1733.

3. Thomas Christie, "The Voyage of the *Anne*—A Daily Record," ed. Robert G. McPherson, *Georgia Historical Quarterly* 44 (June 1960): 224, 227.

4. Oglethorpe to the Trustees, 13 January 1733, Egmont Papers, 14200:13.

5. *Gentleman's Magazine* 55, Part 2 (July 1785): 573. The "correspondent" who sent in this selection was, of course, mistaken on the question of Oglethorpe's age. See Phinizy Spalding, "The Death of James Edward Oglethorpe," *Georgia Historical Quarterly* 57 (Summer 1973): 227-34.

6. Amos Aschbach Ettinger, *James Edward Oglethorpe, Imperial Idealist* (Oxford: Clarendon Press, 1936), pp. 81-97. See also Horace Maybray King, *James Edward Oglethorpe's Parliamentary Career* (Milledgeville: Georgia College, 1968).

7. See Historical Manuscripts Commission, *The King's Collection of Stuart Papers,* H.M.C. Reports, 7 vols. (London, 1902-23), vols. 4-7, passim.

8. Historical Manuscripts Commission, *Diary of John Percival, First Earl of Egmont,* H.M.C. Reports, 3 vols. (London, 1920-23), 2:62, 3:244-45. (Hereinafter cited as Egmont, *Diary.*)

9. See especially Benjamin Rand, ed., *Berkeley and Percival* (Cambridge: At the University Press, 1914).

10. [James Oglethorpe], *A New and Accurate Account of the Provinces of South-Carolina and Georgia* (London: J. Roberts, 1733), pp. 17-18.

11. Ibid., pp. i-vii, 21, 24-26, 30-31.

12. Allen D. Candler, Lucian L. Knight, Kenneth Coleman, and Milton Ready, eds., *The Colonial Records of the State of Georgia,* 27 vols. to date (Atlanta and Athens, 1904-16, 1976-), 1:11-26. (Hereinafter cited as *CRG.*)

13. Egmont, *Diary,* 1:232.

14. Ettinger, *Oglethorpe,* pp. 81-84.

15. Egmont, *Diary,* 1:235, 265.

16. Jonathan Belcher to Thomas Coram, 24 April 1732, *Collections of the Massachusetts Historical Society,* 6th ser., 6 (1893): 112.

17. Johnson to Oglethorpe, 28 September 1732, Egmont Papers, 14200:1.

18. *Gentleman's Magazine* 2 (October, November 1732): 1029, 1079-80.

19. Egmont, *Diary,* 1:293.

20. Oglethorpe to the Trustees, 18 November 1732, Egmont Papers, 14200:5.

21. Egmont, *Diary*, 2:325.

22. *CRG*, 2:11.

23. Peter Gordon, *The Journal of Peter Gordon, 1732-1735*, ed. E. Merton Coulter (Athens: University of Georgia Press, 1963), p. 31.

24. "Voyage of the *Anne*," pp. 223-24. Gordon, whose Latin apparently left something to be desired, reported the child's name as "Georgia Marino." *Journal of Peter Gordon*, p. 29.

25. "Voyage of the *Anne*," p. 227.

26. Ibid.; *Journal of Peter Gordon*, pp. 30-31.

27. "Voyage of the *Anne*," p. 227. The crew and passengers had not gotten along very well from the start. It may be that throwing the water had something to do with hazing the landlubbers. An earlier incident concerning payment of a customary fee to the crew had caused dissatisfaction but had been calmed by Oglethorpe. See ibid., p. 226.

28. Ibid., p. 229.

29. Ibid., p. 230; *Journal of Peter Gordon*, p. 31. Gordon says Oglethorpe impatiently set out in a boat with rowers for Charles Town when no pilot answered the signal. Christie flatly reports that "a pilot came aboard." The inclination would be to take Christie's word. Scanty as it is, he wrote in his diary every day, apparently checking the logbook of the *Anne* daily as well. Additionally, he endorsed his work on the day of arrival in Charles Town and sent it immediately to England. Gordon's *Journal* was written later and contains several other contentions that have led some to question the author's complete accuracy.

30. *S.C. Gazette*, 20 January 1733.

31. Oglethorpe to the Trustees, 13 January 1733, Egmont Papers, 14200:13; Phinizy Spalding, "South Carolina and Georgia: The Early Days," *South Carolina Historical Magazine* 59 (April 1968): 83-96.

32. Oglethorpe to the Trustees, 10 February 1733, Egmont Papers, 14200: 33. The view from Yamacraw Bluff was probably not quite as dramatic as Oglethorpe made out, and certainly the site is more than ten miles from the mouth of the river, unless he reckoned as the crow flies.

33. *Journal of Peter Gordon*, pp. 34-35; Thomas Causton to his Wife, 12 March 1733, Egmont Papers, 14200:53.

34. *Journal of Peter Gordon*, p. 35.

35. Causton to his Wife, 12 March 1733, Egmont Papers, 14200:54.

36. *Journal of Peter Gordon*, p. 35.

37. Causton to his Wife, 12 March 1733, Egmont Papers, 14200:54; *Journal of Peter Gordon*, pp. 35-36.

38. *Journal of Peter Gordon*, p. 36. There is no reference to a "Dr. Lyons" in the available sources concerned with the original embarkation of Georgia settlers. Dr. William Cox and his family did, indeed, spend the evening with Gordon at Yamacraw, but there is no reason to believe it was Cox who did the dancing.

39. Causton to his Wife, 12 March 1733, Egmont Papers, 14200:54.

40. Oglethorpe to the Trustees, 10 February 1733, ibid., p. 33.

41. Causton to his Wife, 12 March 1733, ibid., p. 55.

42. *Journal of Peter Gordon*, pp. 37-38; *CRG*, 3:90; *S.C. Gazette*, 31 March 1733. Although the square named for Governor Johnson of South Carolina was marked off at this time, the streets, seemingly, were not named until 7 July. Bull was honored by having the main street named for him.

43. *Journal of Peter Gordon*, p. 38. Actually Oglethorpe had made the first division into tithings on board the *Anne* on 28 November. See ibid., p. 30; "Voyage of the *Anne*," p. 224.

44. *Journal of Peter Gordon*, p. 40.

45. Oglethorpe to the Trustees, 10 February 1733, Egmont Papers, 14200: 34.

46. Oglethorpe to the Trustees, 12 March 1733, ibid., p. 45.

47. Ibid.

48. See especially Peter Gordon's view of Savannah, shown by him to the Trustees in 1734 when he first returned to London. For a clear reproduction of Gordon's view, see Charles Colcock Jones, Jr., *The History of Georgia*, 2 vols. (Boston: Houghton, Mifflin and Company, 1883), vol. 1, facing p. 121. See also John Lord Viscount Percival, *The Journal of the Earl of Egmont*, ed. Robert G. McPherson (Athens: University of Georgia Press, 1962), pp. 43-44.

49. Eveleigh to the Trustees, 6 April 1733, Egmont Papers, 14200:61.

50. *S.C. Gazette*, 24 March 1732 [1733]. See also *CRG*, 3:405-7.

51. Oglethorpe to the Trustees, 12 March 1733, Egmont Papers, 14200: 45-46.

52. *S.C. Gazette*, 2 June 1733. See also "Oglethorpe's Treaty with the Lower Creek Indians," *Georgia Historical Quarterly* 4 (March 1920): 12-16.

53. *Journal of Peter Gordon*, p. 45.

54. Oglethorpe to the Trustees, 14 May 1733, Egmont Papers, 14200:66.

55. *Journal of Peter Gordon*, pp. 49-50. At this time Oglethorpe also formally presented each family with a town lot, named the wards, and administered the oaths of allegiance. See Oglethorpe to the Trustees, 12 August 1733, Egmont Papers, 14200:108. The streets—mainly honoring Carolinians —were also named at this time.

56. *CRG*, 1:83.

57. Francis Moore, *A Voyage to Georgia* (London: Jacob Robinson, 1744), p. 26.

58. *Journal of Peter Gordon*, p. 50.

59. Ibid., p. 51.

60. Samuel Quincy to Oglethorpe, 20 June 1734, Egmont Papers, 14200: 203.

61. Boswell Papers, Yale University (M 208:2); Joseph Foster, *The Register of Admissions to Gray's Inn, 1521-1889* (London, 1889), p. 369. Oglethorpe's jail investigations probably prompted his interest in the law but, as he told Boswell years later, he had learned some law during his years at Oxford and had done a good deal of reading on the subject, including Bracton and Fortescue. Apparently he took a Master and read law at Gray's Inn, but was never a practicing attorney.

62. For his commissions and powers, see *CRG*, 2:9-11. Oglethorpe was to act, wrote a perceptive author, only as an attorney for the Trustees, and a severely circumscribed one at that. See James Ross McCain, *Georgia as a Proprietary Province* (Boston: Richard G. Badger, 1917), pp. 65-69, and passim. In

spite of its misleading title, this book is still one of the most careful works on the history of colonial Georgia.

Chapter 2. FREDERICA AND DEFENSE CONSIDERATIONS

1. Oglethorpe to the Trustees, 14 May 1733, Egmont Papers, 14200: 65.

2. Ibid., p. 66

3. Oglethorpe to the Trustees, 9 June 1733, ibid., p. 83.

4. *S.C. Gazette*, 2 June 1733; Journal of the Commons House of Assembly of South Carolina, 9 June 1733, I, Part 2, 1100-1101, South Carolina Archives Department, Columbia, S.C. (Hereinafter cited as JCHA. The Journals of the Council and Upper House are also located at the Archives, are bound indiscriminately together, and will hereinafter be referred to, respectively, as Council Journal, and JUHA.) See also Thomas Cooper and David J. McCord, eds., *The Statutes at Large of South Carolina*, 14 vols. (Columbia, S.C.: A. S. Johnson, 1838-75), 3:362-64. (Hereinafter cited as *S.C. Statutes.*)

5. JCHA, 2 June 1733, I, Part 2, 1093.

6. Oglethorpe to the Trustees, 12 August 1733, Egmont Papers, 14200: 105-6. The illness which struck so many in the summer of 1733 was apparently malaria complicated by dysentery. Joseph Ioor Waring, "Colonial Medicine in Georgia and South Carolina," *Georgia Historical Quarterly* 59 (Supplement 1975): 145-46.

7. Oglethorpe to the Trustees, 12 August 1733, Egmont Papers, 14200: 107.

8. Oglethorpe to the Trustees, ca. December 1733, ibid., p. 129.

9. Ibid., pp. 125-28; Egmont, *Diary*, 2:112.

10. William Stephens expresses the prejudice against the pine most clearly. See *The Journal of William Stephens 1741-1745*, ed. E. Merton Coulter, 2 vols. (Athens: University of Georgia Press, 1958-59), App. A, 1:241. Johnson in South Carolina faced much the same problem in his township scheme. Johnson's main purpose, as was Oglethorpe's, was defense, and as Eugene Sirmans has said, "settlers often occupied land that was easy to defend but hard to cultivate." M. Eugene Sirmans, *Colonial South Carolina: A Political History, 1663-1763* (Chapel Hill: University of North Carolina Press, 1966), p. 168. See also Richard P. Sherman, *Robert Johnson* (Columbia: University of South Carolina Press, 1966), p. 107 and passim.

11. For a good discussion of agriculture in Trusteeship Georgia, see Milton L. Ready, "An Economic History of Colonial Georgia, 1732-1754," Ph.D. diss., University of Georgia, 1970, pp. 74-124, and the same author's "Land Tenure in Trusteeship Georgia," *Agricultural History* 48 (July 1974): 353-68.

12. Egmont, *Journal*, p. 342.

13. William Bateman to [Egmont?], 3 September 1734, The Colonial Records of the State of Georgia, 14 vols., Georgia Department of Archives and History, Atlanta (Typescript), 20:13-15. (Hereinafter cited as MS, CRG.) See also JCHA, 28 May 1734, No. 2, p. 193; Mary Musgrove to Oglethorpe, 17 July 1734, Egmont Papers, 14200:219; Egmont, *Diary*, II, 199.

14. George Fenwick Jones, ed., *Detailed Reports on the Salzburger Emigrants who Settled in America . . .*, 4 vols. to date (Athens: University of

169 *Notes to Pages 22-27*

Georgia Press, 1968-), 1:57. (Hereinafter cited as *Detailed Reports*.)

15. Henry Newman, postscript to Samuel Urlsperger, in letter to John Vat, 13 November 1733, Society Letters, CS 2/28, 37, and postscript to Newman letter to Urlsperger, 11 June 1735, Society Letters, CS 2/30, 4, SPCK Archives, London.

16. *Detailed Reports*, 1:57, 61, 67.

17. John Martin Boltzius to Newman, 22 March 1734, in George Fenwick Jones, ed., *Henry Newman's Salzburger Letterbooks* (Athens: University of Georgia Press, 1966), p. 461. (Hereinafter cited as *Newman's Letterbooks*.)

18. *S.C. Gazette*, 11 May 1734.

19. Stephens, *Journal*, App. A, 1:243-44.

20. Egmont, *Journal*, p. 44.

21. Moore, *A Voyage to Georgia*, p. 23; John Martin Boltzius to Cretin de Munch, 6 May 1747, *CRG*, 25:174.

22. Moore, *A Voyage to Georgia*, pp. 10-11.

23. Oglethorpe to Samuel Wesley, 19 November 1734, *Newman's Letterbooks*, p. 514.

24. Oglethorpe to Samuel Wesley, 25 December 1734, ibid., p. 519.

25. Oglethorpe to Harman Verelst, 29 October and 2 November 1735, *CRG*, 21:34, 36.

26. Oglethorpe to Verelst, 10 December 1735, ibid., p. 53.

27. Moore, *A Voyage to Georgia*, p. 12.

28. Ibid., pp. 14-15.

29. John Wesley, *The Journal of the Rev. John Wesley*, ed. Nehemiah Curnock, 8 vols. (London: Epworth Press, reissued 1938), 1:123-24, and passim; Adelaide Fries, *The Moravians in Georgia* (Raleigh, 1905), pp. 110-19; "The Journal of Reverend Benjamin Ingham," in Luke Tyerman, *The Oxford Methodists* (London, 1873), pp. 61-81; and Charles Wesley, *The Journal of the Rev. Charles Wesley*, ed. John Telford (London, [1909]).

30. Ingham, "Journal," pp. 72-74; Moore, *A Voyage to Georgia*, pp. 16-17.

31. Moore, *A Voyage to Georgia*, p. 16.

32. John Brownfield to the Trustees, 6 March 1736, John Brownfield's Copy Book, 1735-40, Archives of the Moravian Church, Bethlehem, Pa. (Microfilm, University of Georgia Library).

33. Moore, *A Voyage to Georgia*, pp. 21-23.

34. Brownfield to the Trustees, 6 March 1736, Brownfield's Copy Book.

35. Boltzius to Oglethorpe, 7 February 1735, *Newman's Letterbooks*, pp. 546-47; George Fenwick Jones, ed., "The Secret Diary of Pastor Johann Martin Boltzius," *Georgia Historical Quarterly* 53 (March 1969): 78-110.

36. Moore, *A Voyage to Georgia*, pp. 33-34; "The Secret Diary of . . . Boltzius," p. 87; Oglethorpe to the Trustees, 13 February 1736, "Letters from General Oglethorpe," *Collections of the Georgia Historical Society* 3 (Savannah, 1873): 13. (Hereinafter cited as "Oglethorpe Letters.") See also *Detailed Reports*, 3:36-40.

37. Moore, *A Voyage to Georgia*, p. 43. The date was 18 February 1736.

38. Oglethorpe to [the Trustees], 27 February 1736, "Oglethorpe Letters," p. 15.

39. Eveleigh to Verelst, 24 March 1735 [1736], *CRG*, 21:115.

40. Moore, *A Voyage to Georgia*, p. 45. Moore is actually citing a companion who went with Oglethorpe to Darien.
41. Oglethorpe to [the Trustees], 27 February 1736, "Oglethorpe Letters," p. 15.
42. Moore, *A Voyage to Georgia*, pp. 47-49, 51-52.
43. Oglethorpe to the Trustees, 28 April 1741, "Oglethorpe Letters," p. 113.
44. Oglethorpe to the Trustees, 24 January 1740, ibid., p. 104. See also Oglethorpe to the Trustees, 29 June 1741, ibid., p. 117.
45. Oglethorpe to the Trustees, 28 April 1741, ibid., p. 113.
46. See Richard S. Dunn, "The Trustees of Georgia and the House of Commons, 1732-1752," *William and Mary Quarterly*, 3d ser., 11 (October 1954): 551-65.
47. Oglethorpe to Field Marshal James Keith, 3 May 1756, Historical Manuscripts Commission, *Manuscripts of Lord Elphinstone*, 9, Part 2 (1883): 229.
48. *CRG*, 2:513-14.

Chapter 3. CORRESPONDENCE AND FINANCES

1. David Bertelson, *The Lazy South* (New York: Oxford University Press, 1967), p. 90. For an excellent account of the Georgia promotional literature, see Verner W. Crane, "The Promotion Literature of Georgia," in *Bibliographical Essays: A Tribute to Wilberforce Eames* (Cambridge: Harvard University Press, 1925), pp. 281-98.
2. Oglethorpe to the Trustees, 10 February 1733, Egmont Papers, 14200: 34.
3. Oglethorpe to Sir Hans Sloane, 19 September 1733, Sloane MSS, 4053, fol. 53, British Library.
4. *Journal of Peter Gordon*, p. 63.
5. Egmont, *Diary*, 2:41. Vernon also complained at the same time about certain "young members" on the Board who paid too little heed to religion. Their leader was reputed to be the secretary of the Trust, Benjamin Martyn.
6. Ibid., p. 55. Such a person was to be assured proper payment.
7. Oglethorpe to Verelst, 3 December 1735. "Oglethorpe Letters," pp. 6-7.
8. See a series of letters by Oglethorpe to Jean Vat, John Wesley, Boltzius, Baron Philipp von Reck, all dated 16 March 1736, ibid., pp. 22-25. For a fuller understanding of this complex affair consult *Detailed Reports*, vol. 3, and "The Secret Diary of . . . Boltzius," pp. 78-110.
9. Oglethorpe to [the Trustees], 28 March 1736, "Oglethorpe Letters," pp. 27-28.
10. Oglethorpe to the Trustees, 11 May 1736, ibid., p. 33.
11. Oglethorpe to [the Trustees], June 1736, Egmont Papers, 14201: 517-22, 523-24.
12. Oglethorpe to the Trustees, 1 July 1736, "Oglethorpe Letters," p. 37.
13. Moore to [Verelst], 20 September 1736, *CRG*, 21:224.
14. Egmont, *Diary*, 2:302.
15. Stephens, *Journal*, 1:xiii-xv.
16. *CRG*, 2:190.

17. Ibid., 4:10. This volume and a supplementary one contain Stephens's journal from October 1737 through 28 October 1741.

18. Ibid., p. 215.

19. Egmont, *Diary*, 3:4; Causton to his Wife, 12 March 1733, Egmont Papers, 14200:53.

20. Oglethorpe to Verelst, received 29 March 1742, Public Record Office, TI/307, fol. 210 (copies in the University of Georgia Library).

21. Oglethorpe to the Trustees, 4 July 1739, *CRG*, 22, Part 2: 163-74.

22. Ibid., p. 171.

23. Ibid., 4:369, 371.

24. Ibid., p. 371.

25. Boltzius to ——, 19 July 1739, ibid., 22, Part 2:182.

26. Ibid., 4:376.

27. Christie to the Trustees, 3 August 1739, ibid., 22, Part 2:198.

28. Causton to his Wife, 12 March 1733, Egmont Papers, 14200:53.

29. *CRG*, 4:421-33.

30. Ibid., p. 425.

31. Oglethorpe to the Trustees, 11 October 1739, "Oglethorpe Letters," pp. 83-84.

32. *CRG*, 4:549.

33. William Stephens to Verelst, 4 August 1740, ibid., 22, Part 2: 409.

34. Ibid., 4:637.

35. Ibid., Supplement: 19, 20, 42, 55, 61, 62, 83-84, 87, 88.

36. Ibid., pp. 83-84.

37. Stephens, *Journal*, 1:115.

38. Ibid., pp. 115, 116, 119, 124-25.

39. Ibid., pp. 179-80. See also Stephens to Verelst, 19 March 1743, *CRG*, 24:5-6, concerning a more than ten-month delay in fulfilling certain Trustee orders for the southern reaches of Georgia.

40. The Loseley Manuscripts, Puttenham Papers, Guildford Muniment Room, Guildford, Surrey. The Molyneux and Oglethorpe families were not often on good terms in Surrey.

41. *CRG*, 2:27; Egmont, *Diary*, 2:29.

42. Ettinger, *Oglethorpe*, pp. 177-78.

43. Oglethorpe to the Trustees, 12 March 1733, Egmont Papers, 14200:45.

44. Oglethorpe to the Trustees, 17 September 1733, ibid., pp. 113-14.

45. Oglethorpe to the Trustees, 15 November 1733, ibid., p. 121.

46. *CRG*, 2:113-14; Egmont, *Journal*, pp. 98-100.

47. There is a difference of opinion among authors as to Oglethorpe's fiscal powers. Ettinger, *Oglethorpe*, pp. 177-78, maintains that the Trustees specifically gave him authority "to draw bills on the Trustees," and "the sole right to draw bills of credit." McCain, *Georgia as a Proprietary Province*, p. 66, presents the opposite picture: "none of the records indicate that he was authorized to draw on the Trustees for money." After looking into the sources, I am more inclined to accept McCain's position.

48. Egmont, *Diary*, 2:278.

49. Ibid., p. 279.

50. Ibid., p. 292.

51. Eveleigh to Verelst, 16 October 1736, *CRG,* 21:212-13.
52. Thomas Wilson, *The Diaries of Thomas Wilson, D.D., 1731-37 and 1750,* ed. Charles L. S. Linnell (London: SPCK, 1964), p. 172.
53. John Wesley to Oglethorpe, 24 February 1737, *The Works of John Wesley,* 12:42.
54. Egmont, *Diary,* 2:424. For Oglethorpe's ideas on the relative benefits of wine, beer, and rum to England and the colonies, see his letter to the Trustees, 12 February 1743, "Oglethorpe Letters," p. 143.
55. Egmont, *Diary,* 2:472-74.
56. Ibid., p. 483.
57. Oglethorpe to Thomas Tower, 19 September 1738, Tower Collection (Photostats), Essex Records Office, Chelmsford.
58. Oglethorpe to the Trustees, 7 October 1738, "Oglethorpe Letters," p. 54.
59. Oglethorpe to the Trustees, 19 October 1738, ibid., p. 59.
60. Oglethorpe to the Trustees, 12 March 1739, ibid., p. 71.
61. Oglethorpe to Egmont, 20 November 1738, Egmont Papers, 14203: 326.
62. Trevor R. Reese, *Colonial Georgia* (Athens: University of Georgia Press, 1963), pp. 30-31; Egmont, *Diary,* 2, passim. Richard S. Dunn saw Georgia growing more and more dependent upon Walpole specifically, rather than on Parliament alone, as the years went by. Although many of the Trustees were also MPs, there was never a Georgia Party per se.
63. Egmont, *Diary,* 3:46-47.
64. Oglethorpe to Verelst, 19 October 1739, "Oglethorpe Letters," p. 88.
65. The bounty system was made only partly operational. Patrick Houston received £ 75 for corn he had grown under the bounty's provisions, "others more or less in proportion," but some had received no pay, "the Trustees money not holding out." *CRG,* 5:500.
66. Ibid., p. 266.
67. Ibid., p. 287.
68. Ibid.
69. Ibid., p. 290.
70. Stephens to Verelst, 19 March 1743, ibid., 24:6.

Chapter 4. RUM AND THE INDIAN TRADE

1. Egmont, *Diary,* 1:295.
2. Egmont, *Journal,* p. 83; *CRG,* 1:31-54, 2:96-97.
3. *CRG,* 1:44.
4. Ibid., p. 45.
5. For the three acts in their entirety, see ibid., pp. 31-54.
6. G. Barnett Smith, *History of the English Parliament* (London, 1892), 2: 255-56.
7. Ettinger, *Oglethorpe,* p. 148; Arthur Pierce Middleton, "The Strange Story of Job Ben Solomon," *William and Mary Quarterly,* 3d ser., 5 (July 1948): 342-50.
8. Oglethorpe to the Trustees, 17 January 1739, Egmont Papers, 14203: 380.

9. See Reese, *Colonial Georgia*, pp. 47–50; E. Merton Coulter, *Georgia: A Short History*, rev. and enlarged ed. (Chapel Hill: University of North Carolina Press, 1960), pp. 57–58; Ralph Betts Flanders, *Plantation Slavery in Georgia* (Chapel Hill: University of North Carolina Press, 1933), pp. 7–8, 15; Ettinger, *Oglethorpe*, p. 150 n. 6.

10. *CRG*, 1:45; Thomas Penn to Oglethorpe, 4 August 1734, Egmont Papers, 14200:227. Beer and wine were not included in the interdict.

11. *CRG*, 1:31–42.

12. MS, CRG, 32:406–7; *CRG*, 2:120, 123.

13. *S. C. Statutes*, 3:327–34, 371–72.

14. *CRG*, 1:50–51.

15. Christie to the Trustees, 28 May 1735, MS, CRG, 20:328–29; Causton to the Trustees, 8 September 1735, ibid., p. 300.

16. Samuel Marcer to the Trustees, 25 April 1735, ibid., p. 348.

17. For Mackay's commission, dated 27 April 1734, see Miscellaneous Records, Book EE, 1741–1743, S.C. Archives Department, Columbia, S.C.

18. Choctaw Talks, Egmont Papers, 14200:207–10; Mary Musgrove to Oglethorpe, 17 July 1734, ibid., p. 219.

19. Patrick Mackay to Causton, 8 July 1734, ibid., 212.

20. *S.C. Statutes*, 4:399–400.

21. Eveleigh to [Oglethorpe], 20 November 1734, MS, CRG, 20:50–52.

22. Mackay to the Trustees, 20 November 1734, ibid., pp. 55–57.

23. Johnson to Oglethorpe, 28 January 1735, ibid., pp. 178–79; Eveleigh to Oglethorpe, 7 July 1735, ibid., p. 653.

24. Sirmans, *Colonial South Carolina*, p. 188; Sherman, *Robert Johnson*, pp. 188–90.

25. Fenwicke to Oglethorpe, 3 April 1735, MS, CRG, 20:582–83.

26. Fenwicke to Mackay, 12 June 1735, ibid., pp. 439–41. See also *ibid.*, pp. 441–45 for representations of Carolina traders.

27. Eveleigh to William Jeffreys, 4 July 1735, ibid., p. 212.

28. Martyn to Mackay, 10 October 1735, ibid., 29:206.

29. Remonstrance, Records in the Public Record Office, London, relating to South Carolina, 36 vols., S.C. Archives Department (Microfilm), 17:227, 399, 400, 401, 403, and passim. (Hereinafter cited as PRSC.) See also Broughton to Egmont, October 1735, ibid., pp. 442–43.

30. Moore, *A Voyage to Georgia*, p. 26.

31. *S.C. Statutes*, 4:448–49; JUHA, No. 6, Part 2, 283–85; *S.C. Gazette*, 3 July 1736; Oglethorpe to Lord ——, 26 July 1736, "Oglethorpe Letters," pp. 39–40.

32. *S.C. Gazette*, 7 August 1736; *Virginia Gazette*, 22 October 1736; *Gentleman's Magazine* 6 (November 1736): 686; Oglethorpe to the Committee of both Houses, [3 or 4] August 1736, Egmont Papers, 14202:141.

33. Eveleigh to Verelst, 9 August 1736, *CRG*, 21:206; Paul Jenys to the Trustees, 10 September 1736, ibid., pp. 209–10.

34. *S.C. Gazette*, 18 September 1736; Egmont, *Journal*, p. 201.

35. *Report of the Committee Appointed to examine into the Proceedings of the People of Georgia . . . And the Disputes Subsisting between the Two Colonies* (Charles Town: Lewis Timothy, 1736).

36. James Harold Easterby, Ruth Green, and R. Nicholas Olsberg, eds., *The*

Colonial Records of South Carolina. The Journal of the Commons House of Assembly, 1736-1749, 10 vols. to date (Columbia, 1951-). *The Journal of the Commons House of Assembly, November 10, 1736-June 7, 1739,* pp. 95, 100, 146. (*The Colonial Records* hereinafter cited as *SCCR.*) The citation problem is complicated by the fact that there are no volume numbers in the set.

37. Sirmans, *Colonial South Carolina,* p. 190.

38. Joseph Wragg to Isaac Hobhouse, 30 June 1736, George C. Rogers, Jr., ed., "Two Joseph Wragg Letters," *South Carolina Historical Magazine* 65 (January 1964): 17-18.

39. Egmont Papers, 14209:85-90; *Journal of the Commissioners for Trade and Plantations, 1729 to 1749, Preserved in the Public Record Office,* 8 vols. (London, 1928-31), 7:213.

40. James Munro and William L. Grant, eds., *Acts of the Privy Council of England, Colonial Series,* 6 vols. (Hereford, 1908-12), 5:513-14. See also *Journal of the Board of Trade,* 7:165, 181-82, 191-92, 201-2; Egmont, *Diary,* 2:466 and passim; John Pitts Corry, *Indian Affairs in Georgia, 1732-1756* (Philadelphia: George S. Ferguson Co., 1936).

41. Egmont, *Diary,* 2:368; Egmont, *Journal,* p. 243.

42. *CRG,* 5:63-64, 66.

43. Ibid., p. 233; Oglethorpe to the Trustees, 11 October 1739, "Oglethorpe Letters," p. 84.

44. Oglethorpe to the Trustees, 28 May 1742, ibid., pp. 120-22; Oglethorpe to the Trustees, 12 February 1743, ibid., p. 142.

45. Oglethorpe to the Trustees, 28 May 1742, ibid., p. 121.

46. Oglethorpe to Samuel Wesley, 19 November 1734, *Newman's Letterbooks,* p. 514.

47. John Brownfield to the Trustees, 2 May 1737, and to Messrs. Pyll and Tuckwell, March 1737, John Brownfield's Copy Book.

Chapter 5. Land Grants, Negroes, and Slavery

1. *CRG,* 3:373-75. For the best available secondary account of the land system see McCain, *Georgia as a Proprietary Province,* pp. 228-32. A brief and lucid recent treatment of early Trustee land policy can be found in Kenneth Coleman, *Colonial Georgia: A History* (New York: Charles Scribner's Sons, 1976), pp. 121-23.

2. *CRG,* 1:22; *SCCR, 1739-41,* pp. 27, 31, 32, 34, 41, 43, and passim; Stephens, *Journal,* 1:236-37; Egmont, *Journal,* p. 212. Nowhere in his own correspondence does Oglethorpe allude to his Carolina property holding, which was extensive.

3. Belcher to Oglethorpe, 25 May 1734, *Collections of the Massachusetts Historical Society,* 6th ser., 7 (1894):70. Belcher understood the inheritance provision imperfectly. He thought the land would be entailed to the oldest son, but this was not literally the case. The phrasing is as follows: "All lots are granted in Tail Male, and descend to the Heirs Male of their Bodies for ever." See Moore, *A Voyage to Georgia,* p. 7. The original settlers had shown misgivings about the land provisions since 24 October 1732 when they met with the Trustees in Old Palace Yard. See *CRG,* 2:7; Egmont, *Journal,* p. 6.

4. Egmont, *Journal*, p. 7.

5. *Journal of Peter Gordon*, pp. 42–43.

6. Eveleigh to the Trustees, 6 April 1733, Egmont Papers, 14200:61. This approach is the "non-rational attitude toward work" mentioned by Bertelson in *The Lazy South*, p. 91.

7. Oglethorpe to the Trustees, 12 August 1733, Egmont Papers, 14200: 106.

8. Vernon to Verelst, 25 May 1734, Egmont Papers, 14207:213. See also Dr. Dumont to Martyn, 21 May 1734, ibid., pp. 209–12; Edward Digby to Martyn, 25 May 1734, ibid., pp. 217–20; John Lord Viscount Tyrconnel to Verelst, 25 May 1734, ibid., p. 221. Tyrconnel wrote that he "zealously opposed" tail male from the start and that the "pernicious clause" must be repealed.

9. Eveleigh to Oglethorpe, 19 October 1734, MS, CRG, 20:644.

10. Christie to Oglethorpe, 14 December 1734, Egmont Papers, 14200: 321.

11. Eveleigh to Martyn, 20 January 1735, ibid., p. 383.

12. Ibid. In Charles Town in 1737, John Tobler wrote: "everything here is overcrowded with negroes." "The John Tobler Manuscripts: An Account of German-Swiss Emigrants in South Carolina, 1737," ed. Charles G. Cordle, *Journal of Southern History* 5 (February 1939): 89.

13. Eveleigh to Martyn, 20 January 1735, Egmont Papers, 14200:384.

14. Martyn to Eveleigh, 1 May 1735, ibid., 14207:372–73.

15. Egmont, *Diary*, 2:184.

16. In addition to the usual references in the newspapers and magazines of the day see also Lewis Morris to James Alexander, 13 April 1735, "A New York Mission to England: The London Letters of Lewis Morris to James Alexander, 1735 to 1736," ed. Stanley N. Katz, *William and Mary Quarterly*, 3d ser., 28 (July 1971): 465–66. Oglethorpe is reported by Morris as "a Sencible man [and] a friend to the Plantations" who, rumor had it, might be soon elevated to the Board of Trade.

17. Egmont, *Journal*, p. 99.

18. Tailfer and Others to the Trustees, undated but received by the Trust 27 August 1735, Egmont Papers, 14201:173–75.

19. Eveleigh to Martyn, 10 September 1735, ibid., p. 189.

20. Ibid., pp. 190–91.

21. Ettinger, *Oglethorpe*, pp. 185–86, 192–94.

22. Egmont, *Diary*, 2:478–79; Egmont, *Journal*, pp. 345–47.

23. Egmont, *Diary*, 2:482.

24. Ibid., p. 483.

25. Ibid., pp. 484–85. See also *CRG*, 2:234–39.

26. *CRG*, 1:345–46; 5:134; McCain, *Georgia as a Proprietary Province*, p. 182.

27. *CRG*, 5:212–13, and passim.

28. Oglethorpe to the Trustees, 4 July 1739, *CRG*, 22, Part 2:172.

29. Ibid., p. 173.

30. Ibid., 1:543–44. For the gradual breakdown see ibid., pp. 345–46, 398–99, 405; 2:271, 300–301, 336, 338, 340–41, 357–60, 394–95, 500. See also McCain, *Georgia as a Proprietary Province*, pp. 226–79.

31. Sarah B. Gober Temple and Kenneth Coleman, *Georgia Journeys* (Athens: University of Georgia Press, 1961), pp. 139-42, has an excellent account of Anderson and his trials and tribulations.

32. The Plain-Dealer [Hugh Anderson] to Oglethorpe, 6 January 1739, Egmont Papers, 14203:n.p.

33. Oglethorpe to the Trustees, 16 January 1739, ibid., p. 376; Oglethorpe to the Trustees, 20 October 1739, "Oglethorpe Letters," p. 90.

34. Oglethorpe to the Trustees, 17 January 1739, Egmont Papers, 14203: 380.

35. "The John Tobler Manuscripts," *Journal of Southern History* 5 (February 1939): 89.

36. Prince Hoare, *Memoirs of Granville Sharp, Esq.* (London: 1820), pp. 155-59; John A. Woods, "The City of London and Impressment, 1776-1777," *Proceedings of the Leeds Philosophical Society* 8 (December 1956), Part 2: 111-27.

37. The best contemporary account of the insurrection is printed in *CRG*, 22, Part 2: 232-36. See also Sirmans, *Colonial South Carolina*, pp. 207-8, and the recent and dramatic re-creation in Peter H. Wood, *Black Majority: Negroes in Colonial South Carolina from 1670 through the Stono Rebellion* (New York: Alfred A. Knopf, 1974), pp. 308-26.

38. Oglethorpe to Verelst, 9 October 1739, "Oglethorpe Letters," p. 83.

39. *CRG*, 4:523. The slave brought £ 23:5:0 sterling. Ibid., p. 524.

40. Such provisions were found in the Georgia-Creek Indian Treaty of 1733 printed in the *Georgia Historical Quarterly* 4 (March 1920): 14. See also *CRG*, 1:51-52.

41. *CRG*, 4, Supplement: 110.

42. Patrick Tailfer et al., *A True and Historical Narrative of the Colony of Georgia*, ed. and with an Introduction by Clarence L. Ver Steeg (Athens: University of Georgia Press, 1960), p. 5.

43. Stephens to the Trustees, 31 December 1741, *CRG*, 23:185-86. The literary reference is to a character, Bayes, in George Villiers's play of 1671, "The Rehearsal."

44. Oglethorpe to Walpole, 28 April 1741, Cholmondeley (Houghton) Manuscripts, Correspondence, Cambridge University Library, No. 3093. Scarcely a year before, he had written Walpole to say that Carolina was "extreamly weak by reason of its Negroes." The figure was about seven to one. Oglethorpe to Walpole, 2 April 1740, ibid., No. 2948.

45. Oglethorpe to Walpole, 12 May 1741, ibid., No. 3095.

46. Petition of the Settlers and Freeholders at Darien against the introducing Negroes into Georgia, 3 January 1739, Egmont Papers, 14203:368. The Salzburger petition, outspoken in its fear and dislike of blacks, is printed in *CRG*, 3:428-31.

47. Oglethorpe to the Trustees, 28 May 1742, "Oglethorpe Letters," p. 121.

48. Ibid., p. 120.

49. Ibid., p. 121.

50. *CRG*, 1:56-62, 550-51.

51. Richard Dunn, "The Trustees of Georgia," *William and Mary Quarterly* 3d ser., 11 (October 1954): 551.

52. For a sampling of such literature see Reese, *Colonial Georgia*, pp. 46-50; Milton Sydney Heath, *Constructive Liberalism: The Role of the State in Economic Development in Georgia to 1860* (Cambridge: Harvard University Press, 1954), pp. 37-41; Daniel Boorstin, *The Americans: The Colonial Experience* (New York: Random House, 1958), pp. 71-96; Samuel Eliot Morison, *The Oxford History of the American People* (New York: Oxford University Press, 1965), pp. 154-55.

Chapter 6. OGLETHORPE AND THE INDIANS

1. John Tate Lanning, *The Spanish Missions of Georgia* (Chapel Hill: University of North Carolina Press, 1935), contains the best full account of the Spanish period of Georgia history. See also Fred Lamar Pearson, Jr., "Early Anglo-Spanish Rivalry in Southeastern North America," *Georgia Historical Quarterly* 58 (Supplement 1974): 157-71.
2. For a thorough handling of the subject see Verner W. Crane, *The Southern Frontier* (Ann Arbor: University of Michigan Press, reissued 1956).
3. *Journal of Peter Gordon*, pp. 35-36.
4. Oglethorpe to the Trustees, 10 February 1733, Egmont Papers, 14200: 34.
5. *S.C. Gazette*, 2 June 1733.
6. *Journal of Peter Gordon*, p. 48.
7. Ibid., pp. 48-49.
8. *A Brief Account of the Establishment of the Colony of Georgia, under Gen. James Oglethorpe* (Washington: Peter Force, 1835), p. 11. This is primarily a compilation by Force of reports taken from the *S.C. Gazette;* it has value in that it brings many of the earliest accounts of the settlement of Georgia together in one volume.
9. *S.C. Gazette*, 2 June 1733.
10. *A Brief Account*, pp. 12-13.
11. *Gentleman's Magazine* 3 (July 1733): 384.
12. "Oglethorpe's Treaty with the Lower Creek Indians," *Georgia Historical Quarterly* 4 (March 1920): 12.
13. Ibid., pp. 12-13.
14. Ibid., p. 14.
15. *S.C. Gazette*, 2 June 1733.
16. JCHA, from the 7th day of February 1733/4 to the 31st of May 1734, No. 2, pp. 57-58; Isaac Chardon to the Trustees, 14 March 1734, Egmont Papers, 14200:165.
17. JCHA, 8 April 1734, No. 2, p. 146.
18. [Thomas Christie], "A Description of Georgia, by a Gentleman who has Resided there Upwards of Seven Years and was One of the First Settlers" (London, 1741), p. 6.
19. Mary Musgrove to Oglethorpe, 14 July 1734, Egmont Papers, 14200: 219-20.
20. Egmont, *Journal*, p. 57.
21. Egmont, *Diary*, 2:117.
22. Ibid., p. 118.
23. Egmont, *Journal*, pp. 60-61. Tomochichi at first thought the arch-

bishop to be "a Conjurer" and refused to answer a series of questions put to him, but he soon warmed to the clergyman and they got along nicely.

24. Oglethorpe to Walpole [August 1734], Cholmondeley MSS, No. 2324.
25. Horace Walpole to Sir Charles Hanbury Williams, 7 September 1745, in W. S. Lewis and Robert A. Smith, eds., *Horace Walpole's Correspondence,* vol. 30 (New Haven: Yale University Press, 1961), p. 94.
26. *Gentleman's Magazine* 4 (September 1734): 505. For a fuller account of the Indians' trip see Charles C. Jones, Jr., *Historical Sketch of Tomo-Chi-Chi, Mico of the Yamacraws* (Albany, N.Y., 1868), pp. 58-72.
27. Oglethorpe to Samuel Wesley, 19 November 1734, *Newman's Letterbooks,* p. 515.
28. Wesley to Oglethorpe, 7 December 1734, ibid., p. 517.
29. Oglethorpe to Wesley, 25 December 1734, ibid., pp. 519-20.
30. Ibid., p. 520.
31. Ibid., p. 521.
32. "A Curious Account of the Indians. By an Honorable Person," *Collections of the Georgia Historical Society* 2 (Savannah, 1842): 61-62. Oglethorpe is the "Honorable Person."
33. Verelst to Newman, 18 October 1734, *Newman's Letterbooks,* pp. 496-97; and five letters from Oglethorpe to Verelst, 29 October-10 December 1735, "Oglethorpe Letters," pp. 1-9.
34. Oglethorpe to the Trustees, 13 February 1736, "Oglethorpe Letters," p. 13.
35. Oglethorpe to the Trustees, 16 March 1736, ibid., p. 19.
36. Oglethorpe to Broughton, 28 March 1736, Egmont Papers, 14201:379.
37. Oglethorpe to the Governor of St. Augustine, 22 May 1736, ibid., pp. 507-8; Oglethorpe to Captain Charles Dempsey, about May 1736, ibid., p. 483.
38. Egmont, *Journal,* pp. 172, 175, 179-80; John Wesley's *Journal,* 1:35-36.
39. Creek Indian Talk, 27 June 1736, 1st Audience, Egmont Papers, 14202:29-31.
40. Creek Indian Talk, 3 July 1736, 2d Audience, ibid., pp. 49-56.
41. Ibid., p. 56.
42. At an Audience of the Chickasaws at Savannah in Georgia July 1736, W. R. Coe Papers, South Carolina Historical Society, Charleston, S.C.
43. Ibid.; Egmont Papers, 14202:77-78; Egmont, *Journal,* p. 179.
44. Egmont, *Journal,* p. 179.
45. Coe Papers.
46. Ibid.; Egmont Papers, 14202:82.
47. Coe Papers.
48. Ibid.
49. The Trustees immediately informed the government of the Chickasaws' request. See Trustees to Newcastle, 24 December 1736, ibid.
50. Oglethorpe to the Trustees, 7 October 1738, "Oglethorpe Letters," p. 55.
51. Oglethorpe to [Verelst], 22 November 1738, ibid., p. 65.
52. *CRG,* 4:279.

53. Ibid., pp. 279-80; Thomas Jones to Verelst, 17 February 1738/9, *CRG*, 22, Part 2: 79. Jones mentions thirty-six Indians.

54. *CRG*, 4:294. Oglethorpe finally got to Savannah on 5 March. The Choctaws, who had arrived 13 February, had been gone for some time.

55. Jones to Verelst, 17 February 1738/9, *CRG*, 22, Part 2: 80.

56. *CRG*, 4:284.

57. Ibid., pp. 294-99; Oglethorpe to the Trustees, 9, 12 March 1739, "Oglethorpe Letters," pp. 69-71.

58. [Oglethorpe] to [Verelst], 15 June 1739, Cholmondeley MSS, No. 2881.

59. Proceedings of Gen. Oglethorpe, 1740-1742, Stowe MSS, 792, fols. 1-2, British Library. (Hereinafter cited as Proceedings.)

60. Ibid., fol. 3.

61. Memorial of Thomas Bosomworth, *CRG*, 26:485.

62. Proceedings, fol. 4.

63. —— to [Verelst], 11 September 1739, *CRG*, 22, Part 2: 215. The anonymous writer, whose terse and sensible account bears the ring of accuracy, also reported that Oglethorpe "was ill with a burning fever in the Indian Town."

64. *CRG*, 26:487-89; Proceedings, fol. 4.

65. Oglethorpe to Verelst, 5 September 1739, *CRG*, 22, Part 2: 208; —— to [Verelst], 11 September 1739, ibid., p. 214. Proceedings mistakenly cites his arrival date as 12 September, an error repeated in Newton D. Mereness, ed., *Travels in the North American Colonies* (New York, 1916), p. 222.

66. Oglethorpe to Verelst, 5 September 1739, *CRG*, 22, Part 2: 208.

67. Ibid.

68. Corry, *Indian Affairs in Georgia*, p. 73.

69. Ibid. The full agreement is found in *Georgia Historical Quarterly* 4 (March 1920): 5-8.

70. Proceedings, fols. 4-5.

71. Oglethorpe to the Trustees, 5 October 1739, *CRG*, 22, Part 2: 218.

72. Oglethorpe to Verelst, 19 October 1739, "Oglethorpe Letters," p. 87.

73. Proceedings, fol. 5.

74. *CRG*, 4:421. Proceedings gives 24 September as his arrival date.

75. *CRG*, 4:421-22.

76. Proceedings, fols. 5-6.

77. *CRG*, 4:428. Stephens was also a pallbearer. For an unusual treatment of Tomochichi see Bernard W. Sheehan, "Paradise and the Noble Savage in Jeffersonian Thought," *William and Mary Quarterly*, 3d ser., 26 (July 1969): 327-59.

78. Egmont, *Diary*, 2:132.

79. *CRG*, 4:518. See also E. Merton Coulter, "Mary Musgrove, 'Queen of the Creeks': A Chapter of Early Georgia Troubles," *Georgia Historical Quarterly* 11 (March 1927): 1-30.

80. Coulter, "Mary Musgrove," p. 5; Corry, *Indian Affairs in Georgia*, pp. 73-74.

81. Boltzius, "Secret Diary," p. 99.

82. Thomas Jenys to Verelst, 9 July 1744, *CRG*, 24:245.

83. Proceedings, fol. 6.
84. Henry Parker to James Glen, 16 April 1751, *CRG*, 26:193.
85. Egmont, *Diary*, 2:368.
86. Governor George Clarke to Oglethorpe, 9 January 1742, *CRG*, 23:226.
87. Oglethorpe to the Trustees, 3 March 1742, "Oglethorpe Letters," pp. 118-19.
88. Ibid., p. 119.
89. Representation of Edmund Gray, *CRG*, 26:354.
90. John Harris, *Navigantium atque Itinerantium Bibliotheca*, 2 vols. (London, 1748), 2:334-35. The long fifteen-page section on Georgia was apparently done by Oglethorpe, or dictated by him to another. See James Boswell, *Boswell in Extremes*, ed. Charles McC. Weis and Frederick A. Pottle (New York: McGraw-Hill, 1970), pp. 306-7.

Chapter 7. ALARUMS AND EXCURSIONS: WAR COMES TO THE
           SOUTHERN FRONTIER

1. Verne Elmo Chatelain, *The Defenses of Spanish Florida, 1565 to 1763* Carnegie Institution Publication 511 (Washington, 1941), pp. 14 n. 1, 111-12; Herbert E. Bolton and Mary Ross, "The Debatable Land," Introduction to *Arredondo's Historical Proof of Spain's Title to Georgia* (Berkeley: University of California Press, 1925), pp. 58-60; Verner Crane, *The Southern Frontier*, pp. 78-82, 246, 247-48, 254-55; Charles W. Arnade, "The English Invasion of Spanish Florida, 1700-1706," *Florida Historical Quarterly* 41 (July 1962): 29-37; Albert C. Manucy, *The History of Castillo de San Marcos & Fort Matanzas* (Washington: National Park Service, 1955 reprint), p. 22; John M. Goggin, "Fort Pupo: A Spanish Frontier Outpost," *Florida Historical Quarterly* 30 (October 1951): 139-92.
2. Newcastle to Broughton, 10 October 1735, PRSC, 17:378-80.
3. Bolton and Ross, "Debatable Land," pp. 72-74; John Tate Lanning, *The Diplomatic History of Georgia* (Chapel Hill: University of North Carolina Press, 1936), pp. 46-47; Ettinger, *Oglethorpe*, pp. 172-77; Reese, *Colonial Georgia*, pp. 55-56, 58. For the text of the agreement, see Egmont Papers, 14202:197-203.
4. Eveleigh to George Morley, begun 31 May and continued 4 June 1736, Egmont Papers, 14201:526.
5. Ettinger, *Oglethorpe*, pp. 192-200; Egmont, *Diary*, 2:334, 339-41, 364-65, 368, 416-17; Colonial Office, PRO, 324/37, fols. 71-73, 74-75 (copies in University of Georgia Library); PRSC, 15:329-30.
6. Oglethorpe to Jekyll, 19 September 1738, "Oglethorpe Letters," p. 49.
7. Thomas Jones to Verelst, 12 November 1738, *CRG*, 22, Part 1: 303.
8. Robert Pringle to Andrew Lessly, 25 November 1738, Robert Pringle, *The Letterbook of Robert Pringle*, ed. Walter B. Edgar, 2 vols. (Columbia: University of South Carolina Press, 1972), 1:43.
9. Oglethorpe's Account of the Mutiny at St. Andrew's, 1738, Photostat at Essex County Records Office, Chelmsford; Egmont Papers, 14203:318-20.
10. Oglethorpe to George Heathcote, 20 November 1738, "Oglethorpe Letters," p. 62.
11. "Captn. James Howell's Affidavit of the Spaniards design to attack

Georgea," dated 21 April 1738, South Carolina Council Chamber, Egmont Papers, 14203:115.

12. Oglethorpe to Newcastle, 23 February 1739, MS, CRG, 35:197; See also Egmont, *Journal*, p. 349.

13. Bull to Newcastle, 9 May 1739, PRSC, 20:40-41.

14. Governor Don Manuel de Montiano to Don Juan Francisco de Güemes y Horcasitas, postscript to letter of 3 January 1739 (N.S.), trans. C. de Witt Willcox, *Collections of the Georgia Historical Society* 7, Part 1 (1909): 29. (Hereinafter cited as "Montiano Letters.") See also John J. TePaske, "The Fugitive Slave: Intercolonial Rivalry and Spanish Slave Policy, 1687-1764," in *Eighteenth-Century Florida and Its Borderlands*, ed. Samuel Proctor (Gainesville: University Presses of Florida, 1975), p. 7.

15. Montiano to Güemes, 14 August 1739 (N.S.), "Montiano Letters," p. 31.

16. Ettinger, *Oglethorpe*, p. 225.

17. *London Magazine*, February 1739, pp. 83-85; Ettinger, *Oglethorpe*, p. 225; *S.C. Gazette*, 3 May 1739, reprints the Convention.

18. Trevor R. Reese, "Georgia in Anglo-Spanish Diplomacy, 1736-1739," *William and Mary Quarterly*, 3d ser., 15 (April 1958): 168-90; Harold William Vazeille Temperley, "The Causes of the War of Jenkins' Ear, 1739," *Transactions of the Royal Historical Society*, 3d ser., 3 (1909): 197-236; Lanning, *Diplomatic History of Georgia*.

19. *The Champion; or, the Evening Advertiser*, 27 December 1739; *S.C. Gazette*, 29 December 1739 and 8 March 1740; Egmont, *Diary*, 3:86.

20. *London Magazine*, December 1739, pp. 652-54; *The Champion*, 27 December 1739.

21. *CRG*, 4:426-27.

22. Oglethorpe to the Trustees, 5 October 1739, "Oglethorpe Letters," p. 82.

23. *S.C. Gazette*, 3 May 1740.

24. Oglethorpe to Robert Walpole, 8 October 1739, Cholmondeley MSS, No. 2926.

25. Extract of Oglethorpe's letter to Lt. Governor William Bull, 27 September 1739, *The St. Augustine Expedition of 1740*, with an Introduction by John Tate Lanning (Columbia: S.C. Archives Department, 1954), p. 91. This volume is a reprint of the lengthy investigation made into the expedition by the Carolina legislature and can also be found printed in *SCCR*. (Hereinafter cited as *Report*.)

26. Oglethorpe to Bull, 7 October 1739, ibid.

27. Oglethorpe to Bull, 20 October 1739, ibid.

28. *CRG*, 4:433-34. The job was not wholly completed on 17 October, and so Oglethorpe designated 5 November as a second cleanup day. The task was then easily finished, and Oglethorpe left about three in the afternoon for Frederica, having been in Savannah for six weeks. Ibid., p. 447.

29. Oglethorpe to Bull, 27 September and 7, 20 October 1739, *Report*, p. 91. See also *SCCR*, *1739-41*, p. 16; Council Journal, 7 December 1737-11 December 1741, No. 7, p. 253.

30. *SCCR*, *1739-41*, pp. 100, 116.

31. *Proceedings*, fol. 6.

32. Oglethorpe to the Trustees, 16 November 1739, "Oglethorpe Letters," pp. 93-94.

33. Proceedings, fols. 7-8; Oglethorpe to the Trustees, 29 December 1739, "Oglethorpe Letters," pp. 100-101; New-York *Weekly Journal,* 28 January 1740.

34. Oglethorpe to Bull, 29 December 1739, *SCCR, 1739-41,* pp. 160, 177.

35. Ibid., p. 179.

36. Ibid., pp. 184, 187.

37. Ibid., pp. 190, 196-97, 199-200, 202-3; JUHA, 9 February 1740, 292, 294-96; *Report,* pp. 103-4.

38. Proceedings, fols. 8-9; Oglethorpe to William Stephens, 1 February 1740, "Oglethorpe Letters," pp. 105-7; Oglethorpe to Bull, 23 January 1740, *Report,* p. 94.

39. Oglethorpe to Stephens, 1 February 1740, "Oglethorpe Letters," p. 108.

40. Proceedings, fol. 10.

41. Oglethorpe to Walpole, 23 January 1740, Cholmondeley MSS, No. 2941.

42. Extract of Oglethorpe's letter to Bull, 24 January 1740, *Report,* p. 95.

43. Montiano to Güemes, 23 February 1740 (N.S.), "Montiano Letters," p. 43.

44. *CRG,* 4:536.

45. Oglethorpe to Bull, 26 March 1740, *Report,* p. 105.

46. *SCCR, 1739-41,* pp. 270-72.

47. Oglethorpe to Newcastle, 1 April 1740, MS, CRG, 35:249-50.

48. Pringle to Captain Samuel Saunders, 2 April 1740, *Pringle Letterbook,* 1:175.

49. *SCCR, 1739-41,* pp. 296-97. Vander Dussen's commission, dated 2 April, is found in Commissions and Instructions, Book DD, 1732-42, S.C. Archives Department, Columbia, p. 347. For Oglethorpe's grant of powers of courts martial, command, and so on, see also *S.C. Gazette,* 4 April 1740, which reprints his concessions to the Assembly's demands.

Chapter 8. THE ST. AUGUSTINE EXPEDITION OF 1740

1. Proceedings, fol. 11; Oglethorpe's Journal, *Report,* pp. 108-9; "Fort San Diego," *El Escribano* 8 (October 1971): 139-48.

2. Proceedings, fol. 11; Oglethorpe's Journal, *Report,* pp. 109-10.

3. *Report,* p. 133. See also Larry E. Ivers, *British Drums on the Southern Frontier* (Chapel Hill: University of North Carolina Press, 1974), p. 109.

4. *Report,* pp. 125, 128-29.

5. Montiano to Güemes, 6 July 1740 (N.S.), "Montiano Letters," pp. 56-57; Ivers, *Drums,* pp. 119-20.

6. Montiano to Güemes, 6 July 1740 (N.S.), "Montiano Letters," pp. 56-58. The Spanish losses, Montiano said, amounted to ten men killed. The Carolina Assembly reported that the English suffered fifty killed and more than twenty taken prisoner. See *Report,* p. 40. Considering that Montiano was making an exhaustive report to his immediate superior it seems reasonable to believe that he was being as accurate as he could. His other casualty estimates

have the ring of truth too. William Stephens in Savannah, upon first hearing news of the defeat, reported: "we lost about seventy Men." See *CRG*, 4:607. Ivers, *Drums*, p. 123, concluded that sixty-three British and English-allied Indians were killed. (Chapter 9 of Ivers, *Drums*, first appeared in *Georgia Historical Quarterly* 51 [June 1967]: 135-53, as "The Battle of Fort Mosa").

7. *Report*, p. 41.

8. Ibid., pp. 43, 114.

9. Ibid., pp. 45-46, 148.

10. Ibid., p. 48.

11. Oglethorpe to Bull, 24 June 1740, ibid., p. 149.

12. For the various letters, requests, councils of war, etc. see ibid., Apps. 85-106, pp. 150-59.

13. Oglethorpe to Bull, 30 June 1740, ibid., p. 154; Oglethorpe to Commodore Vincent Pearse, 2 July 1740, ibid., pp. 157-58.

14. Vander Dussen to Bull, 3 July 1740, ibid., p. 158.

15. Ibid., pp. 59, 159-61.

16. [Joseph] Wragg to ———, 2 July 1740, Egmont Papers, 14205:17-20.

17. Oglethorpe to Charles Pinckney, 30 June 1740, ibid., p. 90.

18. Pinckney to Peregrine Fury, 1 August 1740, ibid., pp. 87-89.

19. *The Champion*, 16, 28 August 1740.

20. Capt. Hugh Mackay's letter upon Sight of Wrags Scandalous letter from Charlestown of 2 July, reflecting on Col. Oglethorpe, 29 November 1740, Egmont Papers, 14205:25-26. See also *CRG*, 5:342. As an antidote to the Oglethorpe critics, Mackay's letter was inserted in *Gentleman's Magazine* 10 (November 1740): 575.

21. Oglethorpe to Bull, 19 July 1740, *Report*, pp. 169-70.

22. *CRG*, 5:395. Stephens took "a bottle of Savannah wine" with him on 31 August when he went to visit Oglethorpe on St. Simons.

23. Ibid., 4:635.

24. Ibid., pp. 653-54. See also Thomas Jones to Verelst, 8 July 1741, ibid., 23:60; New-York *Weekly Journal*, 8 September 1740. An April 1741 rumor reached Egmont that Oglethorpe was so chagrined at his failure to take St. Augustine that he "locks himself up for a fortnight together, and will not be seen by any, and has taken to drinking." Egmont, *Diary*, 3:213.

25. Oglethorpe to the Trustees, 24 January 1741, Egmont Papers, 14205: 233-34.

26. Oglethorpe to Walpole, 25 January 1740, Cholmondeley MSS, No. 2942.

27. Oglethorpe to the Trustees, 12 February 1743, "Oglethorpe Letters," p. 143. See also Oglethorpe to Verelst, 10 February 1743, *CRG*, 23:488.

28. *Report*, p. 76; *SCCR, 1739-41*, pp. 358-59, 369.

29. See John Tate Lanning, Introduction to the *Report*, pp. i-xxviii.

30. B. Phinizy Spalding, "Georgia and South Carolina during the Oglethorpe Period, 1732-1743," Ph.D. diss., University of North Carolina, 1963, pp. 292-332.

31. *The Champion*, 2 October 1740.

32. Oglethorpe to Bull, 19 July 1740, *Report*, p. 170.

33. James Boswell, *Boswell's Life of Johnson*, ed. George Birkbeck Hill, rev. L. F. Powell, 6 vols. (Oxford: Clarendon Press, 1934), 2:181.

34. Pringle to John Richards, 14 July 1740, *Pringle Letterbook*, 1:231; Pringle to Andrew Pringle, 14 July 1740, ibid., p. 230.

35. Vander Dussen to Bull, 27 May 1740, *Report*, p. 115.

36. [Benjamin Martyn], "An Account, Showing the Progress of the Colony of Georgia, in America, from its First Establishment," *Collections of the Georgia Historical Society* 2 (1842): 268-69.

37. H. W. Richmond, *The Navy in the War of 1739-1748* (Cambridge: Cambridge University Press, 1920), 1:50-51.

38. Montiano to Güemes, 28 July 1740 (N.S.), and Postscript, "Montiano Letters," pp. 59, 60, 62-63.

39. Deposition of Edw. Lyng, 8 September 1743, Council Journal, No. 10, pp. 331-33. Two other depositions follow Lyng's.

40. Ibid., 8 October 1742, No. 8, pp. 297-302. Oglethorpe sent Argular to England to be questioned by Newcastle.

41. Montiano to Güemes, postscript to letter of 28 July 1740 (N.S.), "Montiano Letters," p. 62.

42. Chatelain, *Defenses of Spanish Florida*, p. 91. For maps that clearly show the strengthened defenses of the Spanish stronghold, see ibid., Maps 10 and 22.

43. David Ramsay, *The History of South-Carolina, from Its First Establishment in 1670, to the Year 1808*, 2 vols. (Charleston: David Longworth, 1809), 1:144. Ramsay also noted that Oglethorpe had "no confidence in the provincials."

44. Jack P. Greene, *The Quest for Power* (Chapel Hill: University of North Carolina Press, 1963), p. 89. See also Howard Grady Roberts III, "James Edward Oglethorpe and the South Carolina Legislature: Politics on the Southern Frontier" (Master's Thesis, University of Georgia, 1976).

45. William Byrd to Egmont, 8 August 1738, Egmont Papers, 14203:218.

46. Belcher to Egmont, 14 May 1741, *Collections of the Massachusetts Historical Society*, 6th ser., 7 (1894): 391.

47. *The Champion*, 11 February 1742. Specifically Burrington would have added four companies of troops stationed in New York, the North Carolina militia, and other spare contingents where found and available.

48. Belcher to Egmont, 14 May 1741, *Collections of the Massachusetts Historical Society*, 6th ser., 7 (1894): 391.

Chapter 9. THE SPANISH INVASION OF GEORGIA

1. Montiano to Güemes, postscript to letters of 28 July and 7 August 1740 (N.S.), "Montiano Letters," pp. 62-63, 65.

2. Montiano to Güemes, 14 August 1739 (N.S.), ibid., p. 31; Affidavit of Juan Castelnau, Havana, 24 July 1739; "The Spanish Official Account of the Attack on the Colony of Georgia in America, and of Its Defeat on St. Simons Island by General James Oglethorpe," *Collections of the Georgia Historical Society* 7, Part 3 (1913): 7-8. (Hereinafter cited as "Spanish Account.") See also Castelnau's "Declaration" of conditions in Georgia, ibid., pp. 9-14.

3. *S.C. Gazette*, 18 June 1741.

4. Ibid., 2 July 1741.

5. Oglethorpe to Walpole, 29 August 1740, Cholmondeley MSS, No. 2960.

6. Oglethorpe to Walpole, 28 April 1741, ibid., No. 3093.

7. Oglethorpe to Walpole, 12 May 1741, ibid., No. 3095.

8. Oglethorpe to Walpole, 20 July 1741, ibid., No. 3098.

9. Landsdowne MSS, British Library, 820 fols. 61-88. See also Vernon-Wager MSS, 15: 856-71, Library of Congress, Washington, D.C.

10. *The Champion*, 28 November 1741.

11. See the correspondence of Campillo, Güemes, and Montiano, "Spanish Account," pp. 20-21, 25-35.

12. *S.C. Gazette*, 27 February 1742. For the best account of the Spanish buildup see John Jay TePaske, *The Governorship of Spanish Florida, 1700-1763* (Durham: Duke University Press, 1964), pp. 146-48.

13. Proceedings, fols. 12-15.

14. *The Country Journal: or, The Craftsman*, 26 June 1742, reporting a 10 February dispatch from Georgia.

15. Güemes to Montiano, 14 May, 2 June 1742 (N.S.), "Spanish Account," pp. 27-35.

16. Güemes to Montiano, 14 May 1742 (N.S.), ibid., p. 30.

17. Oglethorpe to the Trustees, 28 May 1742, "Oglethorpe Letters," p. 122.

18. Oglethorpe to Bull, 8 June 1742, ibid., p. 131.

19. Montiano to the King, 3 August 1742 (N.S.), "Spanish Account," p. 89; Arredondo's Journal, ibid., pp. 52-62.

20. *SCCR, 1741-42*, p. 563.

21. Oglethorpe to Bull, 4 June 1742, Council Journal, 15 March 1742-19 February 1743, No. 8, pp. 81-82. See also ibid., pp. 84-85 for additional warnings.

22. Oglethorpe to the Commander of His Majestys Ships at Charles Town [Captain Charles Hardy], 18 June 1742, MS, CRG, 36:25-26; *S.C. Gazette*, 21 June 1742.

23. Patrick Sutherland, "An Account of the late Invasion of Georgia . . . ," Georgia Miscellaneous Papers, Colony, 1727-1753, Duke Library, Folder 1, p. 1. Sutherland's Account appeared in *The Gazette* (London), 25 December 1742, and was subsequently printed separately as *An Account of the Late Invasion of Georgia* ([London, 1743]).

24. Deposition of Lt. Primrose Maxwell, 1 February 1743, MS, CRG, 36:57-58. Oglethorpe sent a copy of this affidavit to Newcastle.

25. Stephens, *Journal*, 1:100.

26. Narrative of Francis Moore's Journey to Charles Town in South Carolina 1742, MS, CRG, 36:72-74. (Hereinafter cited as Moore, Narrative.) Oglethorpe sent Moore's account as well as Maxwell's to Newcastle.

27. Ibid., pp. 75-76.

28. Ibid., p. 77.

29. *SCCR, 1741-42*, pp. 547-48, 554, 563-64.

30. See, for example, Council Journal, 17 June 1742, No. 8, pp. 77-80.

31. Sirmans, *Colonial South Carolina*, pp. 212-13.

32. JUHA, 10 July 1742, No. 8, pp. 14-15, 103-4, 112, 116-17.

33. Moore, *Narrative*, p. 80.
34. *S.C. Gazette*, 12 July 1742.
35. Alexander Heron, for example, said Oglethorpe had only six hundred under his command. Robert Pringle estimated seven hundred, including one hundred Indians. The New-York *Weekly Journal* reported an army that totaled "but 700." Alexander Heron to a Friend, 24 September 1742, MS, CRG, 35:523, said about six hundred; *Pringle Letterbook*, 1:387, reports seven hundred; New-York *Weekly Journal*, 11 October 1742. On 13 July, the French deserter who fled to Montiano reported Oglethorpe's strength as between nine hundred and one thousand men. Casinas' Journal, "Spanish Account," p. 78. The most recent work on the battle has concluded that Oglethorpe had an effective "total fighting force" of "approximately five hundred men." Ivers, *Drums*, pp. 157-59.
36. Extract from a letter from Mr. J. Smith, on board the *Success* Frigate, 14 July 1742, in Thomas Spalding, "Life of Oglethorpe," *Collections of the Georgia Historical Society* 1 (1840): 276.
37. Montiano to the King, 3 August 1742 (N.S.), "Spanish Account," p. 89. It was, wrote TePaske, "the largest, best equipped force ever assembled in Florida." *Governorship of Spanish Florida*, p. 148.
38. Montiano to the King, 3 August 1742 (N.S.), "Spanish Account," p. 91.
39. Deposition of Stephen Bedon, Jr., 14 July 1742, Council Journal, No. 8, 113; *The Gazette* (London), 25 December 1742. When it sailed from Havana, Sutherland reported its strength as "between 7 and 8000 Men," and fifty-six ships.
40. For helpful information on these perplexing points, see the last two charts included in "Spanish Account," both of which lead the student of the expedition to the conclusion that Montiano was actually fighting with fewer than 2,000 effectives. TePaske, *Governorship of Spanish Florida*, pp. 147-48, estimated 1,800 or 1,900 troops, and Ivers, *Drums*, p. 152, conjectured "about 1,950 officers and men."
41. Spalding, "Life of Oglethorpe," p. 283. Spalding's information came from men who had actually served in the action under Oglethorpe, and Spalding himself knew the ground intimately from childhood.
42. Oglethorpe to [the Trustees], 30 July 1742, "Oglethorpe Letters," p. 136.
43. *The Gazette* (London), 25 December 1742.
44. Montiano to the King, 3 August 1742 (N.S.), "Spanish Account," p. 91.
45. This rendition of the Spanish reaction to the military events of 7 July is taken from Casinas' Journal, ibid., p. 73. The account as printed in *Collections* is faulty at this point; a full page from the manuscript journal was inadvertently omitted. Margaret Davis Cate, when researching the battle, noted the oversight and had a transcript and translation made from the original in Seville. A copy of the missing page, with the translation, was presented by Mrs. Cate to the University of Georgia Library in 1957, and the above excerpt is from the more recent translation. The passage quoted above is actually included in the *Collections* volume, but the recent rendering of the section seemed to catch the mood of desperation more effectively. The printed

volume reads that Barba found "something novel, consisting of a cut-log stockade, and also here and there some brush wood arranged like a parapet."

46. See Oglethorpe's own account, "Oglethorpe Letters," p. 136; Proceedings, fol. 18; *The Gazette* (London), 25 December 1742.

47. Oglethorpe to [the Trustees], 30 July 1742, "Oglethorpe Letters," p. 136.

48. Casinas' Journal, "Spanish Account," p. 73, 1957 transcript translation.

49. Oglethorpe to [the Trustees], 30 July 1742, "Oglethorpe Letters," p. 136.

50. Proceedings, fol. 19.

51. Casinas' Journal, "Spanish Account," p. 73.

52. Oglethorpe to [the Trustees], 30 July 1742, "Oglethorpe Letters," p. 136.

53. Casinas' Journal, "Spanish Account," p. 74.

54. Oglethorpe to [the Trustees], 30 July 1742, "Oglethorpe Letters," p. 137.

55. Casinas' Journal, "Spanish Account," pp. 74-75; Oglethorpe to [the Trustees], 30 July 1742, "Oglethorpe Letters," p. 137.

56. Oglethorpe to [the Trustees], 30 July 1742, "Oglethorpe Letters," pp. 137-38; *The Gazette* (London), 25 December 1742.

57. Oglethorpe to [the Trustees], 30 July 1742, "Oglethorpe Letters," p. 138; *The Gazette* (London), 25 December 1742; Casinas' Journal, "Spanish Account," p. 79.

58. Oglethorpe to [the Trustees], 30 July 1742, "Oglethorpe Letters," pp. 138-39; Proceedings, fol. 19; *The Gazette* (London), 25 December 1742; Casinas' Journal, "Spanish Account," pp. 79-80; Montiano to the King, 3 August 1742 (N.S.), *ibid.*, pp. 94-95.

59. New-York *Weekly Journal*, 4 October 1742. Oglethorpe wrote this dispatch, in the first person, from Frederica on 31 July.

60. *The Gazette* (London), 25 December 1742.

61. Montiano to the King, 3 August 1742 (N.S.), "Spanish Account," p. 91. Casinas, however, reported that thirty-six men were missing from this action. This figure was given to him by a scout on 11 July (O.S.), and before an accurate head count might have been made. See ibid., p. 77. Ivers, *Drums,* pp. 164-65, used the figure of thirty-six Spanish casualties in all.

62. Montiano to the King, 3 August 1742 (N.S.), "Spanish Account," p. 91; Casinas' Journal, ibid., p. 73.

63. Extract of a letter from Mr. J. Smith, 14 July 1742, Spalding, "Life of Oglethorpe," p. 276.

64. Oglethorpe to the Trustees, 5 August 1742, "Oglethorpe Letters," p. 122.

65. Montiano to the King, 3 August 1742 (N.S.), "Spanish Account," p. 96.

66. Oglethorpe to [the Trustees], 30 July 1742, "Oglethorpe Letters," p. 139.

67. *S.C. Gazette,* 26 July 1742.

68. Güemes to Campillo, 18 August 1742 (N.S.), "Spanish Account," pp. 50-51.

69. [Campillo?] to Güemes, 28 October 1742 (N.S.), ibid., p. 52.

70. Montiano to the King, 3 August 1742 (N.S.), ibid., p. 92.

71. Alexander Parris, the pilot in question, later testified in Carolina that he tried to steer the Spanish ships onto shoals where they would be wrecked. See Parris's testimony before the Carolina Council on 16 February 1742, Council Journal, No. 8, p. 491, and the Deposition of Samuel Cloak, 3 August 1742, ibid., pp. 194, 200.

72. [James Killpatrick], *A Full Reply to Lieut. Cadogan's 'Spanish Hireling,' &c. And Lieut. Mackay's Letter, Concerning the Action at Moosa* (London: J. Huggonson, 1743), p. 58.

73. *S.C. Gazette*, 19, 26 July 1742.

74. Stephens, *Journal*, 1:119.

75. Moore to the Trustees, 13 July 1742, MS, CRG, 35:486.

76. John Dobell to the Trustees, 8 August 1742, Egmont Papers, 14206: 254.

77. Oglethorpe to John Fenwicke, 31 July 1742, Council Journal, 13 August 1742, No. 8, p. 190.

78. Copy of Address to General Oglethorpe "from the Principal Freeholders & Inhabitants of Port Royal & places adjacent in South Carolina," 29 July 1742, MS, CRG, 35:477-78.

79. Egmont, *Diary*, 3:265.

80. See, for example, the pleas contained in his letters of 24 November 1742, 22 January, 14, 16, and 22 February, and 12 March 1743, to Newcastle and Andrew Stone, "Oglethorpe Letters," pp. 123-26, 128-30, 145-50.

81. *S.C. Gazette*, 4 April 1743. See also [Edward Kimber], *A Relation or Journal, of a late Expedition to the Gates of St. Augustine ...* (London: T. Astley, 1744).

82. Oglethorpe to Newcastle, 12 March 1743, "Oglethorpe Letters," p. 150.

83. Oglethorpe to Newcastle, 21 March 1743, ibid., p. 151.

84. *S.C. Gazette*, 18 April 1743.

85. Andrew Rutledge to Verelst, 27 April 1743, MS, CRG, 36:152-53.

86. *London Magazine*, July 1743, pp. 356-57.

87. Extract of a Letter "from a considerable Merchant at *Charles Town* in *South Carolina*, to his Correspondent in *London*," dated 10 August 1743, ibid., November 1743, p. 567.

88. *S.C. Gazette*, 25 July 1743.

89. Oglethorpe to Newcastle, 22 January 1743, "Oglethorpe Letters," p. 128.

90. Ibid., p. 129.

91. Oglethorpe to Newcastle, 24 November 1742, ibid., p. 124.

92. Margaret Davis Cate, "Fort Frederica and the Battle of Bloody Marsh," *Georgia Historical Quarterly* 27 (June 1943): 168-69. Mrs. Cate concluded flatly: "As a leader he [Montiano] was a failure."

93. Ettinger, *Oglethorpe*, p. 245.

94. Reese, *Colonial Georgia*, pp. 82-83. Quite correctly Reese has made an effort to fit Georgia into the mainstream of eighteenth-century English colonial policy, but some of his points are strained. For instance, he has exonerated the government for its failure to back Oglethorpe by saying the

Newcastle regime "could not afford to waste money or troops on what was undeniably a minor aspect of the war." For a more recent—and better balanced—assessment by the same author see *Frederica: Colonial Fort and Town* (St. Simons Island: Fort Frederica Association, 1969), pp. 38-43.

95. See particularly the Letterbook of Richard Hill, 1743, Duke University Library, for Hill's and Carolina's fears concerning Oglethorpe's influence with the king and his ministry.

96. Council Journal, No. 8, pp. 158-60, 165-68, 184, 191, 200, is especially informative. Hardy's parting shot was: "I have not been used like a Gentleman nor like An Officer [and] . . . I despise anything [that] may be said against me in Charles Town." Hardy to Fenwicke, 1 August 1742, ibid., pp. 167-68. Eliza Lucas Pinckney reported that Hardy's procedure had "greatly disgusted the Gov. and Council as well as the rest of the Inhabitance." Eliza Lucas Pinckney, *The Letterbook of Eliza Lucas Pinckney, 1739-1762,* ed. Elise Pinckney (Chapel Hill: University of North Carolina Press, 1972), p. 55. W. E. May's article, "Capt. Charles Hardy on the Carolina Station, 1742-1744," *South Carolina Historical Magazine* 70 (January 1969): 1-19, is disappointing in its failure to make judgments.

97. Oglethorpe to Andrew Stone, 24 November 1742, "Oglethorpe Letters," pp. 125-26.

98. Ibid., p. 125.

Epilogue

1. For a consideration of the biographical literature on Oglethorpe, see Phinizy Spalding, "James Edward Oglethorpe: A Biographical Survey," *Georgia Historical Quarterly* 56 (Fall 1972): 332-48.

2. Oglethorpe to Boswell, 1 March 1776, Boswell MSS, Yale (C 2118).

3. *Boswell in Extremes,* p. 266.

4. "A Catalogue of the Valuable Library of Books, Of the late learned Samuel Johnson, Esq: LL.D. Deceased; Which will be Sold by Auction," Boswell Papers, Yale University. This is Oglethorpe's own copy of the Catalogue. See also his unpublished correspondence with Boswell, ibid., and his numerous letters to the editors. Oglethorpe to Samuel Wesley, 25 December 1734, *Newman's Letterbooks,* p. 519, opens with a classical reference and proceeds to a quotation from the *Aeneid.* Oglethorpe was not hesitant to debate and argue classical points with Johnson himself.

5. "A Latin Poem by James Edward Oglethorpe," contributed by Rudolf Kirk, *Georgia Historical Quarterly* 32 (March 1948): 29-31.

6. In addition to Samuel Wesley and Samuel Johnson, Oglethorpe was on friendly terms with Oliver Goldsmith, Hannah More, and others.

7. Coram to Newman, 13 December 1733, *Newman's Letterbooks,* pp. 395-96; Fanny Oglethorpe to the Duke of Mar, 24 November 1717, *Stuart Papers,* 5:232.

8. Boswell Papers, Yale University (M 208:2).

9. Egmont, *Diary,* 3:142.

10. Ibid., p. 146.

11. Add. MS 41064, British Library. This is a certified copy, in the form of an official roll, taken from the Pipe Office. Oglethorpe's accounts were finally

authorized to be "quit" by Chancellor of the Exchequer, William Pitt, in 1792. See also PRO, A.O. 3/119, fols. 98-100, 306-60, concerning Oglethorpe's unpaid accounts (copies, University of Georgia Library). The greater part of the debt, however, was apparently repaid in 1744. Egmont, *Diary,* 3:293.

12. Theophilus Oglethorpe to the Duke of Mar, 12 February 1718, *Stuart Papers,* 5:459.

13. *The Champion,* 5 January 1742.

14. *Boswell in Extremes,* p. 279.

15. Newman to Oglethorpe, 4 June 1736, *Newman's Letterbooks,* p. 193.

16. Oglethorpe to Von Reck, 16 March 1736, "Oglethorpe Letters," p. 25.

17. See particularly Richard C. Boys, "General Oglethorpe and the Muses," *Georgia Historical Quarterly* 31 (March 1947): 19-29.

18. Horace Walpole to George Montagu, 7 September 1769, *Horace Walpole's Correspondence,* ed. W. S. Lewis and Ralph S. Brown, Jr., vol. 10 (New Haven: Yale University Press, 1941), p. 291.

19. Notes for a projected biography, Boswell Papers, Yale (M 208:1).

20. William Horton to Verelst, 20 September 1746, *CRG,* 25:121-22.

21. Oglethorpe to the Trustees, 4 July and 29 December 1739, "Oglethorpe Letters," pp. 77, 98; Oglethorpe to Newcastle, 22 January 1743, ibid., p. 129.

22. Oglethorpe to Samuel Wesley, 19 November 1734, *Newman's Letterbooks,* p. 514.

23. Ettinger, *Oglethorpe,* p. 150.

24. See Boorstin, *The Americans,* pp. 71-96. See also Paul S. Taylor, *Georgia Plan: 1732-1752* (Berkeley: Institute of Business and Economic Research, 1972). Taylor's position is that the Trustees consciously attempted to create a new and distinct society in Georgia.

25. Phinizy Spalding, "James Oglethorpe and the American Revolution," *Journal of Imperial and Commonwealth History* 3 (May 1975): 404.

26. Stephens, *Journal,* 1:223, 225. The clump of trees to which Stephens refers is easily seen on Peter Gordon's 1734 view of Savannah.

Bibliography

PRIMARY SOURCES

Unpublished Material

Athens, Ga. University of Georgia Library. Copy Book of John Brownfield. Microfilm.

———. University of Georgia Library. The Phillipps Collection of Egmont Manuscripts.

———. University of Georgia Library. Keith Read Collection.

———. University of Georgia Library. Copies from the Public Record Office, London, of items not included in the published *Colonial Records of the State of Georgia.*

Atlanta, Ga. State Department of Archives and History. The Colonial Records of the State of Georgia. 14 vols. Typescript.

Cambridge. Cambridge University Library. Cholmondeley (Houghton) Manuscripts.

Charleston, S.C. South Carolina Historical Society. W. R. Coe Collection.

Chelmsford. Essex Records Office. Tower Collection. Photostats of letters concerning Georgia.

Columbia, S.C. South Carolina Archives Department. Council Journal, 1728–44.

———. South Carolina Archives Department. Journal of the Commons House of Assembly, 1728-36.

———. South Carolina Archives Department. Records in the Public Record Office, London, relating to South Carolina. Microfilm.

———. South Carolina Archives Department. Abstracts of Letters of Governor Nicholson—Lyttelton to the Board of Trade, 1721-56.

———. South Carolina Archives Department. Miscellaneous Records, Book EE, 1741-43.

———. South Carolina Archives Department. Commissions and Instructions, Book DD, 1732-42. (Not limited to commissions and instructions.)

———. South Carolina Archives Department. Commissions, Instructions, 1739-55, Public Record Office 422/1. Microfilm.

Durham, N.C. Duke University Library. Georgia (Colony) Papers, 1738–1802.

———. Duke University Library. The Letterbook of Richard Hill, 1743.

———. Duke University Library. Georgia Miscellaneous Papers, Colony, 1727-53.

———. Duke University Library. James Edward Oglethorpe Papers, 1738-85.

————. Duke University Library. Harman Verelst Papers, 1741–45.

Gloucester. County Records Office. Granville Sharp Papers.

Guildford. Guildford Muniment Room, Guildford, Surrey. Loseley Manuscripts.

London. Trinity Church. The Archives of the Society for the Promotion of Christian Knowledge.

————. The Archives of the Society for the Propagation of the Gospel in Foreign Parts, Tufton Street.

————. British Library. Additional Manuscripts.

————. British Library. Landsdowne Manuscripts.

————. British Library. Sloane Manuscripts.

————. British Library. Stowe Manuscripts.

New Haven. The Beinecke Library. Yale University. The Boswell Papers.

Tampa, Fla. Tampa Public Library. [Martyn, Benjamin?], Some Account of the Design of the Trustees for establishing Colonys in America.

Washington, D.C. Library of Congress. Vernon-Wager Manuscripts, 1654–1773.

Published Material

Public or Official Documents

Candler, Allen Daniel, Knight, Lucian Lamar, Coleman, Kenneth, and Ready, Milton, eds. *The Colonial Records of the State of Georgia.* 27 vols. to date. Atlanta and Athens, 1904–16, 1976–.

Cooper, Thomas, and McCord, David J., eds. *The Statutes At Large of South Carolina.* 14 vols. Columbia: A. S. Johnson, 1838–75.

Easterby, James Harold; Green, Ruth; and Olsberg, R. Nicholas, eds. *The Colonial Records of South Carolina.* 10 vols. to date. Columbia, 1951–.

Journal of the Commissioners for Trade and Plantations, 1729 to 1749, Preserved in the Public Record Office. 8 vols. London: H.M. Stationery Office, 1929–31.

Munro, James, and Grant, William Lawson, eds. *Acts of the Privy Council of England. Colonial Series, 1613–1783.* Hereford: H.M. Stationery Office, 1908–12.

Salley, Alexander Samuel, ed. *Journal of the Commons House of Assembly of South Carolina, November 8, 1734–June 7, 1735.* Columbia: State Commercial Printing Company, 1947.

Stock, Leo Francis, ed. *Proceedings and Debates of the British Parliaments respecting North America.* 5 vols. Washington: Carnegie Institution of Washington, 1924–41.

Newspapers and Journals

The Champion: Containing A Series of Papers, Humorous, Moral, Political, and Critical. (Full title varies.)

Charles Town *South-Carolina Gazette.*

The Country Journal; or, The Craftsman.

Gentleman's Magazine: or, Monthly Intelligencer.

The Gazette (London).

London Magazine; or, Gentleman's Monthly Intelligencer.

New-York *Weekly Journal.*

Williamsburgh *Virginia Gazette.*

Books, Pamphlets, Diaries, Collections, and other Published Primary Sources

Arredondo, Antonio de. *Arredondo's Historical Proof of Spain's Title to Georgia.* Edited by Herbert E. Bolton. Berkeley: University of California Press, 1925.

Boltzius, Johann Martin. "The Secret Diary of Pastor Johann Martin Boltzius," Edited by George Fenwick Jones. *Georgia Historical Quarterly* 53 (March 1969): 78-110.

―――. "Johann Martin Bolzius Answers a Questionnaire on Carolina and Georgia." Trans. and ed. by Klaus G. Leowald, Beverly Starika, and Paul S. Taylor. *William and Mary Quarterly* 3d ser., 14 (April 1957): 218-61.

Boswell, James. *Boswell's Life of Johnson.* Edited by George Birkbeck Hill. Rev. and enlarged ed. by L. F. Powell. 6 vols. Oxford: Clarendon Press, 1934.

―――. *Boswell in Extremes, 1776-1778.* Edited by Charles McC. Weis and Frederick A. Pottle. New York: McGraw-Hill, 1970.

Cadogan, George. *The Spanish Hireling Detected: Being a Refutation of the Several Calumnies and Falshoods in a late Pamphlet Entitul'd "An Impartial Account of the Late Expedition against Saint Augustine under General Oglethorpe."* London: J. Roberts, 1743.

[Christie, Thomas]. *A Description of Georgia by a Gentleman who has Resided there upwards of Seven Years, and was One of the First Settlers.* London: C. Corbett, 1741.

―――. "The Voyage of the *Anne*—A Daily Record." Edited by Robert G. McPherson. *Georgia Historical Quarterly* 44 (June 1960): 220-30.

Collections of the Georgia Historical Society. 17 vols. to date. Savannah: Georgia Historical Society, 1840-.

Gordon, Peter. *The Journal of Peter Gordon, 1732-1735.* Edited by E. Merton Coulter. Athens: University of Georgia Press, 1963.

Harris, John. *Navigantium atque Itinerantium Bibliotheca.* 2 vols. London: 1748.

Historical Manuscripts Commission. *Diary of John Percival, First Earl of Egmont.* 3 vols. H.M.C. Reports. London, 1920-23.

―――. *Manuscripts of Lord Elphinstone.* H.M.C. Reports. London, 1883.

―――. *The King's Collection of Stuart Papers.* Vols. 4-7. H.M.C. Reports, London, 1910-23.

[Killpatrick, James.] *A Full Reply to Lieut. Cadogan's "Spanish Hireling,"* &c. *And Lieut Mackay's Letter, Concerning the Action at Moosa.* London: J. Huggonson, 1743.

[―――]. *An Impartial Account of the Late Expedition against St. Augustine under General Oglethorpe.* London: J. Huggonson, 1742.

[Kimber, Edward]. *A Relation, or Journal, of a late Expedition to the Gates of St. Augustine, on Florida: Conducted by the Hon. General James Oglethorpe, with a Detachment of His Regiment, &c from Georgia.* London: T. Astley, 1744.

Lane, Mills, ed. *General Oglethorpe's Georgia: Colonial Letters, 1733-1743.* 2 vols. Savannah: Beehive Press, 1975.

Mackay, Hugh. *A Letter from Lieut Hugh Mackay, of Genl Oglethorpe's*

Regiment, to John Mackay, Esq; in the Shire of Sutherland, in Scotland.
London, 1742.

[———.] *An Impartial Inquiry into the State and Utility of the Province of Georgia.* London: W. Meadows, 1741.

[Martyn, Benjamin]. *An Account, Showing the Progress of the Colony of Georgia, in America, from its First Establishment.* 1741. Annapolis: Reprint of the London edition by Jonas Green, 1742.

Moore, Francis. *A Voyage to Georgia Begun in the Year 1735.* London: Jacob Robinson, 1744.

"A New York Mission to England: The London Letters of Lewis Morris to James Alexander, 1735 to 1736." Edited by Stanley N. Katz. *William and Mary Quarterly* 3d ser., 28 (July 1971): 439-84.

Newman, Henry. *Henry Newman's Salzburger Letterbooks.* Transcribed and edited by George Fenwick Jones. Athens: University of Georgia Press, 1966.

Oglethorpe, James Edward. "A Latin Poem by James Edward Oglethorpe." Contributed by Rudolf Kirk. *Georgia Historical Quarterly* 32 (March 1948): 29-31.

[———.] *A New and Accurate Account of the Provinces of South-Carolina and Georgia.* London: J. Roberts, 1733.

"Oglethorpe's Treaty with the Lower Creek Indians." *Georgia Historical Quarterly* 4 (March 1920): 3-16.

Percival, John, First Earl of Egmont. *The Journal of the Earl of Egmont.* Edited by Robert G. McPherson. Athens: University of Georgia Press, 1962.

Pinckney, Eliza Lucas. *The Letterbook of Eliza Lucas Pinckney.* Edited by Elise Pinckney. Chapel Hill: University of North Carolina Press, 1972.

Pringle, Robert. *The Letterbook of Robert Pringle.* Edited by Walter B. Edgar. 2 vols. Columbia, S.C.: University of South Carolina Press, 1972.

"A Ranger's Report of Travels with General Oglethorpe, 1739-1742." In *Travels in the North American Colonies,* edited by Newton D. Mereness. New York: Macmillan Company, 1916.

Report of the Committee Appointed to examine into the Proceedings of the People of Georgia, with respect to the Province of South-Carolina, And the Disputes Subsisting between the Two Colonies. Charles-Town: Lewis Timothy, 1736.

The St. Augustine Expedition of 1740. Introduction by John Tate Lanning. Columbia, S.C.: South Carolina Archives Department, 1954.

[Stephens, Thomas]. *A Brief account of the Causes that have retarded The Progress of the Colony of Georgia in America; Attested upon Oath.* London, 1743.

[———.] *The Hard Case of the Distressed People of Georgia.* London, 26 April 1742.

Stephens, William. *The Journal of William Stephens, 1741-1745.* Edited by E. Merton Coulter. 2 vols. Athens: University of Georgia Press, 1958-59.

———. *A State of the Province of Georgia, Attested upon Oath in the Court of Savannah, November 10, 1740.* London: W. Meadows, 1742.

Tailfer, Patrick, and others. *A True and Historical Narrative of the Colony of Georgia.* Edited and with an Introduction by Clarence L. Ver Steeg. Athens: University of Georgia Press, 1960. Original book published in Charles Town: Peter Timothy, 1741.

"The John Tobler Manuscripts: An Account of German-Swiss Emigrants in South Carolina, 1737." Edited by Charles G. Cordle. *Journal of Southern History* 5 (February 1939): 83–97.

Tracts and other Papers, relating Principally to the Origin, Settlement, and Progress of the Colonies in North America, from the Discovery of the Country to the Year 1776. Edited by Peter Force. 4 vols. Washington, D.C.: Peter and William Q. Force, 1836–46.

Urlsperger, Samuel, ed. *Detailed Reports on the Salzburger Emigrants Who Settled in America* . . . Edited by George Fenwick Jones. Translated by Hermann J. Lacher, Marie Hahn, and George Fenwick Jones. 4 vols. to date. Athens: University of Georgia Press, 1968–.

Von Reck, Georg Friedrich Philipp. "Von Reck's Second Report from Georgia." Edited by George Fenwick Jones. *William and Mary Quarterly,* 3d ser., 22 (April 1965): 319–33.

Wesley, Charles. *The Journal of the Rev. Charles Wesley M.A. Sometime Student of Christ Church Oxford.* Edited by John Telford. London: Robert Culley, [1909].

Wesley, John. *The Journal of the Rev. John Wesley A.M. sometime fellow of Lincoln College, Oxford.* Edited by Nehemiah Curnock. 8 vols. London: Epworth Press, reissued 1938.

Wilson, Thomas. *The Diaries of Thomas Wilson, D.D., 1731–37 and 1750.* Edited by Charles L. S. Linnell. London: SPCK, 1964.

SECONDARY SOURCES

General Works, Biographies, Monographs

Bertelson, David. *The Lazy South.* New York: Oxford University Press, 1967.

Boorstin, Daniel J. *The Americans: The Colonial Experience.* New York: Random House, 1958.

Chatelain, Verne Elmo. *The Defenses of Spanish Florida, 1565–1763.* Carnegie Institution Publication 511. Washington, D.C., 1941.

Church, Leslie F. *Oglethorpe: A Study of Philanthropy in England and Georgia.* London: Epworth Press, 1932.

Coleman, Kenneth. *Colonial Georgia: A History.* New York: Charles Scribner's, 1976.

Corkran, David H. *The Cherokee Frontier.* Norman: University of Oklahoma Press, 1962.

———. *The Creek Frontier.* Norman: University of Oklahoma Press, 1967.

Corry, John Pitts. *Indian Affairs in Georgia, 1732–1756.* Philadelphia: George S. Ferguson Company, 1936.

Coulter, Ellis Merton. *Georgia: A Short History.* Rev. and enlarged ed. Chapel Hill: University of North Carolina Press, 1960.

———, and Saye, Albert B., eds. *A List of the Early Settlers of Georgia.* Athens: University of Georgia Press, 1967.

Crane, Verner Winslow. *The Southern Frontier.* Ann Arbor: University of Michigan Press, Ann Arbor Books, 1956.

Davis, Harold E. *The Fledgling Province: Social and Cultural Life in Colonial Georgia, 1733–1776.* Chapel Hill: University of North Carolina Press for Institute of Early American History and Culture, 1976.

Ettinger, Amos Aschbach. *James Edward Oglethorpe: Imperial Idealist.* Oxford: Clarendon Press, 1936.

Fairbanks, George R. *The History and Antiquities of the City of St. Augustine, Florida, founded A.D. 1565.* New York: Charles B. Norton, 1858.

Flanders, Ralph Betts. *Plantation Slavery in Georgia.* Chapel Hill: University of North Carolina Press, 1933.

Foster, Joseph. *The Register of Admissions to Gray's Inn, 1521-1889.* London, 1889.

Fries, Adelaide. *The Moravians in Georgia.* Raleigh, 1905.

Greene, Jack. *The Quest for Power.* Chapel Hill: University of North Carolina Press, 1963.

Heath, Milton Sydney. *Constructive Liberalism: The Role of the State in Economic Development in Georgia to 1860.* Cambridge: Harvard University Press, 1954.

Hewatt, Alexander. *An Historical Account of the Rise and Progress of the Colonies of South Carolina and Georgia.* London: Alexander Donaldson, 1779.

Hoare, Prince. *Memoirs of Granville Sharp, Esq.* London, 1870.

Ivers, Larry E. *British Drums on the Southern Frontier.* Chapel Hill: University of North Carolina Press, 1974.

Jones, Charles Colcock, Jr. *Historical Sketch of Tomo-Chi-Chi, Mico of the Yamacraws.* Albany, N.Y., 1868.

———. *The History of Georgia.* 2 vols. Boston: Houghton, Mifflin and Company, 1883.

King, Horace Maybray. *James Edward Oglethorpe's Parliamentary Career.* Milledgeville, Ga.: Georgia College, 1968.

Lanning, John Tate. *The Diplomatic History of Georgia.* Chapel Hill: University of North Carolina Press, 1936.

———. *The Spanish Missions of Georgia.* Chapel Hill: University of North Carolina Press, 1935.

McCain, James Ross. *Georgia as a Proprietary Province.* Boston: Richard G. Badger, 1917.

McCrady, Edward. *The History of South Carolina under the Royal Government, 1719-1776.* New York: Macmillan Company, 1899.

Manucy, Albert C. *The Fort at Frederica.* University of Florida, Department of Anthropology Notes in Anthropology, Vol. 5. Tallahassee, 1962.

Pares, Richard. *War and Trade in the West Indies, 1739-1763.* Oxford: Clarendon Press, 1936.

Rabun, James Zachary. "Georgia and the Creek Indians." Master's Thesis, University of North Carolina, 1937.

Ramsay, David. *The History of South-Carolina, from Its First Establishment in 1670, to the Year 1808.* 2 vols. Charleston: David Longworth, 1809.

Rand, Benjamin, ed. *Berkeley and Percival.* Cambridge: Cambridge University Press, 1914.

Ready, Milton L. "An Economic History of Colonial Georgia, 1732-1754." Ph.D. dissertation, University of Georgia, 1970.

Reese, Trevor R. *Colonial Georgia.* Athens: University of Georgia Press, 1963.

———. *Frederica: Colonial Fort and Town.* St. Simons Island, Ga.: Fort Frederica Association, 1969.

Richmond, Sir Herbert William. *The Navy in the War of 1739-48.* 3 vols. Cambridge: Cambridge University Press, 1920.

Saye, Albert B. *New Viewpoints in Georgia History.* Athens: University of Georgia Press, 1943.

Sherman, Richard P. *Robert Johnson.* Columbia, S.C.: University of South Carolina Press, 1966.

Sirmans, M. Eugene. *Colonial South Carolina: A Political History, 1663-1763.* Chapel Hill: University of North Carolina Press, 1966.

Smith, W. Roy. *South Carolina as a Royal Province.* New York: Macmillan Company, 1903.

Spalding, Billups Phinizy. "Georgia and South Carolina during the Oglethorpe Period, 1732-1743." Ph.D. dissertation, University of North Carolina, 1963.

Stevens, William Bacon. *A History of Georgia, from Its First Discovery by Europeans to the Adoption of the Present Constitution in 1798.* 2 vols. 1847. New ed. with an Introduction by E. Merton Coulter. Savannah: Beehive Press, 1972.

Strickland, Reba Carolyn. *Religion and the State of Georgia in the Eighteenth Century.* New York: Columbia University Press, 1939.

Strobel, P. A. *The Salzburgers and Their Descendants.* 1855. Facsimile reprint. Athens: University of Georgia Press, 1953.

Taylor, Paul S. *Georgia Plan: 1732-1752.* Berkeley: Institute of Business and Economic Research, 1972.

Temple, Sarah B. Gober, and Coleman, Kenneth. *Georgia Journeys.* Athens: University of Georgia Press, 1961.

TePaske, John Jay. *The Governorship of Spanish Florida, 1700-1763.* Durham, N.C.: Duke University Press, 1964.

Tyerman, Luke. *The Oxford Methodists.* London, 1873.

Wood, Peter H. *Black Majority: Negroes in Colonial South Carolina from 1670 through the Stono Rebellion.* New York: Alfred A. Knopf, 1974.

Wright, Robert. *A Memoir of General James Oglethorpe, One of the Earliest Reformers of Prison Discipline in England, and the Founder of Georgia, in America.* London: Chapman and Hall, 1867.

Articles

Arnade, Charles W. "The English Invasion of Spanish Florida, 1700-1706." *Florida Historical Quarterly* 41 (July 1962): 29-37.

Bolton, Herbert E. "Spanish Resistance to the Carolina Traders in Western Georgia (1680-1704)." *Georgia Historical Quarterly* 9 (June 1925): 115-30.

Boys, Richard C. "General Oglethorpe and the Muses." *Georgia Historical Quarterly* 31 (March 1947): 19-29.

Cate, Margaret Davis. "Fort Frederica and the Battle of Bloody Marsh." *Georgia Historical Quarterly* 27 (June 1943): 111-74.

Coleman, Kenneth. "The Southern Frontier: Georgia's Founding and the Expansion of South Carolina." *Georgia Historical Quarterly* 56 (Summer 1972): 163-74.

Corry, John Pitts. "Education in Colonial Georgia." *Georgia Historical Quarterly* 16 (June 1932): 136-45.

Coulter, Ellis Merton. "Mary Musgrove, 'Queen of the Creeks:' A Chapter of Early Georgia Troubles." *Georgia Historical Quarterly* 11 (March 1927): 1-30.

———. "When John Wesley Preached in Georgia." *Georgia Historical Quarterly* 9 (December 1925): 317-51.

Crane, Verner Winslow. "Dr. Thomas Bray and the Charitable Colony Project, 1730." *William and Mary Quarterly*, 3d ser., 19 (January 1962): 49-63.

———. "The Origins of Georgia." *Georgia Historical Quarterly* 14 (June 1930): 93-110.

———. "The Philanthropists and the Genesis of Georgia." *American Historical Review* 27 (October 1921): 63-69.

———. "The Promotion Literature of Georgia." In *Bibliographical Essays: A Tribute to Wilberforce Eames.* Cambridge: Harvard University Press, 1924, pp. 281-98.

———. "The Southern Frontier in Queen Anne's War." *American Historical Review* 24 (April 1919): 379-95.

Dunn, Richard S. "The Trustees of Georgia and the House of Commons, 1732-1752." *William and Mary Quarterly*, 3d ser., 11 (October 1954), 551-65.

Fant, Handy Bruce. "Financing the Colonization of Georgia." *Georgia Historical Quarterly* 20 (March 1936): 1-29.

———. "The Indian Trade Policy of the Trustees for Establishing the Colony of Georgia in America." *Georgia Historical Quarterly* 15 (September 1931): 207-22.

———. "The Labor Policy of the Trustees for Establishing the Colony of Georgia in America." *Georgia Historical Quarterly* 16 (March 1932): 1-16.

———. "The Prohibition Policy of the Trustees for Establishing the Colony of Georgia in America." *Georgia Historical Quarterly* 17 (December 1933): 286-92.

"Fort San Diego." *El Escribano* 8 (October 1971): 139-48.

Goggin, John M. "Fort Pupo: A Spanish Frontier Outpost." *Florida Historical Quarterly* 30 (October 1951): 139-92.

Herndon, G. Melvin. "Timber Products of Colonial Georgia." *Georgia Historical Quarterly* 57 (Spring 1973): 56-62.

Lanning, John Tate. "The American Colonies in the Preliminaries of the War of Jenkins' Ear." *Georgia Historical Quarterly* 11 (June 1927): 129-55.

———. "American Participation in the War of Jenkins' Ear." *Georgia Historical Quarterly* 11 (September 1927): 191-215.

Meroney, Geraldine. "The London Entrepôt Merchants and the Georgia Colony." *William and Mary Quarterly*, 3d ser., 25 (April 1968): 230-44.

Middleton, Arthur Pierce. "The Strange Story of Job Ben Solomon." *William and Mary Quarterly*, 3d ser., 5 (July 1948): 342-50.

Morgan, David T. "Judaism in Eighteenth-Century Georgia." *Georgia Historical Quarterly* 58 (Spring 1974): 41-54.

Pearson, Fred Lamar. "Early Anglo-Spanish Rivalry in Southeastern North America." *Georgia Historical Quarterly* 58 (Supplement 1974): 157-71.

Potter, David Morris, Jr. "The Rise of the Plantation System in Georgia." *Georgia Historial Quarterly* 16 (June 1932): 114-35.

Ready, Milton L. "Land Tenure in Trusteeship Georgia." *Agricultural History* 48 (July 1974): 353-68.

Reese, Trevor R. "Britain's Military Support of Georgia in the War of 1739-1748." *Georgia Historical Quarterly* 43 (March 1959): 1-10.

———. "Georgia in Anglo-Spanish Diplomacy, 1736-1739." *William and Mary Quarterly,* 3d ser., 15 (April 1958): 168-90.

Ross, Mary. "The Restoration of the Spanish Missions in Georgia, 1598-1606." *Georgia Historical Quarterly* 10 (September 1926): 171-99.

Saye, Albert Berry. "Was Georgia a Debtor Colony?" *Georgia Historical Quarterly* 24 (December 1940): 323-52.

Sheehan, Bernard W. "Paradise and the Noble Savage in Jeffersonian Thought." *William and Mary Quarterly,* 3d ser., 26 (July 1969): 327-59.

Sirmans, M. Eugene. "The South Carolina Royal Council, 1720-1762." *William and Mary Quarterly,* 3d ser., 18 (July 1961): 373-92.

Spalding, Phinizy. "The Death of James Edward Oglethorpe." *Georgia Historical Quarterly* 57 (Summer 1973): 227-34.

———. "James Edward Oglethorpe: A Biographical Survey." *Georgia Historical Quarterly* 56 (Fall 1972): 332-48.

———. "James Oglethorpe and the American Revolution." *Journal of Imperial and Commonwealth History* 3 (May 1975 [1976]), 398-407.

———. "Oglethorpe and Johnson: A Cordial Connection." *Johnson Society Transactions,* December 1974, pp. 52-61.

———. "Some Sermons before the Trustees of Colonial Georgia." *Georgia Historical Quarterly* 57 (Fall 1973): 332-46.

———. "South Carolina and Georgia: The Early Days." *South Carolina Historical Magazine* 69 (April 1968): 83-96.

Taylor, Paul S. "Colonizing Georgia, 1732-1752: A Statistical Note." *William and Mary Quarterly,* 3d ser., 22 (January 1965): 119-27.

Temperley, Harold William Vazeille. "The Causes of the War of Jenkins' Ear, 1739." *Transactions of the Royal Historical Society,* 3d ser., 3 (1909): 197-236.

TePaske, John Jay. "The Fugitive Slave: Intercolonial Rivalry and Spanish Slave Policy, 1687-1764." In *Eighteenth-Century Florida and Its Borderlands,* ed. Samuel Proctor. Gainesville: University Presses of Florida, 1975.

Wood, Betty. "Thomas Stephens and the Introduction of Black Slavery in Georgia." *Georgia Historical Quarterly* 58 (Spring 1974): 24-40.

Woods, John A. "The City of London and Impressment, 1776-1777." *Proceedings of the Leeds Philosophical Society* 8, Part 2 (December 1956): 111-27.

Index